IS THERE PURPOSE IN BIOLOGY?

THE COST OF EXISTENCE
AND THE GOD OF LOVE

BY
DENIS R. ALEXANDER

*This book is dedicated to my many colleagues
in the biological sciences with whom I have enjoyed
working purposefully over the years.*

Also by Denis Alexander:

Beyond Science (Lion Publishing, 1972)

Rebuilding the Matrix: Science and Faith in the 21st Century (Lion Publishing, 2001)

(with Robert White) *Beyond Belief: Science, Faith and Ethical Challenges* (Lion Publishing, 2004)

Creation or Evolution: Do We Have to Choose? 2nd edition (Monarch, 2014)

The Language of Genetics: An Introduction (Templeton Foundation Press, 2011)

Genes, Determinism and God (Cambridge University Press, 2017)

"In this thoroughly engaging and highly informative book, Dr Denis Alexander writes with great clarity and accessible scholarship to bring us face to face with the latest understanding of the mechanisms underlying evolution. The surprise is that 'random' processes driven by 'chance' are actually constrained by the underlying mechanisms and innate properties of matter. Such inherent 'fine-tuning' inevitably results in a biological world of immense variety and complexity that gives every suggestion of being designed for a purpose; one which we can both marvel at and explore through science.

The author argues that the most coherent explanation for this fine-tuning is that it reflects the activity of a divine creator, who does indeed create with a purpose. Key to this is that human beings, the pinnacle of the evolutionary process, can have a relationship with their creator, and so fulfil their purpose.

This book will have a wide appeal. It will help Christians who struggle to reconcile the randomness of evolutionary theory with a purposeful creator God, but also provides an ideal starting point for those who believe evolution is incompatible with God yet are open to exploring further."

Andrew Halestrap, Emeritus Professor of Biochemistry, University of Bristol, UK

"There is perhaps no issue in contemporary science as challenging as the question of whether commitment to evolution is consistent with the idea that life has a purpose, and perhaps no author as well-equipped to shed light on this question as the distinguished molecular biologist Denis Alexander.

In this approachable, insightful, and wide-ranging book, Alexander brings his expertise in biology, history, and theology to bear on this most difficult of questions. While evolutionary biology has routinely been appropriated by pessimistic prophets of a purposeless universe, Alexander makes a careful and convincing case that modern biology is also consistent with belief in a world imbued with divine meaning and purpose."

Peter Harrison, Director, Institute for Advanced Studies in the Humanities, University of Queensland, Australia

"What a wonderful book this is! Some might think the title of the book provocative, as most biologists consider it a settled issue that evolutionary biology does not exhibit any purpose. Yet Denis Alexander examines this very question of purpose in biology.

First, using his in-depth knowledge of evolutionary biology and genetics, as well as his broad familiarity with the relevant discussions in philosophy and theology, he calmly examines the arguments and deconstructs the notion that evolutionary history must necessarily be without purpose. In the second part of the book, Alexander shifts the focus to world views and convincingly shows that evolution fits the Christian understanding of creation particularly well.

Finally, he addresses the problem of pain and suffering, arguing that these are necessarily part of a world that will produce beings of free will and moral responsibility who are equipped to enter into a loving relationship with the creator, who is a Trinitarian God of love. Written in an engaging style, with tongue-in-cheek British humor, this book corrects the popular bleak view of a pitiless, indifferent universe, and instead presents the most welcome view of a world of purpose."

Cees Dekker, Professor of Nanobiology, Delft University of Technology, the Netherlands

"This is a compelling argument for the conclusion that Christian belief in divine purpose and evolutionary theory are fully compatible. It is historically informed, philosophically sensitive, and more science-based than any other argument for this conclusion I have seen before. Alexander's book breathes wonder for God's creation, and love for the science that studies it."

René van Woudenberg, Professor of Epistemology and Metaphysics, Free University of Amsterdam

"Denis Alexander has written a book that clears away a great deal of woolly-headed thinking about a crucial topic. On the one hand, does what we know about the biological world indicate that at bottom the world lacks purpose, as New Atheists claim? If on the other, as Christians affirm, a loving God is the creator of all, how are we to think well about how He interacts with the world He has created? Is the evolutionary history of life really as driven by 'random chance' as so many would have us believe?

As in his other writings, *Is There Purpose in Biology?* addresses these challenging questions in an honest, accessible way that Christians, and those curious about Christian faith and the remarkable world of biology, will find immensely helpful."

Jeff Hardin, Professor of Zoology, University of Wisconsin, USA

Published by
Lion Hudson Limited
Wilkinson House, Jordan Hill Business Park,
Banbury Road, Oxford OX2 8DR, England
www.lionhudson.com

ISBN 978 0 85721 714 1
e-ISBN 978 0 85721 715 8

First edition 2018

Text acknowledgments
p. 22, Quotes from *Creationism and its Critics in Antiquity*, D. N. Sedley, published
by University of California Press. Copyright © 2007 D. N. Sedley. Used by
permission of the copyright holder through Rightslink.

pp. 29, 31, Quotes from *Islam's Quantum Question: Reconciling Muslim Tradition and
Modern Science*, N. Guessoum, published by I.B. Tauris. Copyright © 2011
N. Guessoum. Used by permission of the copyright holder through PLSClear.

pp. 31–32, 36–40, 43–46, Quotes from *The Bible, Protestantism, and the Rise of
Natural Science*, P. Harrison, published by Cambridge University Press. Copyright
© 1998 P. Harrison. Used by permission of Cambridge University Press.

Scripture quotations taken from the New International Version, copyright ©
1973, 1978, 1984 International Bible Society. Used by permission of Zondervan
and Hodder & Stoughton Limited. All rights reserved. The 'NIV' and 'New
International Version' trademarks are registered in the United States Patent
and Trademark Office by International Bible Society. Use of either trademark
requires the permission of International Bible Society. UK trademark number
1448790.

Figure acknowledgments
Can be found on pp. 286–287.

A catalogue record for this book is available from the British Library

Printed and bound in the UK, May 2018, LH26

Contents

FIGURES

Preface

This book started life as a series of three Herrmann Lectures given in honour of Bob Herrmann at Gordon College, USA, in November 2014. Bob Herrmann was a close friend of the late Sir John Templeton and they wrote books together (Templeton and Herrmann, 1989, 1994). Bob Herrmann lectured in biochemistry to medical students for 22 years and was one of the founder members of the John Templeton Foundation, also writing the biography of Sir John (Herrmann, 2004). It was an honour to have Professor Herrmann present at the lectures, and I am most grateful to the Foundation for their financial support for this lecture series.

I am also grateful to those who kindly provided comments and corrections on an earlier complete draft of this book: Graeme Finlay, Keith Fox, Andrew Jackson, Simon Conway Morris, and Alexander Massmann, together with those who commented on particular sections: Robert Asher, Ruth Bancewicz, Nidhal Guessoum, and Rodney Holder. The errors and opinions that remain are of course solely the responsibility of the author.

In addition, I would like to thank Jessica Tinker, Joy Tibbs, and Lawrence Osborn at Lion Publishing for all their help in the preparation of the manuscript.

Introduction

To head off any possible misunderstandings concerning the interpretations of the title, let me say immediately that there are many good reasons for studying biology and its incredibly important applications – but that kind of "purpose" is not what this book is about!

Reactions to the question "Is There Purpose in Biology?" are likely to vary greatly. One reaction will be "of course not": watch your favourite natural history programme and it's obvious that chance rules. Some animals get lucky and do well, others get eaten young, and there's no overall rhyme nor reason to it. We humans are just a lucky accident. Others responding to the same question, most likely coming from a religious worldview, will respond "of course": God has an overall purpose for everything, including biology. Others, perhaps the majority, are more likely to say: "Well it all depends on what you mean by purpose…"

Finding defenders of the first view, that the natural world is necessarily purposeless, is not difficult, especially those who have the evolutionary history of life in mind. For example, Professor Peter Atkins, Emeritus Professor of Chemistry at Oxford University, states that "A gross contamination of the reductionist ethic is the idea of purpose. Science has no need of purpose." The evolutionary biologist Richard Dawkins, perhaps on a rainy day in Oxford, writes that "The universe we observe had precisely the properties we should expect if there is, at bottom, no design, no purpose, no evil and no good, nothing but blind pitiless indifference" (Dawkins, 1995, p. 133). There does seem to be something about the weather in Oxford that nurtures gloomy philosophies.

The American philosopher Daniel Dennett agrees with Atkins and Dawkins – asking whether the complexity of biological diversity can "really be the outcome of nothing but a cascade of algorithmic processes feeding on chance? And if so, who designed that cascade?" Dennett answers his own rhetorical question by saying: "Nobody. It is itself the product of a blind, algorithmic process" (Dennett, 1995, p. 59), adding that "Evolution is not a process that was designed to produce us." The American philosopher Alex Rosenberg, in an article entitled "Darwin's Nihilistic Idea", declares that "Darwinism... puts the capstone on a process which since Newton's time has driven teleology[1] to the explanatory sidelines. In short it has made Darwinians into metaphysical Nihilists denying that there is any meaning or purpose to the universe, its contents and its cosmic history" (Sommers and Rosenberg, 2003).[2] And here is how one textbook of biology portrays the situation:

By coupling undirected, purposeless variation to the blind, uncaring process of natural selection, Darwin made theological or spiritual explanations of the life processes superfluous. (Futuyma, 1998, p. 5)

Fortunately, more recent biology textbooks tend to be more nuanced or, sensibly, just stick to the science and avoid philosophical comments altogether.

In any event, the question I wish to address in this book is this one: Is it *necessarily* the case, as these and other commentators are suggesting, that biology in general, and the evolutionary process in particular, tells us that it has no purpose? The question is carefully worded. If I were asked the question: "Does evolutionary history necessarily demonstrate that there must be a purpose in biology?", then I would answer simply that I don't think that such metaphysical conclusions, referring to questions concerning ultimate goals, can be derived so readily from the study of science. The scientific observations might make an affirmative answer more or less plausible, a point to which we will return later. But science alone is not up to the herculean task of demonstrating Purpose in any metaphysical sense. It can render certain metaphysical inferences less plausible, but trying to establish metaphysical worldviews based on science quickly leads to problems.

To tackle the question further: "Is biology necessarily purposeless?", it is clearly important to first ask what we mean by "purpose". It helps to discriminate between purpose with a small "p" and Purpose with a big "P". Unlike physics and chemistry, biology is full of the teleological language of purpose and has been ever since Aristotle. The beaver builds its dam in order to protect its home from predators. The male peacock displays its plumage in order to attract a mate. Camels have humps for the purpose of food storage. This is purpose with a small "p". All biologists use such language all the time, but no biologist today would be tempted to extract any metaphysical inferences from the use of such language. That has not always been the case. As we will see in Chapter 1, for many centuries it was commonplace to draw theological inferences from purpose with a small "p". Chapter 1 will also recount how that climate of opinion changed.

But in any case, looking at the quotes cited above from the likes of Atkins, Dawkins, Dennett, and others, it is clear that their denial of the "small p" purpose is not what they have in mind, but rather a denial of Purpose, a denial of any ultimate reason for the existence of a biological process such as evolution. When Dawkins writes that "there is, at bottom, no design, no purpose…" and Dennett boldly proclaims that "Evolution is not a process that was designed to produce us", these are clearly metaphysical claims, assertions about Purpose with a big "P". Evolutionary biology itself, so the argument goes, renders it impossible that evolutionary history, taken overall, could have any rhyme or reason. Chance rules. Our own existence is a lucky accident. Things could have turned out very differently.

Biology is necessarily Purposeless. It is this metaphysical inference from the biological account that this book wishes to challenge.

Before embarking on that challenge, there is one further matter to discuss: how would we know that a process is necessarily purposeless? The kind of static that would sometimes fuzz up old-fashioned TV screens would seem to be a good candidate. Rocks of various kinds scattered randomly across a beach, likewise. It is hard to see how these facets of the world around us could be endowed with some deeper overarching purpose. But what about systems that start simple and gradually become more complex? That in itself does not demonstrate purpose. On the other hand, it might make it more difficult for us to conclude that such systems are necessarily purposeless.

And what about systems that are clearly under strong physical constraints so that they can only operate or develop in a single direction? Let's say we are hiking in the mountains with no one else around and we come across two streams. The first is just winding its way down the valley in a haphazard kind of way. But the second is constrained by a series of dams so that the water is directed towards some fruit trees where it is further divided into smaller streams to water the trees. The first stream we might readily describe as necessarily without any particular purpose, but that conclusion would clearly be difficult to make for the second stream. The reason is the physical constraints that we observe – the water could do no other than be channelled by those constraints.

What about our own lives? We could in principle, albeit not in practice, track that very sperm that fertilized that very egg that became us. Out of the millions of sperm on that day, it was that particular sperm that won the race to fertilize the egg, thereby determining that we would be male and not female, or vice versa. And then we could track our development from that moment on, with all the complex gene–environment interactions involved, with thousands of chance events contributing to the person that we are today. Yet would an intimate knowledge of all those apparently random events, together with a detailed history of how our own decisions had changed the course of our lives, lead to the conclusion that our lives are necessarily Purposeless? It is hard to see why that should be the case.

One last example: what about the history of a country? We might observe many random and stochastic events during its long history: the leading politician who was assassinated that changed the course of the nation's history; the invasion in another century that devastated its economic infrastructure; the series of droughts at another time that wiped out half its population. Yet despite all that, as a historian we might also be able to detect certain common threads running through the years, shaped by that country's language, culture, religion, and political choices. At the least, it might be hard to conclude that, taken overall, the history of that country was necessarily Purposeless.

Considering these various uses of the "Purpose" word at least highlights some of the problems in using it unthinkingly. Chapter 1 will track some of the historical background that has entangled purpose and Purpose so thoroughly with biology over the centuries. Chapters 2 and 3 will then pick up the challenge of those authors cited above who propose that biology is necessarily purposeless, reviewing examples from contemporary biology, some of them very recent discoveries, that do not seem consistent with such a claim. Chapter 4 will address the broader questions of what we mean by terms such as "random" and "chance" and how these terms are used in biology in ways often different from their usage in daily speech and even in other branches of science. Chapter 5 then considers how and why biology can readily be incorporated into Christian creation theology, and Chapter 6 tackles the obvious question that arises when you do that: how can an evolutionary history involving so much suffering and death be squared with the Christian understanding of a God of love?

In summary, the book has five main points:

First, as already indicated, some commentators on biology wish to claim that evolutionary history, in particular, must necessarily ("obviously") be without Purpose.

Second, a closer look at biology (Chapters 2 and 3), coupled with an analysis of the meanings of terms such as "chance" and "random" (Chapter 4), does not in fact support the assertion that biology is necessarily Purposeless.

Third, in practice everyone imposes a Purpose upon biology by incorporating it within their particular worldview, a worldview that goes well beyond science (Chapter 5).

Fourth, the "everyone" includes Christians who also claim that the roots of biology in general (Chapter 1), and of evolution in particular, find a natural home within their Christian understanding of creation, especially given the impact of natural theology upon Darwin's thinking (Chapter 5).

Fifth, nevertheless there are theological challenges raised by evolution, not least by the huge scale of suffering of animals and humans. However, it may be argued that the costly price of existence is worth the price (Chapter 6).

1

The Historical Roots of Purpose in Biology

The investigation of Final Causes is barren, and like a virgin consecrated to God produces nothing.
Francis Bacon, *De Augmentis Scientiarum* (1623), Book III, Chapter 5

Providing a complete overview of changing ideas about purpose in biology over the centuries would require a book rather than a chapter. The aim of this chapter is therefore more modest: to highlight some of the main changes in perspectives on the topic that have taken place over the years. In the process we will take a look at some of the key figures who have contributed to the thinking in this area.

First a word about the word "biology" (from the Greek word *bios*, life, and the suffix *-logia*, study of). In earlier centuries, the "study of life" was subsumed under the term "natural history". This was to distinguish it from "natural philosophy", which was deemed, at least until the late seventeenth century, to be superior to natural history because it provided causal and logical demonstrations, whereas natural history was seen as purely descriptive (Harrison, 2010). The word "biology" does not start appearing until the eighteenth century when the Swedish natural philosopher Carl

Linnaeus, famous for his classification system of plants and animals still in use today, used the word in Latin in his *Bibliotheca botanica* (1736). Its first known use in English was by the physician Thomas Beddoes who wrote that "biology is the foundation of ethics and pneumatology" (the study of the mind, in his terminology), maintaining that such knowledge was a prerequisite to "progress in genuine morality" (Harrison, 2015, p. 166). Clearly the nuances of the term are somewhat different today. But it was only in the nineteenth century that the term came into regular use in English and other languages, associated with the emergence of the more specialized study of the natural world.

By the late nineteenth century science was becoming more professionalized, and biology developed further as a distinct discipline in the early twentieth century with its own array of journals and professional societies. The frequency of the term "natural history" still dominated in 1900 in English texts as compared to "biology", but by 1920 the frequency was reversed, and by the year 2000 "biology" dominated over "natural history" in a ratio of 3:1 (Harrison, 2015, p. 166). Already by the late nineteenth century natural history was beginning to be viewed rather disdainfully as a pursuit for amateurs compared to the increasingly specialized discipline of biology.

Irrespective of these various labels, the "study of life" goes all the way back to the Greek philosophers, and it is with them that we should begin. In this book, the word "biology" will be used to encompass any serious attempt at a "study of life", remembering that such usage is somewhat anachronistic when referring to the pre-1800 era.

Aristotle (384–322 BC)

No account of purpose in biology could possibly exclude the writings of Plato's student Aristotle, whose ideas still do much to frame the discussion right up to the present day. In 343 BC Aristotle became the tutor of Alexander, the 13-year-old son of Philip II of Macedon, later known as Alexander the Great.

Aristotle famously taught that there are four causes of things: material, formal, efficient, and final. The "efficient cause" provides the focus for modern science – what makes something happen to something else and how does that work? But Aristotle would have thought such a description by itself to be very impoverished without the *telos*, the final cause, which asks the question "why"? From *telos* we derive our word "teleological", meaning "having an end or purpose", a word that still leads to weighty tomes of essays in which philosophers of biology discuss its various nuances (Allen et al., 1998).

Aristotle made some wonderful biological observations, several of which are described in his *On the Parts of Animals* (written around 350 BC), an investigation into the anatomy and physiology of animals. As Aristotle writes:

> *The causes concerned in the generation of the works of nature are, as we see, more than one. There is the final cause and there is the motor [efficient] cause... Plainly... that cause is the first which we call the final one [telos]. For this is the Reason, and the Reason forms the starting-point, alike in the works of art and in works of nature.*

To avoid any doubt, Aristotle's punchline is that "everything that Nature makes is means to an end" (Aristotle, 2001). *Telos*, for Aristotle, was thoroughly man-centred. As he wrote in his book entitled *Politics*, "If therefore Nature makes nothing without purpose or in vain, it follows that Nature has made all the animals for the sake of man."

Aristotle's other well-known work on biology is entitled *On the Generation of Animals*, again produced sometime in the latter half of the fourth century BC. It is in fact five books each containing multiple chapters, and again the biology is set within a teleological framework, although overall the work is less taken up with such matters in comparison with *On the Parts of Animals*. Much of Book Two consists of embryological observations and discussion, setting the scene for the further study of embryology over the next 2,000 years.

It should not be thought that Aristotle's teleological arguments derive from a belief in God because Aristotle's philosophy contained no room for a creator God. Instead matter is without beginning and its properties are due to its own internal necessity. Much of Aristotle's biological discussions centre around the distinctions between living and inanimate matter: only the former is "ensouled", Aristotle perceiving the soul not in its more Platonic sense of an entity distinct *from* the body, but more as the "internal energizer" which should be identified *with* a living body. Although Aristotle did invoke the idea of an "Unmoved Mover", which was the source of all the motion in the universe, this was quite unlike the creator God of Judeo-Christian thought, and certainly not the kind of involved personal Being that might bestow a *telos* upon some biological organism. Final causes for Aristotle are intrinsic principles of intelligibility, not in any sense active agents of anything. Later commentators have not always been careful enough to distinguish between Aristotle's own writings and the use to which some of them were later put in western Christendom.

The Stoics

The Stoic philosophers who flourished from the beginning of the third century BC are not generally looked on as a source of great biological insights. True though that is, they are mentioned here because of their promotion of the argument from design, an argument that was later to become thoroughly entangled with teleological arguments.

The Stoics drew their prime examples of design not from biology but from the great contemporary feats of engineering. One Stoic argument was a precursor to the metaphor used by Archdeacon William Paley more than 2,000 years later when Paley compared the world to a watch, thereby inferring design by a watchmaker. In its ancient Stoic form, the machine was the wonderful astronomical model built by Posidonius representing the celestial rotations of the sun, moon, and planets. As Sedley summarizes the Stoic argument:

> *Suppose some utterly remote barbarians (the British, for example) were shown one of these sophisticated mechanisms which precisely replicate the motions of sun, moon and planets: would they doubt for a moment that this was the work of an intelligence? Yet what is the world itself, with its celestial motions, if not a vastly superior and more complex version of that very same machine? (Sedley, 2007, p. 207)*

Yet Stoic arguments did not ignore biology altogether, noting for example, the carefully designed structure of animals in which

> *the mouth, through which animals ingest the objects of their appetites, has been located near the eyes and nose, whereas, because excrement is unpleasant, they have diverted the ducts for this and discharge it as far away as possible from the sense organs. When these things have been done in such a providential fashion, are you in doubt whether they are the products of chance or design?*

The interlocutor in the text responds "Indeed not, but when I look at that way they seem like the contrivance of some wise craftsman who loves animals" (Sedley, 2007, p. 215).

The Stoics were pantheists who believed that a divine reality pervades the whole universe. There was no creator – the world has neither beginning nor end. The Stoic philosophy found an effective expositor in the Roman lawyer Cicero (106–43 BC). In his book *The Nature of the Gods* Cicero describes the various ways in which animals catch their food, defend themselves, and reproduce, including the wonderful way in which human physiology and anatomy are designed to make humans at home in the world, seeing all as evidence for design. Cicero was a polytheist, writing that:

> *When we see a mechanism such as a planetary model or a clock, do we doubt that it is the creation of a conscious intelligence? So how can we doubt that the world is the work of the divine intelligence? We may well believe that the world and everything in it has been created for the gods and for mankind. (Emerton, 1989)*

Cicero's arguments were taken up by early Christian thinkers such as Tertullian (AD 160–225) as a way of promoting belief in the one creator God to the surrounding pagan world. Some pagans even wanted Cicero's *The Nature of the Gods* suppressed because it was used so successfully by Christian writers such as Tertullian!

Galen of Pergamon

Galen is remembered more for his medical writings than for his biology, but like many writers of antiquity, his voluminous works cover many biological topics in addition to medicine, philosophy, and what we would now call psychotherapy. Born as a Greek in Pergamon, Asia Minor (modern day Turkey) in AD 129, Galen later moved to Rome where he fell in love with Roman culture, even changing his name to the more Roman sounding Claudius Galenus. Galen studied medicine, first in Corinth and then in Alexandria, eventually becoming the personal physician of the Emperor Marcus Aurelius.

The reason for mentioning Galen here is his strong promotion of a teleological framework for his medicine and biology which was still influential in Europe in the early modern period following its translation into Latin from Greek in the 1530s. The polytheist Galen was widely read in Greek philosophy as he defended Platonic and Aristotelian philosophies against the atomists who wished to deny the providential activities of the gods. In his teleological treatise *On the Usefulness of Parts*, Galen repeatedly points out the excellence of divine craftsmanship. Galen was particularly keen on Plato's *Timaeus* in which a "craftsman demiurge" (not to be confused with the creator God of Judeo-Christian monotheism) forms the often recalcitrant matter of the world into the shapes and forms that we see today, much as a carpenter uses materials to bring about his creations. Galen appears to have had some contact with Jewish thought, since he remarks rather disparagingly that whereas the God of Moses was able to create matter by mere fiat, the demiurge worked skilfully with the properties of his materials, which was more to be praised. For example, the demiurge embedded along the rim of the eyelid a hard layer of cartilage which prevented the eyelashes from growing too long. Only a really good technician would accomplish such a feat (Sedley, 2007, pp. 239–42).

Indeed, in *On the Usefulness of Parts* Galen demonstrates a certain fascination with the teleological roles of hair, pointing out that certain bodily residues result in facial hair which, in the case of beards, also have the aesthetic advantage of providing a dignified adornment for men, appropriate to the character of their souls. Providentially, however, women have been spared beards since their indoor lifestyle does not require this extra protective layer and, in any case, beards are inappropriate to women's souls. Armpit hair, Galen points out, is worthless, a bit like the weeds growing alongside the crops in a field. Teleological explanations have their limits.

While we may smile today at such curious examples, the trope of the divine craftsman proved to be a powerful one, cropping up repeatedly in scientific and medical literature for the next 1,500 years. Here was purpose, not as some ultimate *telos*, but as biological functionality.

Biology in early Muslim sources

Islam's Golden Age of learning began in the ninth century under the rule of the Abbasid Caliphs based in Baghdad. The city became a hive of translation as the texts of the ancient Greek philosophers were translated into Arabic and Syriac (Masood, 2009 pp. 44ff.). The wealthy city, with a population estimated at around 1 million people, by far the biggest city in the world at that time, soon became a centre for trading ancient manuscripts. The Banu Musa brothers, a family of mathematicians and astronomers, paid translators as much as 500 dinars a month, more than £24,000 in today's money.

Muslim thinkers, like their Christian counterparts in Europe several centuries later, both assimilated as well as reacted against this torrent of new learning as it flooded into the *majalis* (salons) in which scholars came together to discuss the latest religious and philosophical ideas. Today, ancient texts are looked upon by scientists mainly for their historical interest, but for those of a previous era the texts themselves revealed the wisdom of the ancients, rather as scientists today would look upon new scientific discoveries. The House of Wisdom in Baghdad of the Caliph al-Mamun centred around a great library: there was a remarkably free exchange of ideas.

It should not be thought that the Islamic world was merely a preserver of Greek natural philosophy through translation. By the end of the heyday of Islamic science from the ninth to thirteenth centuries, great discoveries had been made in mathematics, astronomy, physics, mechanics, and other fields. And some of the writings on medical and biological topics also demonstrated the authors' remarkable abilities in observing and ordering the living world.

Not all the translations were carried out by Muslims. The head of the House of Wisdom in the ninth century was a Nestorian Christian named Hunayn ibn Ishaq (808–73), an Arab descended from an Arab tribe that had converted to Christianity long before the days of Islam (Lindberg, 1992, p. 169). Hunayn and his wider family were brilliant linguists, and many of the translations were collaborative efforts: one might translate a work from Greek to Syriac whereas another might then render the Syriac into Arabic. Most of Hunayn's translations were medical, with an emphasis on Galen and Hippocrates. Altogether Hunayn translated around 90 of Galen's works, thereby transmitting them not only to the Muslim world but eventually to Europe as well. In his spare time, Hunayn produced a Syriac version of the Old Testament. Hunayn and his family provide but one example of dozens of translators who were active in Baghdad and later on in Andalucia as the Islamic world extended into the Iberian Peninsula. As Lindberg reports: "By the year 1000 AD almost the entire known corpus of Greek medicine, natural philosophy, and mathematical sciences had been rendered into usable Arabic versions" (Lindberg, 1992, p. 170).

Hunayn, as with some other translators, did not just translate texts literally, but instead improved them as he saw fit. For example, he expanded on Galen's descriptions of the anatomy of the eye. Hunayn also wrote a brief summary of Galen's work in a question-and-answer form – one of the first Arabic texts to be translated into Latin in the eleventh century, thereby becoming a standard medical text for many centuries (Masood, 2009, p. 47).

Indeed, medicine was of great interest in the Islamic world. Ibn Sina (Avicenna) was born in 980 in Uzbekistan (as it is now) at a time when the Islamic world was no longer under the control of a single Caliph, so he moved around a lot depending on his changing political fortunes. By the age of ten he had memorized the Qur'an and much Arabic poetry. By the age of 16 he had become a physician and established his credentials by successfully treating the Samanid ruler of the eastern Islamic caliphate for a severe diarrhoeal infection (Masood, 2009, p. 103).[3] Ibn Sina was a polymath, his most famous work being *The Canon of Medicine*, a multivolume encyclopedia of medical knowledge amounting to half a million words. Later translated into Latin, it became a standard medical text in Europe for six centuries, with around 60 editions being published between 1500 and 1674. *The Canon of Medicine* contained many novel insights, including the observation that nerves transmit pain and pass signals leading to muscle contraction.

The extent to which design arguments were brought into play varied considerably among the Muslim natural philosophers. Ibn Sina saw the world as Allah's orderly creation that could be understood and practically utilized by human endeavour, beginning his great *Canon*: "In the first place we render thanks to Allah, for the very excellence of the order of His creation, and the abundance of His benefits", followed shortly afterwards by the somewhat daunting advice that any medical student might take to heart, at least the final phrase: "Every follower of my teachings who wishes to use them profitably should memorise most of this work, even though he do not quite understand it all." Avicenna believed in Allah's will being worked out in the whole of his creation and medicine provided one avenue whereby the Purposes of God might be discerned. This was far from the idea of "purpose" in Greek philosophers such as Aristotle, for whom the *telos* was something intrinsic to the very nature of an object's being. In Islamic as well as in Christian thought, "Purpose" was bestowed by God as part of his creation, not something that created matter could display "on its own" as it were.

This same basic idea likewise comes through in those Muslim writers who described the plant and animal world. Long before Ibn Sina came on the scene, al-Jahiz (776–868/9), whom Masood describes as the "Islamic world's first professional science-writer" (Masood, 2009, p. 183), moved to Baghdad from East Africa. Al-Jahiz was good at seeing both sides of a question and for polemical fun (it seems) wrote a book in praise of wine and another one against wine, and then a book in praise of booksellers and one against booksellers (al-Jahiz, 1995, p. xv). The most famous of his 200 books was *The Book of Animals* in which he describes 350 different varieties, where he writes:

> *In sum, no animal can survive without nourishment. The hunting animal cannot escape being hunted. Every weak animal devours those that are weaker; every strong animal cannot avoid being consumed by those that are stronger... God, in sum, made some beings the cause of life to others, and in turn made these the cause of death to yet others. (Palacios, 1930; transl. Robert Asher)*

The idea of purpose and design is even more prominent in a further work attributed to al-Jahiz, translated into English under the title *Chance or Creation? God's Design in the Universe* (al-Jahiz, 1995).[4] There al-Jahiz describes Allah's universe "built and equipped with all that is necessary... Everything has its place and purpose" (p. 4). "Reflect on the design in the creation of carnivorous animals. They were created with sharp teeth, strong claws and wide mouths because it was intended that they should feed on meat" (p. 46). "If chance could explain all this magnificent design, we would have to say that plan and design came about by accident and without thought which would be absurd" (p. 73). Like Galen (from whom some of his ideas may have come – he was very well read), al-Jahiz displayed a special interest in bodily hair, writing sagely that "If the child is male, hair will grow on his chin – a glorious sign of his masculinity – as he leaves the stage of childhood and similarity to women. If the child is female, her face remains free of hair so that its freshness and lustre remain, which moves men to ensure the continuation of the species" (pp. 72–73, plus lots more on hair pp. 89–91). Eight hundred years before Gottfried Leibniz, with his claim that we live in the "best of all possible worlds", al-Jahiz certainly paved the way.

Other biological descriptions from the Islamic world are likewise remarkable for their sense of God's ordering of the whole Great Chain of Being, an idea found in Aristotle and other Greek philosophers, in which the natural world is organized into a great "ladder of life" with rocks at the bottom, plants further up, and then above them animals of increasing complexity and ability to move. For example, the famous Muslim natural philosopher al-Farabi, sometimes known in the Arab philosophical tradition as "The Second Master" after Aristotle, wrote that:

> *Beings start with the least perfect one, then they rise gradually, until each has reached its most perfect form. The classification of these beings starts with the lowliest, then the better and better ones, until one reaches the best; the lowest one is the common matter, then minerals, then plants, then non-speaking animals, and there is no better than the speaking animal (man).*
> *(Guessoum, 2011, pp. 306–7)*

The fourteenth-century North African Muslim philosopher, Ibn Khaldun, made even more striking references to the systematic dynamic organization of the living world, again with man at its peak:

> *Look at the world of creation, how it started from minerals, then plants, then animals, in a beautiful way of gradation and connection... where... each is ready in a strange way to become the first in the line of what comes after it; the animal kingdom is vast and diverse in its species, such that it reached in gradual formation the human being, who distinguishes himself by mind and vision; to it the animal kingdom has risen from apes, which possess conscience and feeling but not vision and thought, and that is the start of the human world; this is what we observe.*
> *(Guessoum, 2011, pp. 307–8)*

The dynamic understanding of the natural order in Ibn Khaldun's descriptions stands in striking contrast to the more static perceptions of the Great Chain of Being which can also be found in other Muslim as well as later Christian sources. The ideas of struggle between animal kinds, of food-chains, and of adapting to different environments are all there in the biological writings of authors such as al-Jahiz and Ibn Khaldun.

Al-Jahiz was certainly not the only Islamic scholar who drew attention to the argument from design. One of the important natural philosophers and translators in the ninth-century Baghdad community was al-Kindi who wrote that "the orderly and wonderful phenomena of nature could not be purposeless and accidental" (Aftab, 2000). Much later the famous philosopher and theologian Abu Hamid al-Ghazali (1058–1111), born in the province of Korasan, now in Iran, wrote a book called *The Wisdom in God's Creation/Creatures*, pointing out the many ways in which structures and aspects of the living world fulfilled God's purposes and intentions. As al-Ghazali writes: "These are clear arguments that point toward their maker, their masterly and eternal design point to the extent of knowledge of their creator, and their arrangement aspects point to the intentions of their producer" (Guessoum, 2011, p. 228).

In our present context, most striking in the writings of these early Islamic natural philosophers is their deep conviction that all things in creation exist by the will of Allah, the pinnacle of creation being humankind. To understand that creation better, it was perfectly acceptable to utilize the imports of "foreign philosophy", such as the ancient Greek texts, provided that they were subservient to the Qur'an and interpreted within its framework. The tacit purpose of the living world, of biology, is to serve humankind, reflected in the great advances in the Islamic world in the applied sciences such as agriculture, crop-breeding, and tree-grafting. Ibn al-Awwan was a twelfth-century agriculturalist who flourished in Spain and his work, *The Book of Agriculture*, contained detailed sections concerning animal husbandry and bee-keeping. But in parallel with these more practical works we find a deep conviction, as illustrated by the writings of Ibn Rushd, al-Kindi, al-Ghazali, and others, that the living world is designed by Allah to demonstrate his wisdom. As Ibn Rushd expressed it: "… the artifact is not a product of nature but rather the creation by an artisan who ordered each thing in its place…" (Guessoum, 2011, p. 219). Purpose is imposed by Allah from outside, not an intrinsic "product of nature" as in much Greek philosophy.

The European Middle Ages

Our focus here will be on the "High Middle Ages", the period 1000–1500. Long gone (hopefully!) is the idea that these centuries were some kind of "dark age" in which nothing much happened of intellectual interest. Down the centuries, people have often been rude about the era preceding their own, sometimes out of ignorance, but mostly to highlight the value of the truth and light now available in their own wonderful century. In any event, the medieval period was a time of great intellectual ferment during which some of the groundwork was laid for the flourishing of the "early modern" scientific movement which characterized the sixteenth and seventeenth centuries (Hannam, 2009).

"Reading the texts" of nature and of Scripture

There was plenty of interest in the living world during the medieval period, but it was not "biology" as we know it. The Latin West had inherited from Augustine a powerful sense that science was the "handmaiden of theology", meaning that theological and moral considerations should always be primary when looking at the natural world. This was accompanied by a strongly allegorical way of reading the "book of nature" which can be traced back long before Augustine to the early church father Origen (c.185–c.254) (Harrison, 1998, pp. 15–20). Drawing on Plato, Origen insisted that "Each of the manifest things is to be related to one of those that are hidden… all things visible have some invisible likeness and pattern." It was by exposing the spiritual realities of the physical world that it could be rendered intelligible. As Harrison summarizes this position: "What becomes important about the features of the visible world is not how they function, nor how they interact causally, but what they signify"; "With Origen, the method of allegory was raised to the level of a science" (Harrison, 1998, pp. 17–18).

This approach to the natural world did not at all deny the usefulness of food, agriculture, animal husbandry, and the like, but all this was deemed good only for the body, something that even pagans could discover. What was far more important, however, for Origen was the spiritual meaning of physical realities that, once uncovered, then became food for the soul. This might not always be apparent, as Origen himself admitted, commenting that the ultimate "purpose" or "intention" of the creator, which had been "concealed in each individual being", could not always be fully known in this present life.

The way in which Origen's allegorical approach impacted on the interpretation of the living world may be seen most clearly in *Physiologus*, written by a contemporary of Origen, which provided a summary of what was then known about animals, plants, and stones. This hugely influential work, translated into many languages, gave living things symbolic interpretations. Pelicans, for example, strike their offspring for being rebellious, but then weep over them for three days lamenting the ones they have killed. On the third day, the mother strikes her side and spills her blood over their dead bodies and the blood itself then awakens them from death. This extraordinary account (to modern ears) then became, in the hands of the author, an enduring symbol of Christ's atonement.[5]

Origen's Platonized version of the Christian interpretation of the world was continued and extended by Augustine in the fifth century, who proposed that knowledge of things in the world, such as animals and plants, was important insofar as they helped the reader to understand Scripture better. Augustine pointed to the serpent, an example found in the *Physiologus*, explaining that unless someone knows something about serpents (snakes), it is hard to interpret their deeper scriptural meanings. Nevertheless, wrote Augustine, reflecting on the description of the pelican in the *Physiologus*, it was "perhaps true, perhaps not", but in any case it was the spiritual truth that mattered. In such ways did Augustine's writings have a huge impact on the thought of the Middle Ages by making a distinction between the literal meaning of Scripture which was to be found in the unambiguous meaning of the words, in contrast to the spiritual sense of Scripture which referred to the various meanings of the objects to which they refer (Harrison, 1998, p. 28). This led to multilayered interpretations of both Scripture and the natural world, and in both contexts it was always the figurative and the allegorical meanings that came out on top, a tradition that continued on into the Middle Ages.

Visit the ancient Kykkos monastery in Cyprus (founded in the eleventh century) and there you will see a beautiful mosaic of the pelican piercing her breast in order to feed her offspring with blood. Go to Norwich Cathedral today and you will see the pelican on the lectern, or visit St Giles-in-the-Fields Anglican church in London and there you will see the pelican above the altar. Its numerous allegorical habitats still remain scattered around. As Hugh of St Victor (c.1078–1141) proclaimed: "the whole sensible world is like a book written by the finger of God" in which each of the creatures is a figure "not invented by human decision, but instituted by the divine will to manifest the invisible things of God's wisdom".[6]

Further illustrations of allegorical interpretations of the natural world may be found during the twelfth and thirteenth centuries in the popular books of birds and beasts, known as bestiaries, which were a mingling of fact and legend. Dragons, unicorns, and griffins can be found together with bears, lions, and elephants. When describing the phoenix, the Aberdeen Bestiary informs us that "Faith in the resurrection to come is no more of a miracle than the resurrection of the phoenix from its ashes."[7] The hard flesh of the peacock represents the mind of teachers who remain unaffected by the flames of lust. The female viper conceives by taking the male's head in her mouth. She then bites off his head and he dies. When the young are ready to be born, they bite through their mother's side, and she dies. From such unpromising beginnings the Aberdeen Bestiary then launches into reflections on marriage, exhorting males that "God wished you to govern the weaker sex, not rule it absolutely. Return her care with attention; return her love with grace."[8] The bestiaries were a lot more entertaining than the biology textbooks I remember from school.

For a thousand years of Christian history, "purpose" in the living world centred around the allegorical and spiritual meanings of its inhabitants. That gave a high value to plants and animals, but more because of what they represented than for their intrinsic value. How attitudes gradually began to change is a fascinating story.

The translation of ancient texts

In the late eleventh century, a Benedictine monk called Constantine made his way to the monastery of Monte Cassino in southern Italy. There he began to translate medical works from Arabic to Latin, the language of European academia – these included the works of Galen and Hippocrates, so supplying the foundations of medical literature on which the West would build for several centuries, along with the great medical treatises from the Muslim world, such as those of Avicenna.

These early translations whetted the European appetite for more just as the translation process had stimulated Islamic thinkers back in ninth-century Baghdad. Beginning in the first half of the twelfth century, translation of ancient classical works into Latin, first from Arabic, later from the original Greek, became a major scholarly activity, with Spain as the main geographical focus. By the thirteenth century a flood of works by Aristotle was translated,[9] and the European academic world reeled before this onslaught of new knowledge. A fourteenth-century natural philosopher had a better library of Greek classics at his fingertips than did Augustine writing back in the early fifth century.

As already mentioned in the Islamic context, our minds are so geared to viewing what is modern as being intrinsically better, in contrast to those things which are "old and irrelevant", that it is difficult to think our way back into the mindset of medieval science. For us, the translation of an ancient text would be of great potential historical significance, but we would be unlikely to look to it as a source of scientific information. For the medieval world, it was the reverse: the ancients were looked to as the supreme authorities in matters of philosophy, and "science" therefore became the analysis and illustration of what the great philosophers taught. Nevertheless, it should not be imagined that the waves of Greek philosophy which flooded into medieval Europe were merely passively accepted. Quite the reverse, new translations became the objects of passionate debate, and occasionally, as in thirteenth-century Paris, the church made some temporary attempts to suppress the newly translated philosophy insofar as it ran counter to central tenets of Christian doctrine.

But what was more common was the attempt to fuse the ancient learning with Christian theology, and the person who perhaps did more than any other to combine Aristotle with Christian teaching was the Italian Dominican friar, St Thomas Aquinas (c.1224–74), whose absorption of Aristotle into medieval theology formed a system which came to be known as "scholasticism" by later philosophers. In the process, Aquinas Christianized Aristotle to a large degree. For example, Aristotle believed that matter was eternal, in contrast to the Christian doctrine that God had created the universe *ex nihilo* (out of nothing), and he had no belief in a God resembling the personal creator God of Christian theology, but Aquinas firmly maintained these key Christian doctrines. The challenge was not how to eradicate Aristotelian influence, but how to domesticate it (Lindberg, 1992, p. 224).

Aristotle's biological writings, including *On the Parts of Animals* and *On the Generation of Animals*, were translated from Arabic into Latin during the second decade of the thirteenth century. These were accompanied by a flood of translations from the great Muslim scholars such as Avicenna's medical works and the works of Ibn al-Haytham during the twelfth and thirteenth centuries (Iqbal, 2002, p. 18). Taken as a corpus together, the new translations contributed to a greater knowledge of the natural world, now shorn of its heavy weight of allegorical interpretation and based more on observation and systematic explanation. In turn, such works inspired the generation of a series of encyclopedias of animals and plants in the thirteenth century. One of these was written by Albertus Magnus (1206–80), Dominican teacher of Thomas Aquinas. Albertus travelled throughout Europe observing and cataloguing a wide range of plants and animals. His 26-volume *De animalibus* is first of all a commentary on Aristotle's works on animals, but Albertus also added his own observations and corrections, pointing out that Aristotle was wrong on whales and adding his own observations gleaned from "experienced fishermen". The "legendary exploits" of the pelican, he added sceptically, "have never been proved by methodical examination in a scientific manner" (Harrison, 1998, p. 65).

Gradually nature began to be seen as like a book which could and should be read alongside the sacred text of Scripture. Aquinas argued that "all our knowledge takes its rise from sensation" and that "it is the knowledge we have of creatures that enables us to use words to refer to God". Study of the world took on a religious significance in its own right, not just because of its allegorical meaning. Hugh of St Victor in the twelfth century maintained that the study of things must be a significant source of truth in its own right. "A speck of dust", wrote Robert Grosseteste, Bishop of Lincoln in the thirteenth century, "is an image of the whole universe" and "a mirror of the creator"; "wherever we look, we find vestiges of God".

Despite such modest moves towards appreciating and understanding the natural world in its own right, the biology of the time was still mostly obtained from the ancient Greek and Islamic texts. As Harrison comments: "medieval intellectual culture was pre-eminently a culture of the book" (Harrison, 1998, p. 65). Writers still tended to interpret the world around them according to the authority of the ancient writers rather than depending on their own observations. Sometimes one ancient authority was used to correct the "facts" found in another rather than by "gathering data" as we would say now. The challenge for the Encyclopedists was not to examine plants and animals themselves, but rather to ensure that all the relevant authorities had been consulted and cited. In 1559, the English physician John Geynes suggested that Galen might be in error on certain points, but for his pains was excluded from the Royal College until he admitted the error of his ways and formally recanted (Hall, 1649).

As far as the study of natural history was concerned, the situation was not helped by the dismissive attitude of some of the leading voices in Renaissance humanism. The fourteenth-century Italian scholar and poet Francesco Petrarch queried the use of "knowing the nature of quadrupeds, fowls, fishes and serpents and not knowing or even neglecting man's nature, the purpose for which we are born..." (Harrison, 2010 p. 11). The Renaissance university curriculum paid little attention to natural history; the classics, philosophy, and history received far more attention. Natural philosophy was deemed to be a more rigorous and worthwhile discipline compared to natural history because it entailed logical descriptions, whereas natural history was not looked upon as demonstrative science. Thankfully, however, change was on the way.

The early modern period (1500–1700)

The historian Peter Harrison has argued persuasively that the Reformation not only changed the way in which many people began to read the text of Scripture, but also as a consequence contributed to a change in the way that people interpreted the text of nature (Harrison, 1998, 2007, 2010). The Reformers insisted that the text of Scripture should be read according to its literal meaning, not according to the layers of allegorical meanings that were added on by its interpreters. Martin Luther wrote that "Scripture without any glosses is the sun and the whole light from which all teachers receive their light, and not vice-versa" (Harrison, 1998, p. 93). On 16 August 1513, Luther began to give a series of lectures in Wittenberg on the Psalms. They started at 6.00 a.m. and continued twice weekly until 20 October the following year. To help with his lectures, Luther had a special edition of the Psalms printed, but this one had wide blank margins on which his students could write their own notes. This might seem like an obviously helpful tool to our modern ears. But in its historical context this was a revolutionary move, because previous editions had also been characterized by wide margins, but this time filled with comments by the religious authorities of the time. Now it was the text itself which became the authority, and the interpreter was the individual student. This was "the symbolic moment of transition between ancient and modern hermeneutics" (Bruns, 1992, p. 139).[10] A further critical step in this transition was the translation of the Bible from Latin, the language of scholarship, into English and other European languages of the common people, coupled with the invention of the printing press which made the newly translated texts widely available.

John Calvin was no less robust in his aim to understand the literal meaning of the biblical text, not in any wooden literalistic way, but rejecting earlier "fanciful" allegorical interpretations. As he wrote in his *Commentary on Genesis* (reflecting on Genesis 2:8 and 6:14): "We must entirely reject the allegories of Origen, and of others like him" which has rendered "the doctrine of Scripture ambiguous and destitute of all certainty and firmness".

This new way of interpreting Scripture, rejecting the authority of the early church fathers such as Origen, went hand in hand with a deep suspicion of all the various forms of authority of the ancients, not least the authority of the early Greek philosophers such as Aristotle. Comments about the "barren Final Causes" of Francis Bacon (see the quote that heads this chapter) were not atypical of this era, the challenge to authority represented by Reformation ideas permeating into natural philosophy and political ideas and movements. Until about 1630 university statutes still prescribed penalties for infidelities to Aristotle (Harrison, 1998, p. 101). In 1654 the cleric John Webster, who wrote on many topics, including theology, chemistry, and medicine, published an influential book called *Academiarum Examen* ("Examination of the Universities") arguing for a complete reformation of the universities, writing that it is not fit "that *Authority* (whether of *Aristotle* or any other) should inchain us, but that there may be general freedom to try all things... so there may be a *Philosophical* liberty to be bound to the authority of none, but truth itself" (Harrison, 1998, p. 102).

It was common for natural philosophers of the seventeenth century to link the new way of reading Scripture with the new way of reading the natural world, both stripped of their allegorical layers of meaning. When Bishop Thomas Sprat, himself a Fellow, came to write the history of the early Royal Society in the late seventeenth century, which had only had a few decades of history at the time of writing (having received its Royal Charter in 1662), he wrote that both reformed churches and the Society "may lay equal claim to the word *Reformation*, the one having compass'd it in *Religion*, the other purposing it in *Philosophy*". Each of them, wrote Sprat, had bypassed the *"corrupt Copies"*, instead "referring themselves to the *perfect Originals* for their instruction; the one to the *Scripture*, the other to the large volume of the *Creatures"* (Harrison, 1998, p. 104). This is an echo of Bishop John Wilkins, one of the founding members of the Royal Society, who wrote that we should not be "so superstitiously devoted to Antiquity"

> *as for to take up everything as Canonical which drops from the pen of a Father, or was approved by the consent of the Ancients… It behoves everyone in the search of Truth, always to preserve a Philosophical liberty; not to be enslaved to the opinion of any man, as to think whatever he says to be infallible. We must labour to find out what things are in themselves by our own experience… not what another says of them. (Alexander, 2001, p. 98)*

Finding out about "things in themselves" became a key aspect of the scientific revolution. As Harrison summarizes this transition of thought:

> *The Protestant insistence on the literal sense of canonical texts had far-reaching, if unintended, consequences… The allegorical methods of interpretation pioneered by Philo and Origen were premised upon the notion that the things in the phenomenal world referred to by words in canonical texts actually represented, through resemblance, other things. To insist now that texts be read literally was to cut short a potentially endless chain of references in which words referred to things, and things in turn referred to other things.*

Harrison goes on to comment that "No longer were objects in the natural world linked to each other by sets of resemblances" (Harrison, 1998, p. 114).

The use of biology for design arguments

This stripping away of the metaphorical meanings of the natural world, with its new interpretation of "things in themselves" worked out "by our own experience", has sometimes been blamed for the demystification of nature or even its "despiritualization", sometimes with the accompanying claim that it was this that led to humanity's abuse of the environment, loss of meaning, and other somewhat speculative extrapolations. But such claims appear less plausible once one realizes that this revolution in thought in no way reduced the emphasis on the overall Purpose that all natural philosophers of this era maintained: that the natural world was there to demonstrate the wisdom and power of God, created for the good of humankind. The allergy towards the idea of Aristotelian final causes, so typical of the natural philosophers of the time, was due to their antipathy towards the idea that such *telos* could be intrinsic to material objects, rather than bestowed upon them by the creator God, and also to the hopelessness, as they saw it, of natural philosophers being able to investigate and come to an agreement on such "final causes", even if they existed. Hence Bacon's rude comment about "final causes" being like unproductive virgins.

The seventeenth century also saw the rise in the "mechanical philosophy", the idea that the universe, and indeed the world and all that is in it, operates on machine-like principles. Today mechanism and meaning are sometimes pitted against each other as if incompatible. Not so in the seventeenth century when the machine was always God's machine. As the Lutheran Johannes Kepler, one of the key founders of modern astronomy, expressed the point: "My aim is to show that the heavenly machine is not a kind of divine, live being, but a kind of clockwork…" (Koestler, 1967, p. 331). The Catholic René Descartes promoted the idea that animals were basically machines that lacked "rational souls". When the first secretary of the Royal Society, Robert Hooke, published his *Micrographia* in 1665, the spontaneous growth of mushrooms was explained by use of the mechanical language of "hammers", "springs", and "pins". The fact that these mechanical analogies are not the most appropriate for describing mushroom growth is beside the point. Rather it was the mechanical analogies which link Hooke's biology of the mid-seventeenth century with the genetic engineering and molecular detail of modern biology. A profound revolution in thought was taking place which eventually swept all before it. Mechanical chains of cause and effect were invoked in place of more mystical modes of thought. With this transition, purpose was switched even more starkly from the internal properties of things to the Purpose for which they were created by God.

The scholarly neglect of natural history that characterized, as already noted, the period before 1600, began to change during the seventeenth century. Theological justification provided social validation of an enterprise that had previously been deemed below the dignity of serious natural philosophers to investigate. John Ray (1627–1705), a key figure in the founding of the discipline that we now know as biology, and the one who first gave us the biological understanding of a "species", well illustrates this by his baptism of natural history into a robust theology of creation. Ray came up to Cambridge as a student at Trinity College at the age of 16, later becoming a Fellow, publishing an immense array of works describing and classifying animals and plants. In his synopsis of British plants (1690), Ray writes in his preface of his gratitude to God that he had been born in an age when, within his own memory, scholasticism had been replaced by a new philosophy based on experiment. His highly popular book *The Wisdom of God Manifested in the Works of Creation* (1691) went through five editions within 20 years of its publication. In it Ray tells us that

> *the treasures of nature are inexhaustible... Some reproach*
> *methinks it is to learned men that there should be so many*

*animals still in the world whose outward shapes is not yet taken
notice of, much less their way of Generation, Food, Manners,
Uses observed... if man ought to reflect upon his Creator the
glory of all his works, then ought he to take notice of them all.
(Harrison, 1998, p. 166)*

And "taking notice of them all" was precisely what John Ray did,
publishing, for example, three great volumes containing 2,610
folios on the classification of 18,600 plants in the years 1686–1704
and cramming his cottage in the little hamlet of Black Notley in
Essex with an immense collection of flora and fauna. At the age
of 77 Ray, now very close to the end of his long and productive
life, struggled on with his descriptions of butterflies, moths,
beetles, wasps, and flies, and recording an astonishing 300 species
of butterflies and moths within the grounds of his own very
modest cottage. The Purpose of biology was very clear for Ray:
the living world was there to bring glory to its creator by its sheer
beauty, fascination, and diversity, declaring that he had published
his *Ornithology* for "the illustration of God's glory, by exciting men
to take notice of, and admire his infinite power and wisdom" (Ray
and Willughby, 1678, p. 105).

When Hooke popularized the world of the flea to a fascinated
reading public in his *Micrographia*, he declared that the more objects
are magnified with the microscope, "the more we discover the
imperfections of our senses, and the Omnipotency and Infinite
perfections of the great Creatour" (Hooke, 1665, p. 8). The new
world revealed by the microscope made quite an impact, the French
priest Nicolas Malebranche exclaiming in a glorious example of
seventeenth-century hyperbole that "One insect is more in touch
with Divine wisdom than the whole of Greek and Roman history"
(Edwards, 1696, pt 1, pp. 204f.). But seventeenth-century writers
and beyond were not content simply to draw attention to the
wisdom of God in creation based on its wonderful properties – the

"distal Purpose" of creation. In addition, they replaced the more allegorical interpretive framework of their predecessors with strong narratives of purpose and design, in so doing providing narratives of "proximal purpose". These were no allegories but the actual purported reasons why God had brought various creatures into being, and it was up to humanity to discern what these purposes might be, purposes which might be to teach people important lessons in life. Abbé Pluche maintained that worms and flies "are employed by the Almighty to humble the Pride of Men". The Scottish preacher John Cockburn maintained that locusts and caterpillars "are a Party of the Army of the Lord of hosts, which he sends out at his Pleasure, to chastise the Pride, Wantonness, Ingratitude, and Forgetfulness of man, who is the only disorderly Part of the Creation" (Harrison, 1998, p. 162). (They were keen on spelling words with Capitals in this era.) This does seem a rather heavy responsibility for flies, locusts, etc. to bear, but such ideas were widespread at the time.

Other writers drew attention to the practical uses of living things. As the theologian and philosopher Henry More pointed out, "those *Herbs* that the rude and ignorant would call *Weeds* are the Materials of very sovereign Medicines" (Harrison, 1998, p. 164). Opium was previously looked upon as a poison, wrote the chemist Robert Boyle, but was "now imploy'd as a noble remedy" (Harrison, 1998, p. 166). Everything had its purpose in God's good creation. The idea that toads, serpents, flies, and other living things that humans find obnoxious could be used to extract poisons from the ground or air was commonly expressed. Archbishop William King pointed out that serpents "tho a Race hateful to us" nevertheless "gather Poison out of the Earth", rendering it more habitable (Harrison, 1998, p. 165). The idea that everything must be designed for a purpose led Sir John Colbatch in 1719 to discover the medical use of mistletoe, writing later of his discovery that he felt "that there must be something extraordinary in that uncommon beautiful plant;

that the Almighty had design'd it for farther and more noble uses than barely to feed thrushes… I concluded, *a priori*, that it was… very likely to subdue… epilepsy" (Thomas, 1984, p. 27). (Author's note: don't try it for anything, it's quite toxic, especially the berries.)

As Harrison comments: "While it has been maintained that teleological explanations hindered the progress of the natural sciences, in reality, the search for the 'ends' of natural things proceeded on the very practical assumption that everything in nature was in some way useful", also pointing out that whereas seventeenth-century natural philosophers vigorously rejected Aristotelian notions of final causes, they "were happy to conflate Aristotle's final causes with the 'divine purposes' of Judaeo-Christian tradition. 'Final cause' thus came to be understood not as a *telos* immanent in the natural object, but rather the purpose for which God had designed the thing" (Harrison, 1998, p. 169). The study of nature was therefore just as much a religious activity as it had been in the twelfth century, but instead of representing a vast array of symbolic meanings, God's creation was now seen as an ordered and well-designed scheme of things from which God's wisdom and providence could readily be inferred.

When Robert Boyle died in 1691 he left money in his will to endow an annual series of eight lectures to be delivered in London churches. The lectures did much to maintain the tenets of natural theology, with an emphasis on God's "design" in the universe, right up to the late nineteenth century.[11] The lectures were given from prestigious Anglican pulpits and drew large crowds. William Derham, an ordained Anglican and Fellow of the Royal Society (a normal joint status for natural philosophers of this era), who collected insects and frogs and dissected worms and fish (Thomas, 1984, p. 282), entitled his 1711–12 Boyle Lectures *Physico-Theology, or a Demonstration of the Being and Attributes of God from his Works of Creation*. "In the seventeenth and eighteenth centuries", Harrison comments, "God came to be understood as a technician, whose intricate designs were everywhere to be investigated, admired, and put to use. As author of creation, God had crafted the things of nature with a purpose rather than a meaning" (Harrison, 1998, pp. 170–71). Such tenets were once more reinforced, in Britain at least, when the Earl of Bridgewater set aside £8,000 in his will in 1829 to fund a series of volumes of natural theology, and these were eventually produced by the top natural philosophers of the day (Topham, 2010). The President of the Royal Society, no less, was designated to choose the authors. Meanwhile generations of Anglican students had the works of Archdeacon William Paley as set texts during the early decades of the nineteenth century, books centred round the tenets of natural theology.

David Hume and beyond

The providentialist natural theology of the seventeenth century, with its focus on the purposes and Purpose of biology, received a potent challenge during the eighteenth century from the Scottish philosopher David Hume (1711–76). Hume's critiques are scattered around several of his works, but receive most attention in his *Dialogues Concerning Natural Religion* (1779, Parts II–VIII, XII; Hume, 1990). In the *Dialogues*, Cleanthes defends the argument from design as a means to infer God's existence and attributes, whereas Philo generally represents Hume's own more critical position. Philo never denies the existence of God but argues that human minds can never be sufficient to infer the attributes of God, particularly starting with reason and observations of the natural world. The details of all the various arguments to and fro need not detain us here,[12] but it is worth noting that Cleanthes set himself up for an obvious and later Darwinian riposte (with the benefit of hindsight) when he claims that:

> *The curious adapting of means to ends, throughout all nature, resembles exactly, though it much exceeds, the productions of*

*human contrivance; of human design, thought, wisdom, and
intelligence. Since, therefore, the effects resemble each other, we
are led to infer, by all the rules of analogy, that the causes also
resemble; and that the Author of Nature is somewhat similar
to the mind of man, though possessed of much larger faculties,
proportioned to the grandeur of the work which he has executed.*[13]

In the context of the *Dialogues*, Philo (Hume) takes Cleanthes to
task on philosophical grounds (successfully or not, let the reader
judge[14]). But the point in our present context is that the argument
is a hostage to fortune once Darwin comes on the scene, and some
of Paley's design arguments were likewise fragile in this respect as
we discuss further below.

While Hume was composing clever dialogues in Scotland, the
so-called *philosophes* were busy attacking institutionalized religion in
France. The *philosophes* were a heterogeneous collection of writers
and philosophers who, during the eighteenth century, popularized
the findings of the natural philosophers to the French public. Most,
but not all, were deists. Francois Arouet, better known under his
pen name of Voltaire (1694–1778), engaged in fiery and satirical
campaigns either for or against particular causes (Voltaire was
not one to sit on the fence). Exiled in London, Voltaire became
deeply influenced by the empirical philosophy of John Locke
and by the natural philosophy of Isaac Newton, whose funeral
Voltaire attended in Westminster Abbey. Returning to France,
Voltaire popularized Newtonianism in his *Elements de la Philosophie
de Newton* (1738). While the great and the good of London life
learned about Newton's theories from the pulpits of respectable
Anglican churches, the French learned about Newton through
Voltaire the anti-Catholic crusader. It should not be thought from
Voltaire's anti-clericalism that he was an atheist. Far from it, Voltaire
campaigned vigorously against atheism, pointing out in the opening
pages of his popularized version of Newton's views that "the

entire philosophy of Newton necessarily leads to the knowledge of a supreme Being, who has created everything and arranged everything freely" (Copleston, 2003, p. 20). Voltaire's arguments for the existence of God were those of traditional natural theology, and in his *Dictionnaire Philosophique* Voltaire carries on an imaginary debate with an atheist in which he maintains that God's intelligent design was demonstrated "as much in the meanest insect as in the planets... The disposition of a fly's wings or of the feelers of a snail is sufficient to confound you" – shades of seventeenth-century English physico-theology. Yet Voltaire's framing for his arguments for design was far from the providentialist accounts of the English natural philosophers in which an active creator God sustains the whole world of biology. Voltaire's deistic concept of God was the remote lawgiver who set up the rational universe governed by Newtonian mechanics, but who then had nothing more to do with the world, convenient as a philosophical construct and to act as a justification for social order, but no more.

Other *philosophes* were ardent materialists, a development hastened by startling scientific discoveries which appeared to undermine the arguments of natural theology. In 1740, it was observed that a hydra behaved like an animal, although it produced buds like a plant. When cut into pieces, new hydra could develop spontaneously out of the pieces. This discovery led to a flurry of speculation about the origins of life and the nature of animal souls. Was the soul of the hydra divisible? Was this an example of matter acting independently of God? The debate was intensified by the findings of John Needham, an English Catholic priest, in 1745, when he thought that he had demonstrated conclusively the emergence of moving microscopic animals by spontaneous generation from a sample of heated gravy inside a sealed vessel. It took a further century before this observation was shown to be incorrect (clearly the air inside had not been as sterile as he thought). Such experiments were threatening to the tenets of natural theology, since they appeared to show that matter could spontaneously organize itself into life, whereas the natural theologians thought that the creation of life could only occur by special divine action. Voltaire poured scorn on Needham, accusing him of atheism and saying that his observations must be mistaken.

A French doctor called Julien de La Mettrie (1709–51) was very impressed by the new data which appeared to support the idea that matter organized itself spontaneously, publishing his *L'Homme Machine* ("Man the Machine") in 1747 anonymously in the Netherlands. La Mettrie concluded that if nature was spontaneously active, then living matter was "nothing but" a machine and there was no need for a god. La Mettrie's book was soon banned in France for its rigorous materialism, and La Mettrie himself (who clearly did not manage to stay anonymous for long) was forced to seek refuge with Frederick the Great of Prussia. Descartes had warned long before that people might extend his theory of animal machines to man, and so promote atheism. La Mettrie fulfilled Descartes' worst forebodings, maintaining that man was just another piece of machinery like the animals, and that priests were motivated only by prejudice and fanaticism in thinking otherwise.

A thoroughgoing materialism was expounded most eloquently during this period by Baron d'Holbach (1723–89), a German who passed most of his life in Paris in the circle of the *philosophes*. D'Holbach's *Système de la Nature* (1770) argued that matter was inherently moving and active, and that no outside force was needed to set it in motion. Just as microscopic animals could spontaneously arise from organic matter, so man also could appear by spontaneous generation. Far from nature being governed by chance, d'Holbach saw matter as being governed by a rigid determinism. The idea of creation was against reason, since the mind could not conceive of a time when nothing had existed, and neither could it conceive of a time when everything would have disappeared. As Goodman comments:

> *D'Holbach's work is remarkable less for its originality than for its extreme opinions. Perhaps as clearly as any other work of the period, it developed that tendency of 18th century French thought to exclude God from Nature. Nothing could be further removed from the type of natural philosophy which was determined to discover God everywhere in Nature.* (Hooykaas, 1974, Block 3 Units 6–8, p. 51)

In Britain, the arguments of the *philosophes* made little headway until the twentieth century and the tenets of natural theology remained popular until at least the middle of the nineteenth century. Materialistic philosophies associated with the French Revolution were generally treated with deep suspicion. But they provided narratives in which biology was no longer an arena in which to demonstrate the power and wisdom of God in creation. Biology still retained its teleological language for the proximal purposes of creatures – all those various purposeful adaptations required for being alive – but the idea that the living world had a broader Purpose faded from view. The philosophy of d'Holbach, which seemed so scandalous in its day, became the "new normal" for many during the course of the twentieth century.

Darwin and Purposeless biology

Charles Darwin (1809–82) was no materialist, at least not of the French radical variety, and was raised a Christian with the tenets of natural theology playing an important role in his university education. As a student at Cambridge it was his parents' expectation that Darwin would end up as a priest of the Anglican church. During the period when Darwin was a student (1828–31) all education at Cambridge (as at Oxford), including the teaching of science, was carried out by ordained Anglican clergy, and more than 50% of the students at that time were destined for the Anglican ministry. In his final exams, Darwin did particularly well on the theology papers, and on his own reckoning it was this that helped him become tenth out of 178 men taking the "ordinary degree" (so-called because it avoided a lot of maths, a subject which Darwin disliked). Both final and earlier exams covered two texts by Archdeacon William Paley, the great proponent of natural theology, and after his final exams were over Darwin proceeded to read for his own enjoyment Paley's *Natural Theology or Evidences of the Existence and Attributes of the Deity*, which set out to refute David Hume's argument that "design" by a creator was merely a human projection onto the forces of nature. In his autobiography Darwin later reflected that:

> *I am convinced that I could have written out the whole of the Evidences with perfect correctness, but not of course in the clear language of Paley. The logic of this book, and, as I may add, of his Natural Theology, gave me as much delight as did Euclid. The careful study of these works... was the only part of the academical course which, as I then felt, and as I still believe, was of the least use to me in the education of my mind.*[15]

One of the passages that Darwin would have read in Paley's *Natural Theology* may, with the benefit of hindsight, be viewed as remarkably prescient of precisely the biological problem that Darwin was later to address so effectively. As Paley mulled over the way in which organisms are well adapted to their environments, he wrote:

> *There is another answer which has the same effect as the resolving of things into chance, which answer would persuade us to believe that the eye, the animal to which it belongs, every other animal, every plant, indeed every organized body which we see are only so many out of the possible varieties and combinations of being which the lapse of infinite ages has brought into existence; that the present world is the relic of that variety; millions of other*

bodily forms and other species having perished, being, by the defect of their constitution, incapable of preservation, or of continuance by generation. (Paley, 1833, p. 449)

Paley rejected such a possibility, partly because he could not conceive of such countless numbers of species disappearing when extant animals in general seemed so adaptable to their environments. Much later, Darwin was to revive a very similar idea, an idea which he called "natural selection". Could there have been some subliminal influence here in Darwin's mind as he mulled over his new theory in the decades after leaving Cambridge? Maybe, especially given Darwin's thorough immersion in Paley's works while a student, although there is no evidence from Darwin's own writings that this was the case. Darwin himself lost his faith in later life, calling himself an "agnostic" after his friend Thomas Henry Huxley had invented the word in 1869. But as the historian and biographer of Darwin, James Moore, comments: "Darwin's understanding of nature never departed from a theological point of view. Always, I believe, until his dying day, at least half of him believed in God."

Darwin always maintained that evolution was compatible with religious belief, pointing to his friend Asa Gray, Professor of Natural History at Harvard and a committed Christian, as an example. Darwin was certainly no atheist (Spencer, 2009). But to a large degree it was his theory that killed off any idea of a broader Purpose for evolution, mainly because of the role that "chance variation" was perceived to play in his theory and, perhaps even more so, because adaptations engineered by natural selection subverted one of the key arguments of a certain form of natural theology, namely, the understanding that complex organs like the eye, the human brain, and so forth were due to God's direct creative action.

As far as "chance" was concerned, Darwin's first readers of *On the Origin of Species* (1859) were quick to spot language that to them seemed to confirm that natural selection was a random and non-directed process. For example, in reflecting on the way that plant breeding occurred in horticulture, Darwin wrote (with my italics added) that "It has consisted in always cultivating the best known variety, sowing its seeds, and, when a slightly better variety has *chanced* to appear, selecting it, and so onwards" (Darwin, 1859, p. 24). In writing about the "struggle for life", Darwin summarized his theory in these words:

> *any variation, however slight and from whatever cause proceeding, if it be in any degree profitable to an individual of any species... will tend to the preservation of that individual, and will generally be inherited by its offspring. The offspring, also, will thus have a better chance of surviving, for, of the many individuals of any species which are periodically born, but a small number can survive. I have called this principle, by which each slight variation, if useful, is preserved, by the term of Natural Selection, in order to mark its relation to man's power of selection. (p. 40)*

"Variation is a very slow process, and natural selection can do nothing until favourable variations *chance to occur*" (p. 114). In another passage, Darwin emphasizes that using the word "chance" to explain the origin of variation is "a wholly incorrect expression", since it simply expresses "our ignorance of the cause of each particular variation" (ch. 5). Nothing was known about genetics as Darwin wrote his great book.

Critics tended to ignore Darwin's cautious use of the word chance when discussing the origins of variation and the survival of some individual organisms over others. John Herschel (1792–1871), mathematician, astronomer, and polymath, was one of the most famous natural philosophers (scientists) of his era and referred to by Darwin himself in the *Origin* as "one of our greatest philosophers", someone for whom Darwin had huge respect. This helps explain why Darwin was so upset when, having read the *Origin*, Herschel referred to his new theory as the "law of higgledy-piggledy" (Carey, 2004). Darwin was deeply disappointed by this comment, writing to his friend the geologist Charles Lyell: "What exactly this means I do not know, but evidently it is very contemptuous. If true this is a great blow and discouragement."[16] To be fair on Herschel, as a brilliant mathematician, the (to him) messy biological theory simply didn't have the mathematical elegance that he expected to see in a physical law. In any case, he had written years earlier to Charles Lyell (in 1836) to say that God does not act by a "miraculous process", but by a "natural" series of "intermediate causes". It was not the natural processes that Herschel was worried about, more that the theory just looked so inelegant.

Much water has flowed under the bridge since Darwin first penned his theory, and it is a distinctly different theory today than it was in 1859. Ironically, given Herschel's mathematically based misgivings, after natural selection as a mechanism for evolution had gone into decline following Darwin's death in 1882, it was mathematicians who came to the rescue, baptizing natural selection into population genetics in a fusion that we now call the "neo-Darwinian synthesis". Three famous figures were associated with this shift in thinking: the British Marxist J.B.S. Haldane, the Anglican British eugenicist R.A. Fisher, and the American Sewall Wright who was a professor at the University of Chicago – an eclectic group indeed. Biologists at that time were so unused to mathematical treatments of their subject that Fisher's first paper submitted to the journal of the London Royal Society was turned down because no one could understand it! However, once explained, it was clear that this new approach was very useful, and it has been so ever since.

The idea of biological adaptations appearing by natural selection in place of God's direct design was clearly a killer blow to those espousing the kind of natural theology that perceived God's direct actions as a kind of "explanation" of certain features of living creatures. If adaptations arose as a result of natural selection operating on chance variations, what room was there for God as an explanation for the specific design features of living creatures? Presumably without realizing it, the enthusiasts for natural theology had ended up viewing the origin of design features as if God were just one more force among many acting in the world, a kind of "designer-of-the-gaps". Or at least as a heavenly engineer who occasionally tinkered around with bits of the creation to make it work better. Both ideas are mistaken as viewed from the perspective of traditional creation theology as we will consider further in Chapter 5. Had the enthusiasts for the "biological design" argument read their Bibles more carefully, perhaps with a bit of Augustine, Aquinas, and Calvin thrown in for good measure, they wouldn't have ended up being such "hostages to fortune" of their own making. For the moment, we may simply note that some Christian theologians were delighted by Darwin's theory precisely because it subverted the rather rationalistic engineering concept of God bequeathed to them by several centuries of biological design arguments. The more such arguments had been deployed in the kind of debates generated by Hume – and Paley saw his works in large part as ripostes to Hume – the less did the God being defended seem like the God portrayed in biblical theology. As the Oxford Anglo-Catholic Aubrey Moore (1843–90), theologian, fellow of St John's College, Oxford, and curator of the Oxford Botanical Gardens, commented: "Darwinism appeared, and, under the guise of a foe, did the work of a friend" (Moore, 1891, p. 73). Precisely how Moore could be so positive, and why it was so easy for the Christian community in general to baptize evolution into the traditional understanding of God as creator, is a topic that we will pursue further in Chapter 5.

But for the moment we note that as far as wider public perceptions were concerned, it was the image of evolution as a "chance process", coupled with the idea that the theory had killed off the design argument, that most reinforced the idea that evolutionary biology must be a purposeless narrative. In the second half of the nineteenth century, the professionalization of science gathered pace and the science and faith, which had previously been so integrated, now increasingly began to go their separate ways. Theological concerns became much less prominent in the teaching of science. At the same time, the mainstream Christian denominations continued to embrace evolution, taught in church schools all round the country (in the UK), but in more secular discourse the assumption that evolution could not have any ultimate Purpose became an implicit or explicit assumption.

As the religious framing of evolution declined, Darwin's theory was utilized in support of virtually every twentieth-century ideology then in vogue, including capitalism, communism, racism, militarism, eugenics, feminism, theism, atheism, and many other "isms" besides (Alexander and Numbers, 2010). As George Bernard Shaw once quipped: Darwin "had the luck to please everybody who had an axe to grind". Evolution has attracted to itself ideologies like barnacles and weeds sticking to a ship's bottom. The "purpose" of biology has too often been transformed into a social or political purpose, often obscuring the real content of the scientific theory in the process. In 1970, the French molecular biologist Jacque Monod published *Chance and Necessity* (Monod, 1997) in which he argued that since evolution was based on chance, so the universe was one in which Chance ruled. Monod concludes: "Man knows now that he is like a gypsy camping on the edge of the universe where he must live. The universe is deaf to his music, indifferent to his hopes, as to his suffering or his crimes" (Alexander, 2001, p. 339). Quite how one can infer all that from molecular biology is not quite clear.

In the early years of the twenty-first century, so-called "new atheists" in the tradition of Monod started making all kinds of ideological extrapolations out of biology, evolutionary biology in particular, in the process tending to alienate large sections of the scientific community who generally don't think this is a good strategy for the public understanding of science (Johnson et al., 2016). And so we come to the "evolution is necessarily purposeless" type of comments already cited in the Introduction. All that's needed now is a bit of clipping of the ideological wings so that the "bird of evolutionary biology" can fly onwards and upwards, unencumbered by such a load of ideological baggage. Fortunately, science itself is of help in that respect as the next two chapters will illustrate. The aim here is definitely not some attempt to reinstate religious arguments derived from biological design or teleology. Nor is our aim, it should once again be emphasized, to suggest that Purpose can be inferred from biology, but rather the more modest claim that when you stand back and look at the evolutionary process as a whole, it just doesn't look "necessarily purposeless". At least if that particular ideological extrapolation out of biology has its wings clipped, it will then be possible to move on and have a more informed discussion about biology and theology.

2

Biology's Grand Narrative

I am impressed by how similarly evolution turns out when it is allowed to run twice.

Richard Dawkins, *The Ancestor's Tale* (2016), p. 600

The brief historical introduction provided in the previous chapter should at least flag up the point that ideas about purpose in biology have been remarkably fluid over the centuries, with various nuances of meaning depending on the era and its cultural, philosophical, and religious context. With that as background, we are now in a better position to return to the question posed in the Introduction: "Is it *necessarily* the case that biology in general, and the evolutionary process in particular, tells us that it has no purpose?" Looked at historically and sociologically, as noted above it is fairly easy to see how the claim that biology is necessarily purposeless came to be made, and even assumed, at this particular time and place in history. But this chapter has a different emphasis. What happens when we look at the general features of biological evolution – the overall "grand narrative" – in the light of the claim that it is necessarily purposeless? What do we actually observe?

Increased complexity

As we consider the 3.8 billion years of evolution as a whole, the striking increase in biological complexity is pretty obvious. For the first 2.5 billion years of life on Earth, things only rarely got bigger than 1 millimetre across, about the size of a pinhead. No birds, no flowers, no animals wandering around, no fish in the sea, but at the genetic level there was lots going on, with the generation of many of the genes and biochemical systems that were later used to such effect to build the bigger, more interesting living things that we see all around us today. As a biochemist, I would love to use a time-machine to travel back to the time when living things were only 1 millimetre across, although I think most people would have found the planet pretty boring at that time. But then gradually the oxygen levels in the atmosphere increased by photosynthesis to the point at which more complex life-forms could be sustained.

Today our atmosphere contains 21% oxygen, but for the first half of the Earth's 4.6 billion years' history there was not much around, generally less than 0.001% (Lyons et al., 2014). A permanent rise in oxygen did not take place until between 2.4 and 2.1 billion years ago, known as the Great Oxidation Event, remembering that the word "event" for geophysicists can be somewhat drawn out. The photosynthesis that takes place in organisms such as green algae in which light energy is converted into chemical energy is the only known process that can generate free oxygen into the Earth's atmosphere. Yet it has proved remarkably difficult to pin down when the first photosynthesizing organisms evolved, with estimates ranging from 3.8 to 2.35 billion years ago (Lyons et al., 2014). Furthermore, metals like iron found in rocks use up the oxygen by becoming oxidized as soon as the oxygen becomes available. Oxygen is also taken up into the oceans (otherwise there would be no fish). So the actual oxygen in the atmosphere depends on a finely tuned balance between production and consumption. This is why the Great Oxidation Event does not necessarily coincide with the time when photosynthesis really got going. Indeed, the whys and wherefores of the Earth's historical oxygen levels are complex, even though the broad picture is now rather well understood (Lyons et al., 2014).

What is clear is that carbon-based living organisms need oxygen if they are going to become more complex because oxygen enables the production of far more usable energy than anaerobic (oxygen-free) metabolic processes. Complexity is energy hungry.

One of the key stages in the development of increased complexity was the transition to multicellularity. Once multicellularity evolves, there is huge scope for increased specialization in cell functions and in the construction of organs. Many bacteria only have one cell-type, but there are seven different types in mushrooms (an evolutionarily ancient fungus), around 50 in fruit flies, and today we humans have more than 200 different tissues – collections of cells with the same specialized functions. There is good evidence that multicellular forms of life have evolved many times independently from all three forms of single-celled life, the bacteria, the archaea and the eukaryotes (Carroll, 2001). This was all beginning to happen around 1.6 billion years ago, although dating such processes is not easy. The earliest fossil evidence for multicellular life-forms, in this case algae, dates from that period (Zhu et al., 2016). By around 1 billion years ago microbial fossils are found on land – until this time all life of any kind was in the sea and the land was barren.

Many people are puzzled by how multicellular life can evolve. It seems a big jump to get from single cells to a multicellular organism. But in fact certain single-celled organisms seem to have evolved in this direction quite often. Multicellularity has evolved at least 20 times since life began and a striking example of this transition is provided by the volvocine algae. Figure 1 shows that multicellular volvocine algae first started appearing around 220 million years ago. Somewhere at some time a single-celled alga divided and the two daughter cells remained embedded in a chemical known as a glycoprotein (extracellular matrix). So from now on this chemical binding meant that different cells had to contribute to the common good, at least as far as that organism was concerned. It is then possible to track through the fossil record what happened next. Different cells became specialized for different functions already by 200 million years ago. Some cells started specializing in motility, in movement, and so they had to sacrifice their own reproduction. As the author of a recent review comments: "The importance of cooperation, conflict and conflict mediation in the early stages of the transition is likely a general principle for origins of multicellularity" (Herron, 2009).

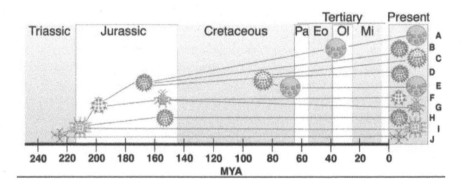

Figure 1. The development of single-cell volvocine algae into multicellular organisms.

Once multicellularity got going in evolutionary history, living things started getting bigger, but initially not by much. With the flourishing of the late Ediacaran fauna (named after the Australian hills where their fossils were first found) during the period 575–543 million years ago, we move into the centimetre scale. Only in the so-called "Cambrian explosion" during the period 525–505 million years ago, and onward from that period, did the size of animals begin to increase dramatically. The Cambrian explosion has drawn particular attention because it refers to that "explosion" of new animal life-forms and body plans that began to appear from about 525 million years ago onwards, and it is from these that virtually all

61

the animals were derived with which we are familiar today. Today we have creatures like ourselves with our brains with 10^{11} neurons[17] with their 10^{14} synaptic connections or more, the most complex known entities in the universe.

As the evolutionary biologist Sean Carroll from the University of Wisconsin-Madison remarks in a *Nature* review:

> *Life's contingent history could be viewed as an argument against any direction or pattern in the course of evolution or the shape of life. But it is obvious that larger and more complex life-forms have evolved from simple unicellular ancestors and that various innovations were necessary for the evolution of new means of living. This raises the possibility that there are trends within evolutionary history that might reflect the existence of general principles governing the evolution of increasingly larger and more complex forms. (Carroll, 2001)*

So the question is whether the evolution of the shapes of life represent a random walk through all possible shapes and sizes, or whether there are physical constraints arising from physics, genetics, and development that channel evolution in certain prescribed directions.

In biology, increased complexity generally refers to a higher number of cell-types or to the number of parts of an animal or plant, leading in both cases to an increase in specialized functions. Complexity can also refer to the variety and interrelationships of species of plants and animals with their accompanying food-chains and competition for similar ecological niches. Figure 2 illustrates the striking increase in the variety of species during the past 540 million years, together with the increase in the number of genera.[18] In fact, the extent of diversification varies rather widely across the living world (Scholl and Wiens, 2016). Species richness, meaning the total number of species within a given group, varies by as much as one millionfold between different groups. But the main point in our present context is that, taken overall, evolutionary history has seen a huge increase in complexity as assessed by the sheer diversity of plants and animals. It is the "big picture" which is so striking.

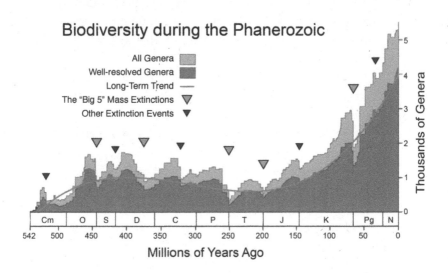

Figure 2. Increase in diversity of biological families over a 545-million-year period since the Cambrian explosion. The term 'Phanerozoic' refers to all the geological eras since the beginning of the Cambrian period. The letters above the numbers of millions refer to the other geological era since the Cambrian.

Increased complexity can also be assessed by studies of the evolutionary development of changes in morphology, referring to the structure and organization of animals. Overall increases in complexity have also been described within specific groups of animals that have continued their evolution since the Cambrian era. For example, the crustaceans are a major group within the arthropods, animals that have no backbone (vertebra). Measuring the number and type of limbs provides a good measure of increased complexity and can be readily assessed from the fossil record. When 66 different taxa[19] of crustaceans were studied over the whole period since the start of the Cambrian, a striking increase in appendage complexity was observed, as measured by the number of limb-types (Adamowicz et al., 2008). Similar increases in complexity have likewise been tracked through evolutionary time in a wide variety of other animal groupings, as widely diverse as molluscan shells (Vermeij, 1973) and parrot head shapes (Tokita et al., 2007).

A further example of increasing complexity in evolutionary time comes from studies on types of skeletal structure. It has been estimated that there are around 180 different types of skeletal structure in the animal kingdom (rigid or pliable, internal or external, etc.). Already by the early stage of the Cambrian explosion, 146 of these different types were in use and have been observed in fossils from the famous Burgess Shale fossil-beds found in the Canadian Rockies (Thomas et al., 2000). This means that more than 80% of the skeletal designs that ever evolved did so within the first 6% of overt animal history (Carroll, 2001).

A quite different approach to the study of increased complexity is by investigating bacterial evolution in real time in the laboratory. Studying major evolutionary change in animals is tricky because we reproduce so slowly. Such is not the case with single-celled organisms like bacteria, which can divide every 20 minutes on a warm sunny day in a cream-bun – something to keep in mind when considering one's next cream-bun. In 1988 Richard Lenski and colleagues, now at Michigan State University, started an experiment on bacterial evolution which continues to the present day, more than 50,000 generations later (Wiser et al., 2013; Tenaillon et al., 2016). The Lenski lab started growing a series of 12 populations of the bacterium *Escherichia coli*, all derived from a single bacterium and fed using glucose. The evolution of different strains of these bacteria from the original parental cells has been tracked ever since. With 6.6 new generations of *E. coli* per day (not quite as fast as in cream-buns), this experiment gives us the equivalent of a year's worth of mouse reproduction, or more than a million years of human evolution. Each day about half a billion new bacteria grow in each flask, involving the replication of the same number of bacterial genomes, and in total about a million mutations occur in each flask as the bacteria divide.[20] Since there are only about 5 million nucleotides in the bacterial genome, this means that every few days virtually the whole genome will be subject to genetic analysis to see whether any of the new mutations might be useful. In practice, the vast majority are not, but new mutations occasionally come along that provide some growth advantages.

During the whole experiment so far, reproductive fitness[21] of the bugs has increased by an average 70%, meaning that they undergo an average 1.7 doublings in the time it took to replicate just once in the original population. But the increased fitness is due to different advantageous mutations in each flask. Most strikingly, after more than a decade of sub-culturing the 12 flasks, something rather extraordinary happened at generation number 33,127. One of the cultures "discovered" how to use citrate as a food source, a chemical used to stabilize the pH and so present in all the flasks since the beginning. It was like a population of cats suddenly taking a liking to whisky (assuming an unlimited supply), and it gave this population a huge growth advantage as it was no longer dependent upon glucose as a food source. This critical event happened in only one of the 12 flasks, and it took more than ten years to show up (involving a lot of work, see Figure 3). Further analysis revealed that the capacity to use citrate could not evolve all in one step, but took three different mutations to achieve. The two "background" mutations had to occur first, and the third critical mutation then enabled the complete ensemble of three mutations to allow the use of citrate, thereby opening up a whole new way of living for the colony. The key mutation involves the duplication of a stretch of DNA, 2,933 genetic letters long, that activates an otherwise silent gene which encodes for a protein transporter that shuttles citrate into the bugs. The result is that 99% of the colony goes on to use citrate, whereas about 1% have become "glucose specialists", stubbornly refusing to forsake their original food source. This wonderful experiment highlights the need for multiple cooperative variant genes to emerge together in order to generate a selective advantage, and it also shows how one key mutation can open up a whole new landscape of evolutionary possibilities.

Figure 3. Zachary Blount in the Lenski laboratory used all these petri dishes to show how one colony of bacteria evolved to use citrate.

At the beginning of these experiments, many thought that the outcome would be boring – keep bacterial colonies in the same culture media day after day and there would be little chance of significant change. But the sceptics have been proved wrong – evolution just carries on regardless and fitness goes on increasing. In fact, six of the bacterial populations mutated to "hyper-mutable" phenotypes, meaning that their mutation rates went up a hundredfold, thereby greatly increasing their rate of evolution. Furthermore, most of the mutations that occurred were beneficial, showing that they bestowed adaptive benefits to that particular population, and new mutations open up new opportunities for new advances (Tenaillon et al., 2016).

So whether at the level of single-celled organisms such as bacteria, or in the tendency for single-celled organisms to become multicellular, or at the level of the number of interacting components of plants and animals, or when considering the huge diversification of species, increased complexity is a striking feature of the living world. Zoom out to look at the big picture, and this is what one observes. Zoom in to look at specific groups of animals or plants, and it depends where you look. The point in giving the examples above is not to infer that every group of animals and plants invariably or inevitably becomes more complex during evolutionary history, because many do not. Some parasites tend to become simpler with time because their host supplies many of their nutritional needs, so they can afford to shed unwanted parts of their anatomy, whereas other parasites become more complex. Neither do particular groups of living organisms invariably become more diverse. Occasionally mass extinctions dramatically reduce diversity. For example, the Permian mass extinction, which took place about 251 million years ago, led to as many as 80% of marine species going extinct, although increased diversity bounced back again soon afterwards (Stanley, 2016). The point is that when taken overall, looking at the evolutionary system as a whole, the increases in complexity and diversity are, as Carroll points out, "obvious".

Earth started as a very hot planet 4.6 million years ago being bombarded by meteorites. Had judicious observers been around at the time, it is unlikely that they would have predicted that a few billion years later the land mass of the planet would turn green and become the home for billions of thinking humans able to ponder (or not) on the meaning of their existence. Evolutionary history gives every appearance of being a drama with the late entry of intelligent minds upon the stage, able to investigate and to some extent understand their own history, providing a striking denouement. As Paul Davies, cosmologist and popular science writer, comments: "If we take as a measure of complexity change, not successive instantaneous sums over all extant species, but the directionality of branching, then there is clearly, for unexceptional reasons, a growth of complexity with time" (Davies, 2013, p. 30). Molecular systems and physical constraints are clearly set up, as will be discussed further below, without which the evolutionary process could not occur. It does not look like a process that is necessarily purposeless.

It is worth emphasizing in this context that such conclusions do not depend on a particular view of how the evolutionary process operates. The scientific community is currently divided on this issue (Laland et al., 2014). Some biologists think that the classic explanations provided by the so-called neo-Darwinian synthesis – genetic variation plus natural selection as assessed by the output of reproductive success – are sufficient to explain how evolution works. Others think that the theory needs a major overhaul and that other key factors, such as cooperation (Nowak and Highfield, 2011), should be incorporated as essential parts of the theory rather than as "sub-texts".[22] For our present discussion, the eventual outcome of this discussion (and the jury is still out) makes no difference. Evolutionary history is what it is – its dramatic features will not go away by explaining the mechanisms of its operation more precisely.

Biological laws

Biologists don't generally spend much time looking for "laws of nature", feeling that this is really the task of mathematical physicists. Living organisms are far more complex than relatively simple objects like stars and do not lend themselves easily to the kind of broad generalizations concerning the properties of matter that we associate with the term "law". Having said that, the word "law" does pop up occasionally in biology, even though its usage is then often followed by listing the various exceptions to the law, which is not quite what physicists have in mind when they use the term. Mendel's two "Laws of Inheritance" are a case in point, useful in rather strict circumstances in plant and animal breeding experiments, but in need of considerable modification in most biological contexts. There are other "laws of biology", however, that are of greater interest in our present context because they highlight the tight constraints on the ways in which carbon-based living organisms evolve on a planet with these particular properties of gravity, light, dark, temperature, and so forth. As evolutionary diversification and specialization continue, there are certain physical constraints that generate some remarkable morphological and scaling rules, known as allometric laws.

To pick just one example, consider Kleiber's law: the metabolic rate scales in proportion to the three-quarter power, first proposed by the Swiss biologist Max Kleiber in 1932. Since that time there have been literally hundreds of papers disputing, qualifying, and in fact mostly confirming this value, at least for many taxa of animals and plants. As it happens for our present purposes the precise scaling value doesn't really matter as everyone is agreed that a scaling law does indeed exist that relates the basal metabolic rate of an organism with its size. A particularly striking example is shown in Figure 4 illustrating the scaling law for trees in the upper panel and for animals in the lower panel (Banavar et al., 2014). The data fit the three-quarter power scaling rather well: metabolism does scale in proportion to the three-quarter power. What is really striking about this finding is that it fits with both plants and animal species that have evolved over a huge range of geographically and climatically different environments. Furthermore, the authors of the present paper also confirm Kleiber's law not just from the empirical data as shown here, but also mathematically by making various assumptions that impinge on the energetic efficiencies of these organisms. Even though animals can move, whereas plants cannot, the stringent constraints of energy control in both cases have ensured that the size and shapes of both plants and animals have evolved in response to the same mathematical and physical principles.

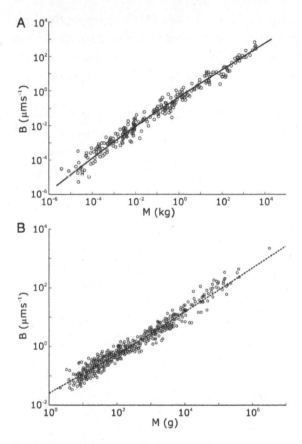

Figure 4. Kleiber's law: metabolism scales in proportion to the three-quarter power. Panel A shows the scaling law for trees and Panel B for animals. M (*x*-axis) refers to the mass of the animal or plant and B (*y*-axis) to the basal metabolic rate. Each dot represents one particular species of tree or animal.

Other allometric scaling values for biological structures are no less impressive. Body mass in relation to the cross-sectional areas of both mammalian aorta and tree-trunks scales at three-quarters, as in Kleiber's law. Sophisticated models have been proposed to explain such relationships, based on the fact, for example, that living things are sustained by the transport of materials through linear networks that branch to supply all parts of the organism – which in turn constrains the basic parameters of being alive, such as body mass and metabolic rates (West et al., 1997).

Further biological trends are broader in scope than allometric scaling, although clearly related to scaling factors. For example, "Cope's rule" points out that there is a tendency for size in organisms to increase over geological time, not always, but very often (Alroy, 1998). Based on fossil tooth data, horses increased in size by about 10% for every million years of evolutionary time, equivalent to 500,000 generations (McFadden, 1992). Marine animals are particularly useful in such studies because there is a good fossil record and sizes are easy to measure. In one such investigation 17,208 genera of marine animals spanning the last 542 million years since the Cambrian explosion were found to increase in average size by a factor of 150, whereas the maximum size increased by a factor of more than 100,000 (Heim et al., 2015). Most of the size increase reflects diversification across the various classes of animal. In other words, as new species appear in the evolutionary bush of life, the species that come later have a tendency to be bigger. Basic chemistry and physiology are thought to play key roles in the shaping of size. It is much easier to be big when breathing oxygen from air rather than extracting it out of seawater. For example, when the cetaceans (such as whales) returned to the sea from the land during the Eocene period about 48 million years ago, they carried on breathing air (which is why they return to the surface generally every few minutes to take in fresh air), quickly becoming the biggest marine animals. Relative to water, air has 20 to 30 times the concentration of oxygen and has diffusion rates through membranes that are some 300,000 times faster, of particular importance in the processes leading to oxygenation of the blood (Pauly, 2010). So it is much easier for large animals to meet their metabolic needs by breathing air rather than water.

As we stand back and look at the whole sweep of evolutionary history, we see huge creativity in life, immense diversity, but in a highly organized way, in which the ways of being alive for both animals and plants are constrained by the physical necessities of living on a planet with light and darkness, with this particular gravity, with particular atmospheric conditions at particular times, with particular temperature ranges. So, given carbon-based life, there do seem to be only so many ways of being alive on planet Earth.

Convergence in evolution

It is often thought that evolution is a purely random process and that over the billions of years since life began the process might have gone in any direction, not necessarily resulting in the kind of intelligent life-forms that we see on the planet today. The late Harvard evolutionary biologist Stephen Jay Gould famously likened evolution to a drunk on a sidewalk staggering around in a random manner. In fact, words such as "random" and "chance" in the context of biology are often misunderstood and are used without clear definition: we shall unpackage their meanings in greater detail in Chapter 4.

For the moment, it is worth considering the remarkable ways in which the same or very similar adaptive solutions to life's challenges are found again and again during the history of evolution in a phenomenon known as "convergence". This refers to the repeated but independent development of the same biochemical pathway, or organ, or structure in different biological lineages. In other words, as animals or plants face the challenges of adapting to particular environments, so at independent times and in independent circumstances the evolutionary process has converged on the same adaptive solution, in hundreds of cases generating remarkably similar ways of meeting the challenge. Some of these adaptations are so spookily similar that it's difficult to believe that a particular species with the adaptive structure did not evolve from the other, but such is not the case. In the examples that follow, it is clear that convergence to the same solution occurred independently, not least because in many cases the species in question were living on separate continents separated by thousands of miles of water and millions of years of evolutionary history. To use Gould's analogy in a slightly different way, the sidewalk is a really narrow space in comparison with the breadth of a multi-lane highway. The evolutionary process is very often constrained to the sidewalk for the simple reason that all the other possible options down the multi-lane highway simply won't work.

The phenomenon of convergence has long been known in biology, but only in more recent years has the full scale of convergence in evolution been adequately recognized. Richard Dawkins has a helpful section explaining convergence in his fine book *The Ancestor's Tale* (Dawkins, 2016, pp. 671–82), but without doubt the person who has done most to investigate and popularize the idea in recent years is Simon Conway Morris, Professor of Evolutionary Palaeobiology at Cambridge (Conway Morris, 2003, 2015), whose research group has also developed the remarkable Map-of-Life website highlighting many examples of convergence.[23]

Convergence operates as much at the molecular level as it does at the level of morphology, and some of the examples below contain both types of information. The next chapter will focus particularly on some remarkable examples of molecular convergence in the evolutionary process. Here we outline a few striking examples of convergence at the level of the structure and function of animal anatomy.

The eyes have it

One of the most famous examples of convergence is the evolution of the eye, Darwin's "organ of extreme perfection" (Darwin, 1859).

Ninety-six per cent of all animal species contain a complex optical system (Land and Fernald, 1992). There are ten main types of eye, but most fall into two categories: camera eyes or compound eyes. Despite their complexity, both types have evolved independently multiple times in quite different evolutionary lineages, perhaps more than 40 times (Salvini-Plawen and Mayr, 1977). Compound eyes, typical of arthropods like crabs and of insects like bees, generally consist of thousands of individual photoreceptor units arranged on a convex surface pointing outwards, and the image perceived is a composite of all the signals received from each separate unit. The net result is a pattern of light and dark, a bit like the halftone illustrations in a newspaper or magazine. Compound eyes are good at detecting movement, but overall camera eyes are much more efficient. For example, if we humans had compound eyes instead of the camera eyes we in fact have, our eyes would each need a radius of around 30 feet to obtain the same visual acuity, which would be inconvenient to say the least. It was the Lutheran astronomer Johannes Kepler back in the early seventeenth century who first understood how the human eye works, described in a publication generally considered to be the foundation of modern optics (Kepler, 1604). As the name suggests, camera eyes work on the same principle as a pinhole camera, with light entering the eye via the pupil and passing through the gel inside to then focus on the retina, a network of light-sensitive photoreceptor cells that then send the messages to the brain where they are integrated to construct a composite image. Animals that have camera eyes, such as squid, jellyfish, spiders, and vertebrates like us, are typically predatory and very active, requiring good visual acuity to catch their prey.

An example of convergence that has been recognized now for more than a century is that between the camera eyes of cephalopods like squid and octopus and the eyes of vertebrates, as Figure 5 illustrates. The similarities are striking, with some interesting differences also. In our eyes, we have a "blind spot" due to the exit of the nerves from the retinal photoreceptors in a bundle in the middle of the retina so that light cannot be detected in that particular area. The camera eyes of the squid and octopus are better arranged in this respect in that the nerves leave the retina from the back-side before being gathered into a bundle so there is no "blind spot". In practice, our brains fill in the missing information, so it doesn't make much difference either way. In the present context, the important point to note is that the evolution of cephalopod and vertebrate eyes has occurred in evolutionary lineages separated by millions of years of evolutionary time (Fernald, 2006).

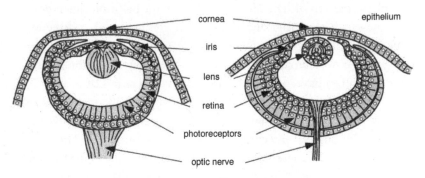

Figure 5. A comparison between the structure of a cephalopod eye on the left and a vertebrate eye on the right.

It should not be thought that convergence to a very similar structure, in this case a form of camera eye, entails building the eye from ground zero, as it were. Around 729 genes have been conserved between human and octopus eyes (Ogura et al., 2004); in other words, these are genes that presumably have been passed down from their last common ancestor more than 110 million years previously, although the way such estimates are made means that most of the genes in common are involved in all cells of the body, not just for building eyes. When the need to see more clearly becomes acute during evolutionary history, there is strong pressure to evolve eyes using whatever genomic resources are around to help in the process – it just keeps on happening.

For example, a group of marine annelids (known as alciopids), close relatives of earthworms, have camera eyes that are very similar to those of both cephalopods (such as the octopus) and vertebrates (Conway Morris, 2003, p. 154). Among snails a camera-like eye has evolved at least three times independently, a snail known as *Strombus* providing one striking example. There is even a very toxic jellyfish, known as the box jellyfish (Cubozoa), which you definitely want to avoid if swimming in tropical or semi-tropical waters, that has refined camera eyes. These are no doubt useful in helping it to dart rapidly towards its prey – speeds of up to six metres per minute have been recorded, something to bear in mind if you spot one while swimming (I have seen bottles of vinegar on Australian beaches, there at the ready in case you get stung by one). The box jellyfish has no fewer than 24 eyes of which 8 are camera eyes, so is excessively blessed with vision. Yet it has no brain, but instead a distributed complex neural network, so its developed visual abilities must depend on the interpretation of the light signals received by this neuronal system. The main point here is that the camera eye of the box jellyfish evolved independently from other species that have such eyes (Bentlage et al., 2010). The jellyfish are not fish and certainly not vertebrates, far too squidgy, but belong to a group of animals known as the cnidarians. They have a different body plan from other animals and have followed their own evolutionary path for around 600 million years. The evolutionary process has once again "converged" on the same adaptive solution to improving vision.

One of the most extraordinary examples of the evolutionary convergence of camera-like eyes comes in three different types of microorganism which are found on three different branches of the tree of life, allowing these microbes to move in response to light. One type of single-celled plankton called the warnowiid dinoflagellates (Figure 6a) has a camera eye which is remarkably similar to the vertebrate eye, with components equivalent to the cornea, lens, and retina of our own eyes, yet formed out of very different cellular materials. In fact, those who first reported seeing the eye in these plankton thought that it must have been scavenged from a jellyfish – but they were wrong. In 1887 Georges Pouchet proclaimed that if we didn't know it was part of a dinoflagellate, we would surely attribute it to an animal (Conway Morris, 2015, p. 95). The eye appears to have evolved to allow these dinoflagellates to prey on other dinoflagellates (Gavelis et al., 2015). The plankton eye is built out of plastids and mitochondria, intracellular components that by themselves have quite different functions: plastids in many dinoflagellates are the locus for photosynthesis, whereas in others, as in the warnowiids, that role has been lost although the remnants remain; mitochondria generate the energy required for cellular metabolism. Both the plastids and the mitochondria in the dinoflagellates originate from separate types of bacteria that were engulfed at different times in their evolutionary history and have remained there ever since. To build their eyes, the clever little creatures have stacked lots of mitochondria together to form a cornea-like surface across a lens structure with a membrane network derived from multiple plastids packed together to make up the retina (Gavelis et al., 2015). The organelles inside the cell initially have quite distinct functions, but are then "co-opted" to collaborate together to bring about a new and useful function.

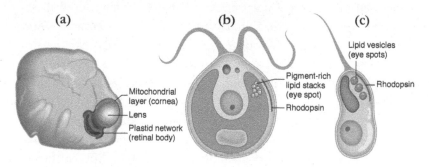

Figure 6. Convergent eyes in different branches of the tree of life. Panel (a) Warnowiid dinoflagellate; Panel (b) Chlamydomonas; Panel (c) Blastocladiella.

The warnowiids are not the only microorganisms to have camera-like eyes, although others are less complex as Figure 6 illustrates, and are best described as "eye-spots", although they still retain certain elements of the camera-eye overall structure. The single-celled green alga *Chlamydomonas* is a relative of plants that live on land and is generally found in locations like stagnant water, most annoyingly in swimming pools. On a quite separate evolutionary branch of the tree from the dinoflagellates, the algae eye-spots consist of a stack of lipid (fat) globules that are rich in specialized pigments. These reflect light on to two different light-sensitive proteins called rhodopsins that act as photoreceptors that then trigger movement in response to light (Richards and Gomes, 2015). It is fascinating to note that the rhodopsin family of proteins is used both here and in eyes all over the living world, including our own.

Yet another type of eye-spot is found in a further separate evolutionary branch, the swimming spores of the Blastocladiomycota fungi illustrated in Figure 6c (Richards and Gomes, 2015). In this case, lipid-filled vesicles are used to deflect the light on to rhodopsin proteins, allowing the production of a key chemical (cyclic GMP) that transmits the message to the organism, the same chemical also involved in vertebrate eye function. What is striking in all these examples is the way that similar structures have been assembled independently using very different sets of materials. As Richard Dawkins comments: "It seems that life, at least as we know it on this planet, is almost indecently eager to evolve eyes" (Dawkins, 2004, p. 673).

The multiple independent evolutionary pathways leading to compound eyes are in full support of this contention. The annelids are a very large phylum containing around 17,000 different living species, including well-known friends such as the earthworm, as well as leeches, not seen as so friendly for most people now (though much used in medicine right up to the nineteenth century). Compound eyes are found all over the place among this great collection of species and in a group called the sabellids this type of eye has evolved independently several times; likewise in the bivalve molluscs, of which there are around 9,200 living species, including the well-known oysters that some enjoy for dinner (Conway Morris, 2003, p. 158). Not all arthropods possess compound eyes, but many do, and there is good evidence that they have reappeared more than once in separate lineages (Oakley, 2003), although again it should be noted that convergence does not imply that compound eyes arose *de novo* each time, but rather that the genetic resources, or at least some of the resources, were available when the selection pressure was once more "on" to generate this particularly useful adaptation. For example, compound eyes are often found in arthropods deep down in the ocean where they are useful for collecting very small amounts of light.

This brief section on convergence in eye evolution has only just touched the surface of a huge subject.[24] If you live on a planet of light and darkness, you are very likely to get eyes at some stage of evolution. The adaptive advantages are huge and obvious. This even led Dawkins to suggest that evolution is "progressive", a notion that Darwin himself found problematic, Dawkins writes:

"the cumulative build-up of complex adaptations like eyes, strongly suggests a version of progress – especially when coupled in imagination with some of the wonderful products of convergent evolution" (Dawkins, 2016, p. 681).

Placentals and marsupials

One of the most remarkable, and readily visible, examples of convergence is illustrated by the similarities between the marsupials that have evolved separately in Australia and South America, many of which look very similar to their equivalent placental counterparts in other parts of the world. It was only a few million years ago that the Isthmus of Panama joined together North and South America, whereas Australia started separating from Antarctica about 100 million years ago. "Reproductive isolation" in the evolutionary process refers to the way in which populations are separated from each other so that they cannot interbreed, either because of physical obstacles (such as high mountains or wide oceans) or genetic differences arise that preclude interbreeding. Separation of continents or islands by oceans provides not only great opportunities for the emergence of new species (as Darwin found in his famous voyage round the world on the *Beagle*), but also an opportunity to study evolutionary convergence in species that have been reproductively isolated for millions of years.

Marsupials are animals like kangaroos and wombats that give rise to less developed young and suckle them in an external pouch, whereas placentals are animals that nourish their young to a later developmental stage in the uterus before birth. Many Australian marsupials have placental counterparts in Africa and elsewhere, each species looking quite similar because it has evolved to fill up similar ecological niches. Other marsupials are found in South America and likewise have their counterparts elsewhere. Figure 7 illustrates the striking similarities between the dagger-like teeth of the placental sabre-tooth cat (lower) and the marsupial equivalent found in South

America (upper, known as thylacosmilids), yet the sabre-tooth in both cases has evolved quite independently. Sabre-tooths are found in the fossil record from 34 million years ago onwards until they finally went extinct 9,000 years ago, so these observations are based on fossil data. Their last common ancestor was a small tree-climbing animal like a shrew or an opossum, living during the Jurassic period, certainly not an animal with big sabre teeth. The sabre teeth evolved quite independently. If a big cat is to be an efficient hunter in a particular environment, these are the teeth it might well get.

Figure 7. Evolutionary convergence in the sabre-tooth between the marsupial species (upper panel) and the placental cat (lower panel).

Australia and South America are great places to look for marsupial equivalents of their placental counterparts found in other parts of the world. Here are huge spaces with lots of opportunities for animals living on land to fill up the ecological niches provided, be they underground or above ground – but not flying, because of course a big ocean proves no impenetrable barrier to birds, and not fish either, for obvious reasons! Burrowing animals provide some good examples. Those of us who live in Europe are very familiar with moles, even though we may not see them very often, but rather observe the results of their busy lifestyle with little mounds of earth all over a beautiful golf course or the lawns of manicured gardens. I once had an uncle who was very proud of his lawns and who used to wage perpetual warfare against the moles who turned them into something that looked more like a ploughed field. The moles always won. In Australia, there is a rather rare marsupial mole called *Notorcytes*, which looks strikingly similar to *Talpa*, the European mole, and may be found burrowing in the western deserts (Figure 8). In South America, there are extinct marsupial moles called the *necrolestids*, which are also very similar based on the fossil data. All these moles evolved quite independently in different continents from non-digging ancestors, separated by oceans of water but ended up with similar anatomy, physiology, behaviour and, to some extent, genes (Conway Morris, 2003, p. 139; Dawkins, 2016, pp. 275–76). Anatomical similarities include their powerful forelimbs used for digging, their rudimentary eyes (not really needed down below), and their small testicles (quite wise when thinking about burrowing narrow tunnels). The digging "spade" of European moles is made out of all five fingers, whereas the marsupial paw uses only two fingers. A rather bizarre convergent behaviour noted by Conway Morris and found in 20 different burrowing mammals is that they all prefer to start eating a carrot from its lower tip. The Zambian common mole rat can even identify which end of the carrot is which after both ends have been cut off. All this becomes very understandable when one remembers that burrowing animals first meet a carrot from its bottom end rather than its top.

Figure 8. *Top*: The European placental mole *Talpa*. *Bottom:* The Australian marsupial mole.

Many other marsupials are more or less counterparts to their placental equivalents on other continents. There are marsupial shrews, "cats", "dogs", and "flying squirrels" all of which have evolved independently. The flying squirrels of the American forests look and behave very much like the equivalent gliders of the Australian eucalypt forests (Dawkins, 2016, p. 276). In fact, there are three different types of glider in the Australian forests, all of which have evolved independently from each other – as well as from all other gliders in the rest of the world. Gliding, like flying, is really useful to escape being eaten.

The Tasmanian wolf called *Thylacinus* is perhaps the best-known example of convergent evolution in the category of marsupials (Figure 9). It was the largest known carnivorous marsupial of modern times and one of only two marsupial species where both the males and females have pouches (when you see a kangaroo with a pouch in Australia it is always a female). The wolves were sometimes misleadingly called Tasmanian tigers due to their striped backs, but tigers they were not, being much more like wolves and dogs. They were still alive in Australia and New Guinea within the memory of those still living. The last captive Tasmanian wolf died in captivity in Hobart Zoo in 1936.[25] Their evolution in Australia was quite independent of wolves in other parts of the world, such as the Mexican grey wolf shown in Figure 9, and their fossils have been found going back to the late Oligocene period about 25 million years ago.

Figure 9. *Top*: Marsupial Tasmanian wolf. ***Bottom***: Placental Mexican grey wolf.

As already mentioned, islands provide great opportunities for evolution to take off in creative directions and the island of Madagascar off the east coast of Africa is no exception. The island has 130 species of palm tree, more than found in the whole of the rest of Africa, and it has two-thirds of the world's species of chameleon. More relevant to our immediate topic, the island also has a unique family of shrew-like animals known as tenrecs (Dawkins, 2016, p. 200). These are placentals, not marsupials, but their convergent evolution to phenotypes resembling other animals that have evolved quite independently in other parts of the world is quite striking. There is evidence that they arrived in Madagascar as two founder populations from Africa when there were no other mammals present so they had no competition for filling up the various mammalian ecological niches that mammals are best suited to fill, diversifying in the process – a perfect "laboratory" in which to study convergence. The original tenrecs have now evolved into 27 different species, including some that look like hedgehogs, some like shrews, and others more like otters (Figure 10), but they are not closely related to any of these groups, something that was not clearly recognized until the late 1990s. Look at the hedgehog from Madagascar (Figure 10, *upper left*) and compare it with the hedgehog from Britain (Figure 10, *lower left*) and you will be hard-pressed to tell the difference – yet both have evolved along quite independent evolutionary pathways from different kinds of creatures. There are only so many ways of being a mammal on planet Earth, and the "reserved spaces for mammals" in design hyperspace will continue to be filled up as opportunity arises. There are very many theoretically conceivable ways to live in a niche, but the spots that are actually taken by real organisms with particular adaptations are surprisingly few by comparison. Madagascar has provided some great opportunities to watch the convergent process unfold in evolutionary time.

Figure 10. *Upper left*: The Tenrec "hedgehog". *Upper right*: A shrew Tenrec. *Lower left*: The European hedgehog. *Lower right*: The common shrew.

The mystery of the adipose fin

Those who enjoy catching fish, or perhaps keep fish in an aquarium, will be well aware of the bewildering array of fin types possessed by different types of fish. A small and modest fin, probably missed by all but the aficionados, is called the adipose fin, as illustrated in Figure 11, a fin that is found on more than 6,000 species of fish. "Adipose" means "fat" and the fin originally obtained its name because it was thought that it acted as a store of extra fat. This has long been shown not to be the case, but the name stuck. The adipose fin was also deemed in earlier times to be a vestige, meaning a "leftover" from its previous evolutionary history, now lacking any particular function. But more recently it has been shown that the fin improves swimming in turbulent waters and may also act as a flow-sensor. Fish can swim without it, but in fast-flowing rivers, for example, it helps. Originally it was also thought that it evolved only once, but more recent and careful analysis has demonstrated that it has evolved multiple times independently, hence its interest in the context of convergence (Stewart et al., 2014).

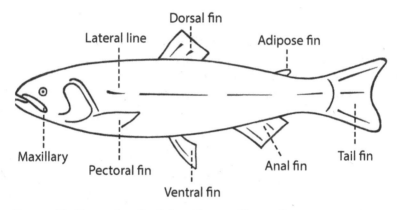

Figure 11. Example of a fish with an adipose fin.

To come to this conclusion, a research group from the University of Chicago studied the skeletal anatomy of adipose fins from 620 different species of fish (Stewart et al., 2014). In the fossil record, the fins first appear as small appendages and then develop greater anatomical and functional complexity. By bringing fossil data into the story, together with some genetic data and anatomical analysis, the authors were able to demonstrate that adipose fins have evolved multiple times over the millions of years since the Cambrian explosion. This by itself does not conclusively demonstrate that the fin is adaptive, but taken together with the other results pointing to its advantages to those fish that have it, it appears that the evolutionary process has converged repeatedly to the same adaptive solution in providing fish in fast-moving or turbulent water with an extra appendage to help them on life's way. What is most remarkable is that adipose fins are found on fishes ranging in size from centimetres in length to several metres, on fish from very different ecosystems, from rivers to deep ocean waters, and on fish with many different diets. If an adipose fin is the need of the hour, then an adipose fin is what you are likely to get (in evolutionary time at least).

Convergence is ubiquitous

In his book *The Ancestor's Tale*, Richard Dawkins runs through a whole collection of examples of convergent evolution (Dawkins, 2016, pp. 676–77). The venomous sting (as in jellyfish and spiders) has evolved independently at least ten times, Dawkins remarking that "it's a good bet that venom, including hypodermic injection, would evolve in reruns" of evolution. Sound production for social purposes has evolved independently in birds, mammals, crickets, cicadas, fish, and frogs. The use of weak electric fields for navigation has evolved several times. True powered flight (not just gliding) has evolved four times – in insects, pterosaurs, bats, and birds. Parachuting and gliding have evolved multiple times in animals such as lizards, frogs, rodents, snakes, and "flying fish". Conway Morris adds many more examples (Conway Morris, 2003, 2015). For example, the convergence of mimicry of insects and spiders to an ant morphology has evolved at least 70 times independently. The technique of retaining the egg in the mother prior to a live birth is thought to have evolved separately about 100 times among lizards and snakes alone.

To add more and more examples of convergence could become tedious but enough illustrations of the principle have been provided here to make the point: convergence is a normal part of the evolutionary process and provides striking confirmation that evolution proceeds in an orderly and constrained way to generate biological diversity. In a commentary on Gould's idea of ultimate randomness in evolutionary history, Conway Morris writes that it is

now widely thought that the history of life is little more than
a contingent muddle punctuated by disastrous mass extinctions
that in spelling the doom of one group so open the doors of
opportunity to some other mob of lucky-chancers... Rerun the
tape of the history of life... and the end result will be an utterly
different biosphere. Most notably there will be nothing remotely
like a human... Yet, what we know of evolution suggests the
exact reverse: convergence is ubiquitous and the constraints of
life make the emergence of the various biological properties (e.g.
intelligence) very probable, if not inevitable.

There is what Conway Morris calls a "hyperspace" of possibilities of being alive on planet Earth and the "task" of evolution is to find those spaces. "Convergence offers a metaphor as to how evolution navigates the combinatorial immensities of biological 'hyperspace'" (Conway Morris, 2003, p. 127). That does not entail convergence in every case – some adaptive responses to the environment are unique as far as one can tell, although their number appears to be relatively few compared to those displaying convergence (Dawkins, 2016, p. 677), but convergence does make the point that evolution is far from being a random or chance process considered overall. In some ways, the more molecular examples of convergence that will be considered in the following chapter provide even more dramatic examples in support of this conclusion.

Grand patterns in animal shapes and sizes

Richard Owen was a famous nineteenth-century anatomist who is remembered as the founder of London's Natural History Museum (opened in 1881) and the inventor of the name for the new order of dinosaurs (Rupke, 2009). At an event full of Victorian melodrama held on New Year's Eve 1853, the great Professor Owen sat at the head of a private dinner held inside a large model dinosaur built as part of the Crystal Palace Exhibition to celebrate the discovery of these wonderful animals. And when Darwin discovered new animals during his voyage on the *Beagle*, he shipped them off to Owen for identification, including the large flightless bird that he ate for Christmas dinner while in South America, only late in the meal realizing that the bird was rather rare.

In our present context, Richard Owen is also remembered for applying the tenets of German Romantic *Naturphilosophie* to his study of anatomy. Although this stream of thought had many strands, it tended to lay emphasis on nature taken as a whole, maintaining that "forms" reflect the ideal structure of nature. Nature, in this view, has a single formative energy or "soul", and its forms are the necessary outcomes. This was a very different kind of philosophy from the natural theology that dominated the world of Oxford and Cambridge in the first half of the nineteenth century, a point already highlighted in the previous chapter, in which a nature devoid of any inner energy or soul, yet full of functionality, reflects the handiwork of the creator God. Form, body plan (or *Bauplan* as it is known in German), not function, was of central importance to Owen. Scientifically in his day the issue was whether there exists a "unity of composition in the animal kingdom" (Rupke, 2009, p. 98). The meaning of a particular anatomical structure for Owen lay not in its function but in its place in the composition of the whole organism. When he published his book *On the Archetype* (1848) it helped to establish him as one of the most influential naturalists of his time.

Why does Owen, and the biological tradition he represents, matter for our present context? In his initial thinking Owen distanced his archetype ideas from Platonic thinking, in which the material forms present in this world are but pale and imperfect reflections of the ideal Forms upon which they are ultimately based. However, as time went on he shifted his ideas and ended up baptizing his views into an overtly Platonic framework in which the archetype became "a divine forethought, a blueprint of design for the formation of animal life" (Rupke, 2009, p. 128).[26] But after Darwin's publication of *On the Origin of Species* the pendulum swung and the adaptive functions of animal parts became central to biological thinking. It was these that were then gradually honed by natural selection to achieve their functions, not some predetermined *Bauplan*. But here is the historical twist in the tail: by the late twentieth century, ideas that were looking remarkably like the *Bauplan*, albeit shorn of its original metaphysical baggage, were once again becoming common within mainstream biology. The main reason was simply the data: advances in evolutionary developmental biology, known as "evo-devo", coupled with the increasing knowledge of genomics, revealed some simple rules leading to a fusion of form and function in which common threads weave their way through the evolution of living organisms. The phrase "deep homology" became trendy, referring to those processes of growth and development which are regulated by genetic processes that are widely conserved across a range of species with deep roots back into their evolutionary history.

Such trends are well described in books such as biologist Sean Carroll's *Endless Forms Most Beautiful* (Carroll, 2005) and what follows also depends heavily on a section in my own book *The Language of Genetics* (Alexander, 2011). First there is the modular system used in building the architecture of living things such as the vertebrates so loved by Richard Owen. The basic bony elements of all vertebrates are more or less the same with proportionality between the parts maintained from the enormous sauropod dinosaurs to small delicate salamanders from the Jurassic period some 150 million years ago. Our own limbs reflect this modular design with each limb consisting of several distinct parts – upper arm, lower arm, and wrist, for example. The five-digit structure of the hand has persisted for 350 million years, although the precise digit number varies greatly between species. Even the complex patterns on a butterfly wing are built upon tiny modules in which the veins demarcate each unit. The body patterns of fish, snakes, and lizards are composed of scales arranged in regular geometric patterns. Animal bodies and their parts are arranged in an orderly fashion, constructed according to certain recognizable themes which keep repeating in species after species through evolutionary history.

Diversity is very often achieved by simply varying the number of modules of similar type. For example, the number of vertebrae varies greatly, ranging from 6 to 10 in the frog, depending on the species, 33 in humans and up to a few hundred in the snake. Similarly, the number of segments in arthropods (such as insects) varies considerably. Groups of segments are organized into modules characterized by the appendages that protrude from them, be they feet, wings, or antennae. Diversity is further extended by the twin characteristics of symmetry and of polarity. Animals often have matching left and right sides with an "axis of symmetry" running down the middle from the head to the tail. Animals also usually display three axes of polarity: from head to tail, from front to back (for us, or top to bottom in animals that walk on four legs), and from the body to the end of a limb sticking out.

The past few decades have seen great strides forward in understanding how these orderly body plans are encoded in the genome. Not that all the instructions are in the genome like an architect's plan, but rather the genome encodes a recipe such that if the "correct" environmental inputs are present at certain crucial times during development, this is the body plan that will eventually emerge. We can take the fruit fly *Drosophila* as our exemplar organism to see how this works out in practice. The fly has a head, a thorax, and an abdomen, as Figure 12 illustrates. The thorax consists of three segments: the first segment carries a pair of legs, the second a pair of wings and a pair of legs, and the third a pair of legs plus what are known as the "halteres". The halteres are a pair of rudimentary wings that help insects maintain stability during flight. The abdomen contains 11 segments. The big challenge for a very early embryo is to establish its general layout and the overall orientation of its polarity. The *Drosophila* embryo starts by sorting out its front/back and top/underside. Then the number and orientation of the body segments are arranged, followed by the assignment of functions to each segment. A different set of genes organizes each of these stages. The polarity gene products work by setting up gradients of "morphogens" along which cell development occurs in either a front/back or up/down orientation. The morphogens are arrayed in a kind of chemical matrix that provides the embryo with precise information about where cells should be in three-dimensional space. At least 12 different genes are involved in the up/down orientation.

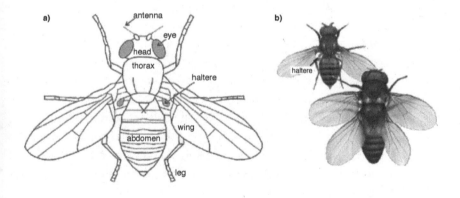

Figure 12. (a) The fruit fly ***Drosophila melanogaster***, one of the first and perhaps the most widely studied model organisms in genetics. (b) Illustrations of two fruit flies, one wild-type, or normal, fly and one ***ultrabithorax*** mutant fly. Note that the halteres in the mutant have been replaced by wings.

Following on from this stage, nine hox genes define which of the fly's segments does what. Eyes normally arise only on the head segment, whereas legs only appear on the thoracic segments. Hox genes are part of a big class of genes known as homeotic genes, first identified by William Bateson, inventor of the term "genetics". Bateson noticed in his botanical studies published in 1894 that different parts of plants, such as the stamens, occasionally grew where the petals ought to be growing. Such changes were called "homeotic" because they involve the change of one thing into something else (from the Greek *homeoiōsis* meaning a "resemblance").

The hox genes encode proteins called transcription factors that together regulate hundreds of other genes, either by switching them on or by silencing them, leading to great cascades of effects. Their role as master-control genes can readily be shown by mutating a single hox gene. For example, mutations in a hox gene called *antennapedia* cause legs to develop on the head of a fly instead of the antenna. Another well-known example is the mutation of *ultrabithorax*, the hox gene responsible for placing a pair of legs and the halteres on the third thoracic segment (see Figure 12). When the gene is mutated so its protein is no longer produced properly, this third segment now develops what rightfully belongs to the segment just in front: a pair of legs plus a pair of fully formed wings. Such *ultrabithorax* gene mutations can occur in flies in the wild, which is what initially drew the attention of geneticists to this amazing family of executive genes.

The hox genes provide the cells in the different segments with a kind of GPS navigator so that they know where they are and what they are supposed to do during development – except this is a GPS system that uses chemical signals rather than radio waves. Mutations in the hox genes are like feeding the GPS system with wrong addresses so the cells start making legs, but at entirely the wrong address. It reminds you of those real-life stories about drivers who trusted the voice of their outdated GPS instructor too much and ended up turning left into a river or right into a building site.

Drosophila have only four pairs of chromosomes, and remarkably the hox genes line up on the third chromosome in the same order as the segments line up in the fly. So the genes responsible for the head are found up at one end, with those responsible for the rear down at the other end. Quite why they should be arranged in this way is not fully understood, but it certainly gives a very neat and orderly appearance to the system.

Reach down and feel your ribs (hopefully you can feel them). The segmental pattern indicated by your ribs is generated by your hox genes. In vertebrates like us, however, the hox gene system is a bit more complex than in flies, and there are usually four clusters of hox genes on the chromosomes, each cluster containing nine to eleven genes. Some but not all vertebrates have the same sequential arrangement of genes along the chromosomes, and the sequence may be correlated to the timing of development as well. The hox genes that encode the head are up one end of the cluster and are switched on first, and then the others are activated in sequence, until finally the hox genes at the other end light up last. It's like playing a wooden flute starting from the top, with the first hole playing the first segment and the bottom hole playing the last segment. Development is literally a question of going head first.

Like the notion of "deep time," a phrase often used when looking back into the earliest history of our universe, deep homology becomes apparent when we peer back into our evolutionary past and find that the same genes and regulatory networks keep cropping up in animal and plant bodies. Ancient regulatory systems both constrain organisms and provide a basis from which novelty can spring. The hox genes were right there in the earliest bilaterians at least 600 million years ago. Bilaterians include all animals that have a recognizable front end and back end, as well as an upside and a downside, which describes 99% of known animal species, including us. In each case, the hox genes are intimately involved in the development of their body plans, just as in the case of the segmentation of *Drosophila*.

What evo-devo tells us is just how orderly the whole evolutionary and development processes really are. Richard Owen had a point – it's just that he overemphasized form at the expense of function, although to be fair on Owen he certainly knew that both were important and often looked for ways of integrating them together. Darwinian evolution does the integrating work very nicely by showing how certain forms bestow such great adaptive advantages that they become the main bodily theme for thousands of species for millions of years. The *Bauplan* is there all right, but not as a result of some "inward driving force" on the part of living organisms, more as the fruit of millions of years of selective advantage, channelled by the constraints of living in this kind of planet with its gravity and other physical demands that determine what forms of life work best.

Cooperation, intelligence, and big brains

There are many other general features of evolution that are relevant to our present topic, although space does not allow their description in any detail. One striking feature of living organisms is their cooperative behaviour. This started with the cooperation between cells that was necessary for the generation of the first multicellular organisms, and it continues today with the widespread cooperation that occurs within species and sometimes between species (Nowak and Highfield, 2011; Nowak and Coakley, 2013). Mathematical analysis of animal populations shows that a population of only cooperators has the highest average fitness (measured by reproductive success), whereas a population consisting only of defectors, those who never cooperate, has the lowest fitness. Yes, there is competition as well, but life only functions properly if cooperation remains a central feature. As one of the leaders in the study of cooperation, Martin Nowak, Professor of Biology and Mathematics at Harvard University, comments: "Genomes, cells, multicellular organisms, social insects, and human society are all based on cooperation" (Nowak, 2006). Professor Nowak has even suggested that cooperation should be recognized as the third "pillar" of evolutionary theory, along with gene variation and natural selection. Humans are the cooperators par excellence. Looking at current wars around the world, that might not seem like it. But in what other species would an adult human in London (for example) jump into the river at the risk of their own life to save a drowning child who was completely unknown to them and who later turned out to be from Beijing? (Yes, it happens.)

Another evolutionary product that we see all over the animal kingdom is intelligence. Parrots and crows are remarkably intelligent. As Emery and Clayton report: "Some bird species make and use tools, can count, remember specific past events and reason about the mental states of individuals, behaviours that some have considered to be unique to humans" (Emery and Clayton, 2005). Tool use has been demonstrated in a wide range of birds, and the New Caledonian crows are perhaps most remarkable in this respect. They can use stick tools in the wild, manufacture tools from leaves, craft both wood and ferns into hooks, and there is even evidence for cumulative cultural evolution whereby tool traditions are passed down the line to the next generations (Hunt and Gray, 2004). They have also been tested on the "Aesop's fable test" whereby a worm floating in a tube half-full of water, so out of reach, has been presented to them and they worked out that the way to obtain the food was to add stones to the tube to bring the floating food within reach (Taylor et al., 2011).[27] Orang-utans likewise have been observed filling tubes with water in order to obtain out-of-reach peanuts ("subjects required an average three mouthfuls of water to get the peanut") (Mendes et al., 2007).

Several species of dolphin are also remarkably intelligent, and their brains are significantly larger in relative terms than that of our close relatives such as the chimpanzee, gorilla, and orang-utan (Conway Morris, 2003, pp. 247ff.). In fact, until 1.5 million years ago dolphins had the largest brains of any creatures on the planet. They have a highly developed social system and can communicate with an extended social network comprising at least 100 individuals. Their Facebook equivalent is provided by whistles and other noises. They can also recognize themselves in the mirror; help humans with fishing by providing hints as to where to cast the net or herd the fish; and they are also good mimics and can learn human words on occasion.

There are hundreds of other examples of animal intelligence, but space does not allow to describe them further. Along with intelligence also comes the ability to have fun. Animals having fun? Well it certainly looks like it as crows sit on a jar lid on a snowy roof in Russia and slide down the roof,[28] and as black swans surf the crests of waves and then go back and do it again (much easier for swans than for humans)[29] (Emery and Clayton, 2015). Watch your own dog chasing its tail or your cat getting tangled in your knitting and that brings it closer to home. Is "having fun" for animals a bit too anthropomorphic? Maybe so, but serious biological attention to this question does suggest that this is exactly what they're doing (Emery and Clayton, 2015).

One of the most striking features of evolutionary history of all time is the rapid increase in brain size in hominids that has taken place over the past 2 million years (Figure 13) in which the brain more than tripled in size from around 400 cc all the way up to an average 1300–1400 cc. Today the brain size of the great apes, who have evolved on separate branches of the evolutionary tree since our last common ancestor some 8–10 million years ago, is in the region of only 300–500 cc, even though their body size is comparable with ours. There continues to be much discussion in the biological literature as to the causes of such a dramatic increase in hominid brain size. Despite very early signs of bipedality (walking on two legs), dating back to 6 million years ago, the brain size of hominins[30] did not start surpassing that of chimpanzees until millions of years later, around 2 million years ago. Furthermore, the first stone tools start appearing at least 3.3 million years ago, somewhat before the onset of the most marked increase in brain size. So clearly bipedality and simple tool use alone were insufficient to drive the "cultural revolution" that was associated with the increase in brain size that occurred over the past 2 million years. The construction and use of more sophisticated tools, together with increasingly complex social structures, are both thought to have played critical roles in expanding brain size (Dunbar, 2004, 2016). Whatever the precise combination of genetic variation and selection pressures might have been that brought about this rapid transition, it is worth reflecting on the fact that it is only because this happened at all that we have authors who write books and people who read them. It is no slur at all on animal intelligence, which is remarkable, to point out the obvious: that this huge increase in processing capacity has led to a "phase transition" and the emergence of minds that can ponder on questions like Purpose and the meaning of their own existence. As Martin Nowak comments: "My position is very simple. Evolution has led to a human brain that can gain access to a Platonic world of forms and ideas."[31]

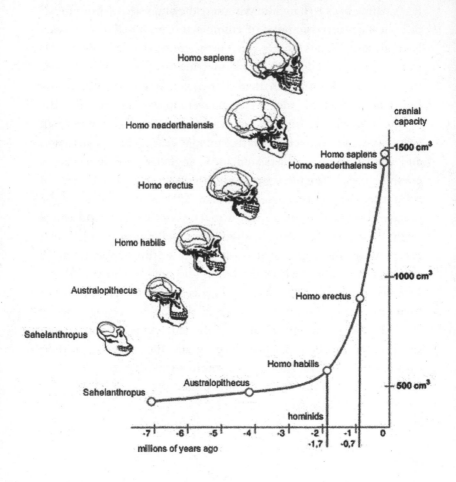

Figure 13. Increasing brain size in hominin evolution over the past 7 million years.

The biological grand narrative

Once again, as we look at the "grand narrative" of evolution, taken as a whole, the claim that it is necessarily Purposeless begins to look increasingly implausible. We cannot escape the obvious arrow of evolutionary time – from ultra-simplicity to incredible complexity. We cannot avoid the constrained features of the evolutionary process, dependent ultimately upon the laws of chemistry and physics. Constraint and convergence are all around us. Nomic (lawlike) regularity is a consistent feature. A barren hot planet bombarded by meteorites that ends up being the home of animals having fun, and humans who have some fun too, but also ponder the question of existence, does seem to cast doubt on the claim that this whole process must, of necessity, be without Purpose. As we drill down from the big and the visible to the molecular world, such conclusions receive even greater support, and it is to that world that we now turn.

3

Biology's Molecular Constraints

The fact that the universe conforms to an orderly scheme, and is not an arbitrary muddle of events, prompts one to wonder — God or no God — whether there is some sort of meaning or purpose behind it all.

Paul Davies, *The Goldilocks Enigma* (2007), p. 16.

Many people feel very much at home talking about animals. After all, our TV screens are full of them and, for many, pets are an important (and sometimes demanding feature) of daily life. But for those without a science background the world of molecules seems alien and difficult, something best left to those "who like that kind of thing". That's a pity, because how the world of molecules relates to the big living things that we see around us every day, like dogs, cats, and birds, can shed much light on why things are the way they are — and indeed on why we are the way we are.

The examples that follow, as in the previous chapter, are just the tip of a large iceberg. But one has to start somewhere, and as with the examples of the "big", the world of the "small" seems inconsistent with the idea that the world of living matter is necessarily Purposeless.

The genetic code

One of the most amazing features of the living world is the genetic
code (Figure 14). Personally, I still receive huge enjoyment by just
looking at it – maybe not everyone's cup of tea, but hopefully this
brief section on it will stimulate your admiration.

Second letter

First letter		U	C	A	G	Third letter
	U	UUU UUC } Phe UUA UUG } Leu	UCU UCC UCA UCG } Ser	UAU UAC } Tyr UAA Stop UAG Stop	UGU UGC } Cys UGA Stop UGG Trp	U C A G
	C	CUU CUC CUA CUG } Leu	CCU CCC CCA CCG } Pro	CAU CAC } His CAA CAG } Gln	CGU CGC CGA CGG } Arg	U C A G
	A	AUU AUC } Ile AUA AUG Met	ACU ACC ACA ACG } Thr	AAU AAC } Asn AAA AAG } Lys	AGU AGC } Ser AGA AGG } Arg	U C A G
	G	GUU GUC GUA GUG } Val	GCU GCC GCA GCG } Ala	GAU GAC } Asp GAA GAG } Glu	GGU GGC GGA GGG } Gly	U C A G

Figure 14. The genetic code. Each codon of three "letters"
encodes an amino acid. There are four different letters, known
as bases, in the DNA: thymine = T (transcribed into RNA as U =
uracil); C = cytosine; A = adenine; G = guanine. In the double-
stranded DNA helix, a G binds to a C and an A binds to a T (or U
in RNA). Protein-encoding genes in the DNA are transcribed into
messenger RNA (mRNA), and it is the triplet codon sequences in
the mRNA that are shown here. RNA uses the same nucleotides as
DNA except that uracil is used in place of thymine. Abbreviated

forms of the 20 amino acids are shown e.g. Tyr = tyrosine; Ser = serine; Gly = glycine, etc.

The genetic code is extremely elegant. There are four genetic "letters" in the DNA (see Figure 14 legend for details). Each "genetic word" composed of three letters is known as a codon. Randomly mix up four letters to arrange them into three-letter codons and what you get is the 64 codons shown in Figure 14. The task of the protein-encoding genes in the DNA is to convert the information contained in the long sequences of triplet codons into the precise sequence of amino acids found in proteins. Our bodies are composed, in part, of proteins and they carry out most of the essential functions of our bodies that keep us alive. The functions of the proteins are dependent on getting the amino acid sequence exactly right. So, as Figure 15 illustrates, the information in the DNA is "transcribed" into a mirror-image copy of its sequence known as messenger RNA (mRNA) inside the nucleus of the cell where the DNA is located. The mRNA then moves out of the cell into the surrounding area of the cell known as the cytoplasm where the amino acids are located. Each amino acid is picked up by a "shuttle molecule" or "adaptor" known as a transfer RNA (tRNA). There are about 60 different tRNA molecules that recognize the 20 different amino acids usually used to make proteins (some amino acids are recognized by several tRNAs). Each tRNA includes an acceptor "arm" that attaches by a chemical bond to a specific amino acid, as Figure 15 illustrates. At the other end of the tRNA molecule there is another arm, and right in the middle of it is a triplet sequence of nucleotides known as the anticodon. The anticodon corresponds exactly to the codon in the mRNA sequence, like a plug fits into a complementary socket. So, for example, the UAC codon in the mRNA will bind to the AUG anticodon in the tRNA, and sure enough we find tyrosine bound to the other end of this particular tRNA. There are a total of 20 amino acids specified by the genetic code, but there are more than 20 different tRNA "plugs" because there are more than 20 different mRNA "sockets".

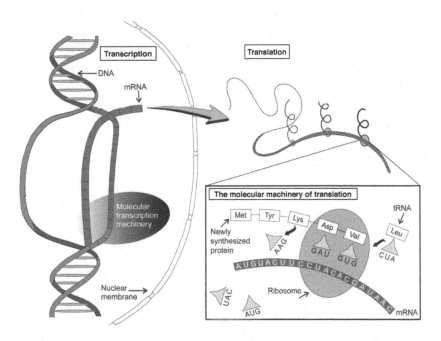

Figure 15. Transcription and translation. Transcription is the process by which RNA is synthesized using a DNA template. Transcription occurs in the nucleus of the cell, and mRNA molecules then move into the cytoplasm, which occupies the main body of the cell, where they are translated into proteins. Translation is the process by which proteins are synthesized from individual amino acids using mRNA as a template. Translation occurs on ribosomes, which bring together the mRNA and amino acids bound to tRNAs.

The clever ribosome, a complex molecular machine that provides a docking site for protein synthesis, now plugs in the next tRNA, which has UUC as its anticodon, corresponding to AAG in the mRNA, and this time we find the amino acid lysine bound to the acceptor arm of the tRNA. The first two amino acids of our new protein are now next to each other, brought into position like two boats moored side by side. An enzyme then catalyses a peptide bond between the two amino acids, which holds them together quite firmly, and the ribosome shuttles along to pick up the next amino acid in the growing chain until we have the sequence: tyrosine–lysine–aspartate–valine–leucine–leucine. A real protein will be much bigger than this, and so on the machinery goes until it finally reaches a STOP signal, and the completed protein drops off.

The DNA code is redundant, meaning that nearly always more than one codon encodes for each amino acid. For example, inspection of Figure 14 shows that there are six codons that encode for the amino acid serine. There is also one codon that serves as a START signal so that the translational machinery knows where to start reading the mRNA and there are also three STOP codons telling the machinery where the end of the protein should be.

The same basic process of transcription followed by translation, and virtually the same genetic code, are common to all living things: microorganisms, plants, and animals. Now the big question for our present context is: how did such an elegant genetic code ever get established? And did it just happen randomly or are there some chemical and physical underlying principles, associated with systems analysis, which could mean that this particular genetic code might just be the best code that there can be? If each of the 20 amino acids and STOP signals are assigned at random to at least one codon, there are a possible 10^{84} codon tables that could be generated like the one shown in Figure 14 (that's a 1 followed by 84 noughts, which is a mighty big number). Why do we have this particular code out of all the trillions of possible codes?

Now I was brought up (during my education in biochemistry) as a strong believer in the QWERTY phenomenon. Stare at the top line of the letters in your laptop or other electronic device, and that is what you see. As most people know, early typists used a different keyboard, but when they typed fast on the old-fashioned typewriters, certain sets of keys kept getting stuck. In the process of solving the problem, they put the QWERTY letters in a row and there they have remained until this day, fixed by the evolutionary history of the typewriter – and don't you dare change it! (Though many have tried.) By analogy, that might be a very good reason why the genetic code is pretty much the same for all living organisms, with a few minor exceptions sufficiently rare that their discovery tends to get published in the scientific literature. That's also known as the "frozen accident" theory. The genetic code is part of a complex recognition and translation system, as we have just noted – change one component of the system and it no longer works properly. But that still leaves the question as to how the 64-triplet codon system arose in the first place. If we ever find life on other planets, as most scientists think we will (this author included), might it even have the same or a very similar genetic code as the one shown in Figure 14?

We definitely do not yet know the answer to any of these questions for sure. But what we do know is that the genetic code has certain clear advantages as compared to other possible codes that one might derive from a sequence of the bases found in DNA. Study Figure 14 and it is immediately apparent that the genetic code is non-random. In general, codons that differ only by a single genetic letter tend to encode the same or similar amino acids. For example, four out of the six codons that encode serine all have UC as their first two genetic letters. The same principle holds true for many of the other amino acids – the first two letters are the same, only the third varies. This means that if the third nucleotide is mutated in codons starting with UC, you are still going to get a codon that encodes serine – so nothing changes in the protein being made. This is known as a "synonymous" mutation because the resulting amino acid remains the same. But if the third letter in UUU changes to an A, then the resulting amino acid will change from a phenylalanine (Phe) to a leucine (Leu), which is known as a non-synonymous mutation. The more synonymous codons there are for a particular amino acid (like serine or leucine), the more frequently is that amino acid found in proteins (Gilis et al., 2001). Furthermore, codons with U in the second position tend to correspond to bulky water-hating amino acids ("hydrophobic"), which contribute to the eventual three-dimensional structure of the protein – they are generally found on the inside of the protein well away from the water on the outside (Koonin and Novozhilov, 2009). One other point that isn't apparent just by looking at Figure 14 (unless you've memorized the structures of all 20 amino acids) is that the smaller the amino acid, the more codons are committed to encoding it. So small amino acids like serine (Ser) and glycine (Gly) are encoded by six and four different codons, whereas the much larger amino acids called tryptophan (Trp) and histidine (His) are encoded by one and two different codons, respectively. Everything is very carefully arranged.

Theories for the origin of the code tend to fall into three types and it's very possible that all three ideas are relevant to the mystery (Koonin and Novozhilov, 2009). In our present context, what is important to note is that in all cases the idea is that the evolution of the code followed a logical, step-by-step gradual process. Certainly, it may have ended up as a "QWERTY phenomenon", too costly in biological terms to change, but there is plenty of evidence suggesting that the evolution of the particular code we have was no accident.

One type of idea is known as the "error minimization theory" in which selection operates to minimize the deleterious effects of mutations occurring at different places in the codon. A mutation simply refers to a change in one or more base "letters" in the DNA sequence. Mutations generally happen during cell replication when the DNA of the cell also replicates. The fidelity of DNA replication is incredibly high, but occasionally errors in replication get past the rigorous checking and repair machinery that is located in the cell nucleus. A less common cause of mutations is radiation or chemical damage, for example from chemicals that we eat or breathe. We all differ in around 0.5% of our genetic letters. Every newborn baby carries up to 60 new mutations not present in their parents, the precise number dependent upon the age of the father (Kong et al., 2012). Mutations are essential for evolution to occur and essential for the wide genetic variation that exists in human populations. Of course, deleterious mutations can also contribute to disease, which is a bad thing, but mutations also contribute to us all looking and being somewhat different, which I think most people would accept as a good thing (if all humans looked identical, life would be pretty boring). But if we did not have the genetic code we in fact have, then the genetic disease load would be much higher. Why?

In thinking about this question, it should be remembered that when any one of the genetic letters is changed to another, in most situations the codon for one amino acid will most likely be changed to the codon for a different amino acid, in other words the change will be non-synonymous. So in assessing just how deleterious is "deleterious", one needs to think about the chemistry of each amino acid and what will be the consequences of switching one for another in the protein being made. For example, some amino acids are hydrophilic chemicals, which is jargon meaning that they love water, whereas other amino acids are hydrophobic ("water-hating") as already mentioned. So substituting a hydrophobic amino acid in the place of one that is hydrophilic will potentially cause a much greater disruption of protein structure than if the substitute were hydrophilic. Disease may very well be the result. There are also chemical implications entailed in switching one type of genetic letter for another. Bearing all these points in mind, it turns out that out of a million possible sets of randomized 64-triplet codons, only one set turned out to be better than the set that we in fact have. As the authors who made this discovery comment: our genetic code is quite literally "one in a million" (Freeland and Hurst, 1998; Freeland et al., 2003). As with all current ideas about the genetic code there are, needless to say, complications (as discussed in Koonin and Novozhilov, 2009). In any event, such observations, fascinating as they are, do not tell us how the genetic code evolved in the first place.

"Stereochemical theories" represent the second main idea about the genetic code. These ideas suggest that it was the amino acids that originally "chose" the codons and anticodons that are now found in the transfer RNA adaptors that bind to amino acids and bring them into line during protein synthesis. The "Escaped Triplet Theory" (also dubbed the "Direct RNA Template" model) is a good example of this type of idea (Yarus et al., 2005). Amino acids are present in some of the meteorites that bombard the Earth, and many of them can be synthesized under prebiotic conditions (meaning chemically under conditions that do not require the biochemistry of living cells). The "Escaped Triplet Theory" is based on the fact that if we take a large number of randomized RNA sequences (known as "aptamers") and determine experimentally which ones interact preferentially with a certain amino acid (albeit weakly), we are far more likely than mere chance would allow to pick out precisely those RNA molecules that contain the triplet codon, and often the anticodon as well, that today we know specifies that particular amino acid. For example, in one randomized binding study, the amino acids arginine, isoleucine, and tyrosine bound preferentially to RNA molecules containing either their known codons or anticodons (Rodin et al., 2011). In another study six out of eight amino acids rigorously tested displayed such preferential binding (Yarus et al., 2009). In the translation system used by all cells today, such differential binding affinities are irrelevant because the tRNAs act as adaptor molecules to bring each amino acid into its correct position. So the idea in the "Escaped Triplet Theory" is that we are seeing some molecular characteristics that might represent remnants of an earlier, more primitive system for synthesizing proteins using RNA as template. The greater affinities of a subset of amino acids for RNA molecules containing precisely the "correct" codons and/ or anticodons – that is, the coding system now in use – does quite likely represent the vestigial signs of a stage along the way to the more complex system that we have today that translates genetic information into very precise protein structures. "Tantalising hints but no conclusive evidence" is how one reviewer has assessed data concerning these ideas (Koonin and Novozhilov, 2009).

The third main collection of theories that aim to explain the origin of the genetic code are known as "coevolution theories" because they point out that the present genetic code clearly needed to coevolve with the various components of the system as illustrated in Figure 15 (Wong et al., 2016). Beyond the system as shown, there also had to be a plentiful supply of the amino acids used to make proteins. Indeed, it was recognized very early on after the genetic code was worked out during the 1960s, that it had rather special structural relationships to the amino acids. For example, it has long been known that several amino acids are made in the body by the same biosynthetic pathway. After the triplet codons had been identified, it was then noticed that codons specifying the amino acids made by the same biosynthetic pathway tend to have the same first "letter" (nucleotide) in the triplet. Amino acids made by the same pathway are said to belong to the same "family". So codons of the amino acid belonging to the shikimate, pyruvate, aspartate, and glutamate families tend to have U, G, A, and C in the first position, respectively. As with the stereochemical theories, it looks as if there is an intimate relationship between the genetic code and the amino acids that they now encode. The full technical details of coevolution theories are complex (Wong et al., 2016) and beyond the scope of our present discussion. But for those concerned about the question 'which came first, the chicken or the egg?', the answer is clear in this instance: "both". In other words, complex systems need to evolve together if they are to retain functionality, which is why no discussion of the origin of the genetic code is complete without considering the cellular system in which it is embedded taken as a whole. That is what coevolution is about.

The scientific literature on the origins of the genetic code is huge and this brief summary does not do it justice. Furthermore, all the ideas summarized in the three main theories very likely play key roles along the way to the genetic code that we have today. What is important to highlight in our present context is that all these ideas depend on orderly, systematic, biochemical ideas and observations. Were stochastic (chance) events involved in the generation of the genetic code? Of course – no doubt billions of them. But there appear to be good reasons why the code we now have appears to function so well in all living things today on planet Earth: physical and chemical constraints ensured that its generation was shaped by the needs of optimum functionality. If we find life on another planet, as seems very likely (and assuming we don't contaminate it with Earthly molecules), it also seems a reasonable expectation that information-containing molecules like RNA and DNA will be present in its life-forms, and it would not be at all surprising to find a genetic code if not the same, at least similar, to the one we have on planet Earth. Hopefully it will be dissimilar enough so that we can be sure that it belongs to planet Bandril rather than planet Earth.

Physical constraints on RNA molecule selection

The comment above concerning the extent to which "chance" events were involved in the generation of the genetic code raises the question: "Well, how would we know? We weren't there!" Fair point, but as indicated in that discussion, it is natural selection that wins in the end – however many systems are "tried out" in the workshop of life, it is only those that function well in the generation and success of living systems that will be perpetuated. But this also raises a further question: in the "chance" stage of the process, when lots of different systems are being tried out, is natural selection actually presented with every possible version of a molecule that could exist before natural selection weeds out the unfit, and the optimal molecule (in that particular living organism) is then perpetuated to exist in succeeding generations? This question is reminiscent of the experiments of Rick Lenski described in the previous chapter in which there are so many bacteria in the populations being investigated in his experiments that pretty much the whole genome of these bugs is being mutationally checked out every few days to see if it increases the fitness of the bugs under fixed environmental conditions. But when it comes to the structure of molecules, rather than bugs, it turns out that basic physical constraints mean that in some, perhaps most situations, the full range of possibilities generated by randomizing the options is never achieved, and so natural selection can only act with reference to a specific subset of possibilities.

To illustrate how this works in practice, consider an experiment carried out by the laboratory of Professor Ard Louis in the Physics Department at Oxford University (Schaper and Louis, 2014). Understanding the experiment depends on knowing that RNA molecules that encode enzymatic activity (meaning they act as biological catalysts) are known as ribozymes. So these molecules can both self-replicate and catalyse other biochemical transformations. It is partly for this reason that the "RNA world" idea for the origin of life is currently quite popular, because ribozymes potentially get round the chicken-and-egg problem of whether information-containing molecules or enzymes (made of proteins) arose first: ribozymes are both information-bearing and act as enzymes.

The Louis research team synthesized a ribozyme 55 nucleotides long. Using computer modelling programs, it's possible to predict what the structure of any given RNA molecule will be as these molecules are a lot simpler than protein structures. So this research group then generated millions of randomized versions of this particular ribozyme and what they found, astonishingly, was that 25% of all the possible sequences of the four genetic letters produced identical structures representing 50% of all the possible three-dimensional structures, whereas other structures were only generated by a tiny percentage of the randomized sequences. In other words, the system is constrained to select for those structures that are more likely to be available, and in fact the number of possible versions of this string of nucleotides is so huge that there are some structures that natural selection is unlikely ever to see. Mutations provide the target for natural selection, but evolution is biased to select for those physical structures that are generated more frequently. The authors of this work have dubbed this phenomenon "the arrival of the frequent" because the system is biased to "present" to natural selection only a relatively limited repertoire of all theoretically possible randomized 55 nucleotide-containing molecules.

To test these ideas further, the same research group has investigated different structures of a much longer RNA molecule 126 nucleotides long (Dingle et al., 2015). If only a single molecule existed of each possible randomized sequence of this length (remembering that it only contains four different nucleotides), the total mass resulting would be greater than the mass of the known universe. Who ever said that only cosmologists deal in big numbers! But despite this huge number, these researchers discovered that finding the structures that could function "correctly" in living cells was surprisingly easy, despite the vast number of theoretical possibilities. The reason once again is that only a limited number of sequences adopt the type of structure that is potentially functional. As Ard Louis comments: "Strong bias in the arrival of variation may explain why certain phenotypes are repeatedly observed in nature, while others never appear" (Louis, 2016). If you are commuting in London every day by bus to your place of work and bus numbers

10, 22, and 43 will all get you there, but bus number 10 is ten times more frequent than the others, you should not find it surprising that you most often travel to work on bus number 10.

The chemical properties of the periodic table of elements ultimately shape what is available for selection. Most people will remember the periodic table from their school chemistry. All 118 known elements are arranged in a nice neat table according to their atomic numbers, starting with hydrogen, which has an atomic number of 1, all the way up to the most recently discovered element (at the time of writing) ununoctium, which has an atomic number of 118 (ununoctium means one-one-eight in Latin). When I was at school I made up a mnemonic in order to memorize the periodic table. (Why, I can't imagine. Many things one did in one's youth are deeply mysterious when viewed with the advantage of hindsight.) But annoyingly I can still remember the first line: "Horrible Henry Lit a Beryllium Bomb Containing Nice Orange Flavoured Nectar" (you need to look at the table to make sense of that). As far as living organisms are concerned, we really don't need to worry about ununoctium, but rather with the key elements involved in life which have much smaller atomic numbers, such as 6, 7 and 8 (carbon, nitrogen, and oxygen). It is such elements in the nucleotides that make up molecules such as RNA and DNA that define their structures in space which in turn determine their functional properties in living things, in turn helping to explain phenomena such as the "arrival of the frequent".

The constraints on protein evolution

From information-containing molecules like DNA and RNA, let us turn to another class of information-containing molecules: proteins, the building-blocks of life. As already outlined, proteins are polymers built out of 20 different kinds of amino acid. It is the precise sequence of the amino acids, in turn encoded by the genes, that define the properties of each protein.

The fact that just 20 different kinds of amino acid (plus a couple more rare ones on occasion) are used to build all the proteins in all living organisms, is itself remarkable. There are many thousands of possible amino acids. In fact, a computer program has been used to generate around 120,000 possible amino acid structures of which approximately 4,000 could, in principle, be used to build proteins (Meringer et al., 2013).[32] Many of these are known to exist. For example, the famous Murchison meteorite, which landed near Murchison in the state of Victoria in Australia in 1969, contains at least 75 different amino acids. Yet out of the thousands of amino acids that could have potentially been used to make proteins, the 20 that are in actual use have been shown to be just right for the job in terms of their size and chemical properties (Ilardo et al., 2015). To come to this conclusion, the scientists who carried out this study compared the 20 amino acids in actual use with 1,913 other amino acids that lie within the same size range, but found that other sets of 20 amino acids drawn from these 1,913 would not work nearly so well or would cost the cell too much energy in producing them (Ilardo et al., 2015). As the authors of this paper conclude: "The amino acids used for constructing coded proteins may represent a largely global optimum, such that any aqueous biochemistry would use a very similar set." Clearly there has been a very strong selection pressure to end up with the 20 amino acids in current use in all proteins.

Probably no other known polymer displays the huge range of properties found in different kinds of protein. Proteins can be rigid like the collagen present in our bones; they can be soft and mushy, as in the liver; they can be used as enzymes, highly specific catalysts; they can carry oxygen around the body; plus hundreds of other properties and functions. The mean length of proteins is 475 amino acids long. But consider a protein just 100 amino acids long. There are 20^{100} possible sequences for such a protein, a number much larger than the total number of electrons in the universe.

Initially back in the 1960s when the first three-dimensional structures of proteins were being solved, it was thought that they would all be unique. Since evolution was a random process (or so it was thought at the time), each protein would reflect a happy accident, frozen in time due to its gain in function. Once the accident had happened, it would be impossible to change because that protein became one of the "housekeeping proteins" that are essential for life on this planet as we know it. But then the Nobel Prize-winner Max Perutz (in Cambridge) and others started showing that proteins with the same functions in different species had very similar structures, albeit different sequences of amino acid. Perutz recorded how his finding was "met with disbelief among biologists" (Perutz, 1983), even though we now take that fact for granted. Today we know that many different amino acid sequences can fold into the same three-dimensional structure. In some cases, these sequences give no evidence of sequence homology (similarity). Evolution has "discovered" the same functional structures by finding different ways up the mountain and eventually arriving in the same functional space.

And very early on it was recognized that proteins can be classified according to the different folds that they contain, meaning the particular way in which their domains are arranged in three-dimensional space. Indeed, it is that particular ensemble of folds that together specifies a protein's function. Over the years, many classification schemes have been established and the three-dimensional structures of more than 100,000 proteins have now been published. The number of folds in all these proteins is estimated in the range 1,000–10,000. But even if the true number is 10,000, this is still a tiny number compared to 20^{100}. In other words, all living things are united, not only by having the same genetic code, but also by possessing an elegant and highly restricted set of protein structures. Only this particular set, presumably, will carry out all the various functions that are required for proteins to organize the biochemical processes of life.

So how do proteins evolve? There is a vast literature in answer to that question. But in our present context it is the constraints involved that are truly fascinating. One way of envisaging protein evolution is by means of fitness landscapes as illustrated in Figure 16. The peaks represent the amino acid sequences for a particular protein that bestow optimal fitness on a particular organism operating in a particular environment, and the valleys represent less fitness. So the question then is: when mutating step-by-step from low fitness to optimal fitness, are there many paths up the mountain or just a few? One study investigated this question by studying how a bacterial enzyme adapted to the presence of a novel antibiotic (Poelwijk et al., 2007). And to cut a long story short, what the investigators found was that there were 120 theoretically possible ways for the amino acid sequence of the enzyme to move from no resistance to the antibiotic to optimal resistance by means of random mutations, but in practice only 18 of those ways were actually feasible due to various constraints. Based on these and other examples, the authors comment: "That only a few paths are favored... implies that evolution might be more reproducible than is commonly perceived, or even be predictable."

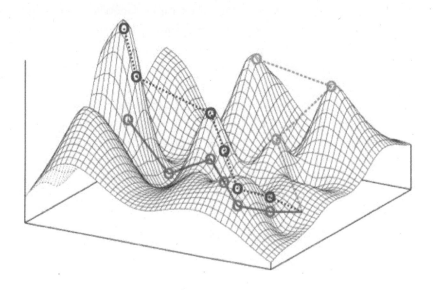

Figure 16. The dotted lines illustrate the various ways in which an enzyme (a protein that acts as a catalyst) can evolve to achieve optimal fitness for a particular task, illustrated by the "mountain peaks". There are only a few ways "up the mountain" to achieve optimal fitness and these can be achieved in small, incremental steps. The figure was designed to illustrate evolutionary fitness as measured by reproductive success, but the same point applies equally well to enzyme evolution.

Convergent evolution also applies just as much to proteins as to other components of living things. As the title of a scientific paper on the topic states "Convergent evolution of enzyme active sites is not a rare phenomenon" (Gherardini et al., 2007). The specific amino acid sequences of proteins that bestow upon them specific enzymatic activities is no accident. This again contrasts sharply with what biologists initially thought would be the case before such structural studies began. For example, Jacques Monod in his famous book *Chance and Necessity* (Monod, 1997) declared that "the biosphere does not contain a predictable class of events" (p. 49) and that amino acid sequences "show no regularity, special feature or restrictive character... but rather appear completely haphazard, each discloses nothing in its structure other than the pure chance of its origin" (pp. 94–97). As already mentioned, Monod extrapolated from such assertions in biology, which we now know to be false, to also assert that Chance with a big "C" also rules over the universe, a claim that we shall consider further in the following chapter.

Genes, evolvability, and sticklebacks

One puzzle people often have about evolution is how a living organism's genome evolves from state A to state B without destroying the organism along the way? It's clearly not possible to change the basic bricks and mortar of a living system that much, meaning the so-called housekeeping genes that are needed to keep the basic physiological functions going. For example, the gene encoding cytochrome c, involved in energy generation in the cell, is very similar right across the plant and animal kingdoms. Change the amino acid sequence of the cytochrome c protein by even a little bit and it no longer functions properly and all you have is a dead plant or a dead animal. Generating energy for the cell is a very basic function. So cytochrome c is a typical "housekeeping" gene.

How evolution gets round this problem of making the transition from genomic state A to state B is a trendy research field known as "evolvability". For example, instead of the lethal option of acting on housekeeping genes, evolution tends to act on regulatory sequences or on genes that act as "input/output genes", encoding key switching proteins that integrate whole sets of information that are then mediated to downstream effectors.

As the authors of a review entitled "Is Genetic Evolution Predictable?" comment:

> *Recent observations indicate that all genes are not equal in the eyes of evolution. Evolutionarily relevant mutations tend to accumulate in hotspot genes and at specific positions within genes. Genetic evolution is constrained by gene function, the structure of genetic networks, and population biology. The genetic basis of evolution may be predictable to some extent. (Stern and Orgogozo, 2009)*

More than 350 such hotspot genes, meaning genes that are more "evolvable" than others, have now been identified.

A single example will serve to illustrate the point. Three-spined stickleback fish have evolved into many distinct forms in different lakes. The original three-spined stickleback lives in coastal seas and, like salmon, swims up rivers to spawn. During the last big retreat of the glaciers 10,000–20,000 years ago, many populations of three-spined sticklebacks were trapped in newly formed lakes, and they have since adapted to those environments (Wray, 2007). Whereas marine sticklebacks are heavily armoured with an array of plates and spines, the freshwater populations all show versions of armour loss. They don't need to be armed like tanks in friendly freshwater lakes.

How could genetic variation evolve in such a short time to generate such different phenotypes without causing changes lethal to the sticklebacks along the way? Investigations into the genetic basis of pelvic spine loss have turned up a gene called *Pitx1*, a protein transcription factor or activator which regulates the developmental programme that leads to spine formation. It turns out that a DNA lesion in freshwater sticklebacks has removed about 500 nucleotides of regulatory sequence that normally upregulates Pitx1 protein production specifically in the pelvis. With the Pitx1 protein expressed normally in all other tissues, but virtually lost in the pelvic region, development proceeds normally in all other respects except for the reduction in body armour.

Most remarkably of all, mutations in the same or closely related *Pitx1* gene regulatory regions have evolved independently multiple times in stickleback populations found in different freshwater lakes around the world. These populations exist in landlocked lakes where there can have been little chance of swapping fish between the lakes. So mutations are not really random: there are regions of the genome where variation is much more likely to occur. In fact, it turns out that the gene *Pitx1* is located in a fragile region of the chromosome that is subject to more deletions of segments of DNA than other regions (Chan et al., 2010).

So sticklebacks are predisposed to remarkably rapid changes in their pelvic spines at multiple levels: the relevant regulatory gene is located in a highly changeable area of the genome; the gene in question can act as a master-control body-armour switching apparatus; and variants that reduce pelvic spines will be rapidly selected in environments where those spines decrease fitness. Without such clever "evolvability" living things wouldn't exist – including us. It's yet another example of "Goldilocks biology" – unless the evolutionary systems have these very particular kinds of property, we certainly wouldn't be here to discuss the question. But isn't that a circular argument – we wouldn't exist to have the discussion unless precisely these kinds of well-organized systems were in place? Precisely so, that's just the point.

Convergence at the molecular level

In the previous chapter we considered some examples of evolutionary convergence from the perspective of "big living things" and their adaptive requirements for existence on this planet. Molecules came into the story on occasion, but they weren't the main focus. We now give some examples of convergence where the molecular aspect is in many ways the most fascinating part of the story. More than 100 examples have already been reported in the scientific literature describing examples of genetic convergence in which genes have been independently adapted or modified in identical or very similar ways to produce adaptive traits (Stern, 2013). In reality, of course, the "big visible changes" and the "small molecular changes" are but two sides of the same coin: both aspects are changing at the same time because the genetic, protein, and morphology (or other adaptive) stories at the "higher" level are intricately entwined together. Living organisms are complete integrated systems – it's just us scientists who find it easier to focus on one or another component of the system to make the explanations (hopefully) a bit more understandable.

Genes that change repeatedly and independently during the course of evolution to produce the same traits are sometimes known as "hotspot genes". One study identified 111 different genes that have repeatedly caused the appearance of similar traits in separate evolutionary lineages (Martin and Orgogozo, 2013). Hot-spot genes can be discovered experimentally by exposing bacteria or fungi to toxic reagents, such as antibiotics, under controlled laboratory culture conditions. For example, in one experiment using yeast exposed to a fungicide (which kills most yeast or at least inhibits their growth), resistance to the fungicide occurred in 33 out of 35 cases in two hotspot genes known as ERG3 and ERG6, reflected in the substitution of different amino acids at different sites in these genes, sufficient to bring about resistance (Gerstein et al., 2012). The genomic scope for adaptation was narrow. As reviewers of this field note: "Overall, the repeated evolution of specific amino acid residues are one of the best illustrations of the constraints that structure the protein adaptive landscape, with a finite number of substitutions allowing a functional and viable effect on the phenotype" (Martin and Orgogozo, 2013). The examples that follow provide some striking examples of this principle.

A molecular story in convergent echolocation

Echolocation is the method that mammals such as bats, porpoises, and dolphins, use for hearing. It involves sending out pings of sound that bounce off objects and are then received back and analysed – an animal sonar system, used not just to detect the presence of objects, but to locate and identify prey. The brain works out how long it takes for the ping of sound to come back, and so how far away is the object. If you've ever watched bats wheeling around the trees at dusk, or perhaps sensed them flying around your head in a dark cave, you'll know that the system has to work incredibly quickly and efficiently to avoid mishaps. Bats can detect the presence of a tiny crawling insect or even a human hair, and can recognize each others' "voices".

A special protein called prestin is key to this sophisticated high-speed process. Prestin is found in the outer hair cells of the inner ear of the mammalian cochlea, a fluid-filled chamber. As the fluid is compressed by the sound waves the ear receives, so the sensory hairs surrounding the chamber move very slightly and convert their movements into nerve impulses via thousands of "hair cells". The outer hair cells that serve as an amplifier in the inner ear refine the sensitivity and frequency selectivity of the mechanical vibrations of the cochlea.

The specialized prestin found in echolocating mammals provides a much faster system for converting air pressure waves into nerve impulses than the prestin found in mammals (like us) that do not use echolocation. The convergent story became apparent when it was discovered that the prestin gene has independently accumulated many of the same mutational changes in bats, porpoises, and dolphins, changes that are essential for prestin to perform its unique functions (Jones, 2010). Similar changes have occurred in unrelated lineages of different bats. Genetic evidence suggests that these changes have undergone natural selection. In other words, here is an adaptation that is of great advantage to the animal that has it, so animals carrying this particular set of mutation in the prestin gene are more likely to reproduce and spread the beneficial gene around an interbreeding population. The particular advantage may well be the necessity to hear very high frequencies, far above the ability of the human ear to hear. The advantage of possessing this fancy piece of echolocation equipment has helped shape the evolution of the prestin gene such that it has converged on the same adaptive solution independently on multiple occasions.

Molecular convergence in photosynthesis

Another dramatic example of molecular convergence is provided by a photosynthetic pathway, known as the C4 pathway (Gowik and Westhoff, 2012). Photosynthesis is the process whereby plants derive energy from the sun, "fixing" carbon dioxide and giving off oxygen at the same time. It normally generates a molecule containing three carbon (C) atoms as its first product, so the process is known as C3 photosynthesis. About 95% of the biomass of all photosynthesizing life on the planet uses this C3 pathway, which is most efficient when relatively abundant carbon dioxide is available, temperatures are moderate, and water is plentiful.

C4 photosynthesis, used by plants that include crops such as maize and sugar cane, generates a molecule containing four atoms of carbon as its first product, and comes into its own under rather different conditions when carbon dioxide levels fall, and the climate is hot and dry. The leaves of plants are organized differently when they photosynthesize this way in order to concentrate the carbon dioxide at a particular spot. The C4 pathway evolved in grasses about 30 million years ago, probably in response to a declining level of carbon dioxide in the atmosphere. What is most striking in the present context is that C4 photosynthesis has evolved independently more than 40 times in at least 18 different plant families, one of the most striking examples of molecular convergence yet described.

This has involved the parallel evolution of several different genes encoding the enzymes that are required for the C4 pathway. One of these genes (known as PEPC) evolved C4 functionality at least 8 times in different grasses independently, involving similar or identical changes in 21 different codons in their genomes. Some of this variation is due to lateral gene transfer from other grasses whereby a species that has already learned the genetic "tricks of the C4 trade" passes on its information by direct transfer (Christin et al., 2012). Whoever said that different grasses don't cooperate.

Similar striking examples of PEPC gene convergence have been found in flowering plants as well. The sedge family contains more than 1,500 species that use C4 photosynthesis, which appears to have evolved five times independently within this family (Besnard et al., 2009). In this case, the PEPC gene has acquired identical or similar sets of mutations in at least 16 different codons that have been under strong natural selection, just like the prestin alleles in the echolocation example. Identical changes in the same codons were also found in various grasses and eudicots, a quite distinct group of flowering plants that includes familiar friends like the buttercup and dandelion. In other words, in many cases precisely the same mutation occurred to convert one amino acid to another at precisely the same spot in the PEPC amino acid sequence.

Crickets under attack

Is evolutionary convergence still happening? The answer is "yes", although the slow speed of evolution generally makes it difficult to observe the process. Occasionally there are exceptions, and a recent example from the world of crickets provides an example (Pascoal et al., 2014). Male crickets sing to attract a mate by vibrating their wings. On two Hawaiian islands, however, they face a challenge. There are killer flies on the prowl that have learned how to home in on the crickets' chirps with deadly precision. Once close to their prey, a pregnant fly will spray baby maggots onto the cricket's back, which then burrow in, feed well, and eventually emerge after about a week, leaving the husk of the hapless cricket behind. Charming. The flies came from North America; the crickets were newcomers from Australia. Fortunately for the crickets, an adaptive mutation came to their rescue not once, but twice, independently in two different cricket populations on two different Hawaiian islands separated by more than 60 miles.

First a mutant population of crickets was discovered on the island of Kauai. The mutation resulted in crickets that can no longer chirp, thereby preventing being a target for the nasty flies. Clearly being a chirpless cricket comes at a cost given that males normally chirp to attract a mate. Yet within 20 generations this mutation had spread through more than 90% of the crickets on this island. Somehow the male chirpless crickets still found their mate – many, it turns out, by the cunning ploy of loitering near crickets that could still chirp and intercepting the females on their way to the chirpers. Now comes the really surprising part of the story. Two years after the discovery in 2003 was made in Kauai, another population of silent crickets was found on the island of Oahu more than 60 miles away. The obvious initial conclusion by researchers was that a cricket carrying the mutation had been blown over to Oahu, or had been transferred on a boat, or perhaps a cricket egg had been transferred on someone's boot – all quite possible explanations. But then it was noticed that the wings of the two silent cricket populations on the island had different shapes. Further chromosomal analysis showed that the mutations which disrupted chirping in the two populations were in the same gene but were different mutations, indicating that they had arisen independently in the two different populations. The idea that the trait had evolved twice, at almost the same time, seemed far-fetched. As the leader of the research group that reported these findings, Nathan Bailey, commented to the BBC: "it still seems amazing to me".[33] But a review of hundreds of examples of evolutionary convergence should render such discoveries less surprising.

Energy-hungry brains and wings

Bats, primates, and cetaceans such as the blue-nosed dolphin have evolved independently for many millions of years, but they all have something important in common. In the case of dolphins and primates, it is because of their large brains. The dolphin brain at 1,500–1,700 gm actually weighs more than the human brain at 1,300–1,500 gm and is four times larger than that of the chimpanzee (400 gm). Some brain cells are called neurons, and they are the most energy hungry of all our cells – hence the need for frequent snacks while carrying out academic work (such as writing books). And bats are energy hungry due to the incredible rate at which they flap their wings. So there is a big evolutionary pressure to come up with the most efficient energy production system. This is provided by the Krebs cycle, the key energy-producing system in the mitochondria of our cells. And one of the key enzymes in that cycle is known as IDH2, a protein 452 amino acids long and folded up in order to carry out its precise enzymatic function.

It was recently shown, as Figure 17 illustrates, that in all three of the independent lineages of dolphins, bats, and primates like us, there is one single change of an amino acid from a valine to an alanine at position 186 (Ai et al., 2014). This makes the enzyme distinct from the IDH2 found in dozens of other species that are less energy-demanding and is very likely related to the efficiency of the enzyme in the Krebs cycle, though this has yet to be formally demonstrated. The main point in the present context is that precisely the same mutation has arisen in three different mammalian lineages independently, representing animals that are particularly energy hungry, in comparison with 28 other vertebrates in which the IDH2 gene was sequenced where valine was found at position 186, not alanine. The darker lines in the diagram below show the precise points at which the alanine 186 mutation originated in these lineages, a striking example of convergent evolution.

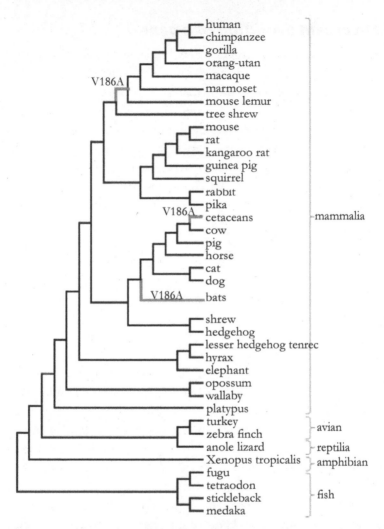

Figure 17. The conversion of a valine to an alanine in the Krebs cycle enzyme IDH2 at position 186 in three independent evolutionary lineages as shown by V186A. Note that the last common ancestors of bats, whales (cetaceans), and primates (humans, chimpanzee, etc.) do not have the V186A mutation in their IDH2, demonstrating that the mutation has arisen independently in these lineages.

Convergent evolution of a gene

Some examples of convergence defy the imagination, though the one that follows, though decidedly unusual, turns out to have an underlying potential mechanism that at least helps us understand how it came about.

Two "background facts" are important to appreciate this story. The first is that there are genes in many living organisms that block the replication of certain types of virus, thereby providing useful protection against viral attack. The second fact is that there are so-called "jumping genes" in the genomes of animals known as "transposons". These represent "copy-and-paste" segments of DNA and the great majority (representing an astounding 45% of our own genome) arise by a molecular mechanism whereby a segment of DNA is copied into RNA and then randomly inserted into some other location in the genome by converting the RNA "message" back into DNA again to make a second copy. Most of the time the copy makes no difference to the function of the genome, but sometimes it does. For example, the "jumping gene" can land right in the middle of a functional gene and disrupt it, causing disease on occasion. Other times, more helpfully, the jumping gene lands right within another gene so that it fuses with it and forms a new gene with new properties. This example of novel gene generation depends on this latter mechanism, something which happened not once, but on at least three different occasions in separate evolutionary lineages.

Geneticists don't always make it easy for the general reader to follow their results, partly because they have to call the different genes something and there are many thousands of genes, so thousands of different names. For example, TRIM5 is a gene that is involved in providing some animals, such as primates, with resistance to viral infection, and it does a good job in adapting to different retroviruses as they come along. If you are wondering about the "retro" aspect of the virus, it also helps to know that the flow of information is generally from DNA to RNA inside the cell, but the retroviral information goes in the opposite direction. A famous example of a retrovirus that infects humans is the HIV that causes AIDS. Once inserted into the genome, its DNA catches a free ride so that every time the cellular DNA replicates, more and more copies are made of the viral DNA.

The transposon part of this story comes from a gene called *Cyclophilin A*, or *CypA1* for short. The role of this gene is to encode the enzyme of that name which helps with the correct folding up of proteins, nothing to do with bestowing resistance to viral infections in animals. But then in a transpositional event around 5 million years ago, a copy of the *CypA1* gene, landed, wham!, right in the middle of the TRIM5 gene in an owl monkey (a large-eyed chiefly nocturnal monkey found in South America) (Sayah et al., 2004). The resulting new "fusion gene" is known, not surprisingly, as *TRIMCypA-1*. Of greater interest, *TRIMCypA-1* provides the owl monkey with a new and powerful resistance to the monkey equivalent of the HIV-1 retrovirus (simian immunodeficiency virus). Truly, the monkey won the National Lottery on this one (as it were).

Also about 5 million years ago, there was a quite separate transpositional event involving the same players to generate *TRIMCypA-2*, but this time it occurred in a macaque monkey, from this one individual spreading through various macaque species as Figure 18 illustrates (Virgen et al., 2008). It is easy to be sure that this fusion event occurred independently from the one in owl monkeys because the insertion involved a different location within the genome. Once again, the new fusion protein brings about resistance to specific retroviruses in the lucky macaques. Even just taking these two examples alone, this provides a remarkable example of convergence in which the same novel gene is generated independently with the same positive consequence. But now we come to the third part of the story, more recently discovered, in which a third fusion event has occurred involving the same genes, generating *TRIMCypA-3*, but this time in primates living about 18–43 million years ago, as Figure 18 illustrates (Malfavon-Borja et al., 2013). This particular fusion gene is still found to the present day in several Old World monkeys. The twist in the tale is that the new gene remained functional for around 10 million years and then degenerated to become a "pseudogene", now present in all simian primates. What this means is that mutations accumulated in the fusion gene to such an extent that it could no longer make the functional protein that bestows viral resistance as previously. Yet resurrection of the original fusion in the laboratory has shown that it exerted a broad and potent activity against many viruses. Why did it lose its function? Presumably because the "viral attack" frequency became less stringent in the environment in which the primates were living. Or perhaps because other viral resistance mechanisms evolved that were even more efficient, so that this one became less important. Maybe both explanations played a role. But in general, functional genes evolve into pseudogenes when their functions become less important and so the "natural selection pressure" is lessened. Pseudogenes can readily be recognized by their highly specific DNA sequence as being a functional gene in other living organisms, but have attained their pseudogene status by accumulating one or more mutations that disable their functionality.

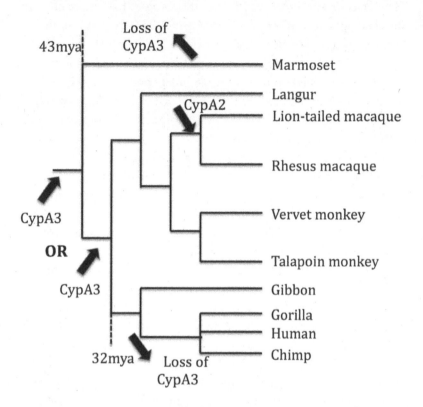

Figure 18. A phylogenetic tree showing when and where *CypA2* and *CypA3* were inserted into the evolutionary history of the species shown. "Loss of *CypA3*" does not mean that this fusion gene was totally lost from our genetic history, but rather it degenerated into a pseudogene around the times shown. Inspection of this diagram explains why the *CypA2* fusion gene is found in macaques but not in, for example, humans. The *CypA3* pseudogene is found in a much wider range of species because the transposition event happened much earlier in evolutionary time.

The take-home message from this somewhat intricate but fascinating series of events is that genes can converge onto the same solutions in order to adapt to the challenges that life throws up – in this case, the challenge of viral attack. The same solution in this case happened on at least three independent occasions. What perhaps makes this less surprising is that transpositional events are occurring all the time in the genome in which sections of DNA are copied and then pasted into other parts of the genome. Furthermore, the genome contains multiple copies of the *CypA* gene, increasing the chances that one of them will be picked up in a transpositional event (Zhang et al., 2003). But as the authors of some of this work described here comment: "Based on the number of CypA retrogenes and their distribution, we found the probability of the three retrogenes in such close proximity (to the TRIM gene) to be highly nonrandom… We therefore conclude that some recurrently acting selective pressure must have preserved CypA retrogenes within the TRIM5 locus" (Malfavon-Borja et al., 2013). With the benefit of hindsight, we now know that the resulting fusion genes provide some protection against viruses, so the selection pressure provided is that caused by the challenge of staying alive long enough to reproduce in the face of viral attack. But when we consider the fact that primate genomes are billions of genetic letters (nucleotides) in length, the fact that different primates on different occasions, over a relatively short period of time (in evolutionary terms), have acquired such resistance via the same convergent mechanism involving precisely the same part of the genome, these findings are indeed remarkable. The take-home message is that if the selection pressure is really powerful, then random molecular events are far more likely to be preserved for succeeding generations if their contribution to fitness is high. Evolution is converting randomness into purpose all the time, a theme further discussed in the following chapter.

Insects converge on resistance

The previous story focused on the acquisition of resistance to viruses over a period of a mere 40 million years or so. By contrast, another example involves insect species spanning 300 million years acquiring resistance to plant toxins (poisons) by evolving identical amino acid changes in the same protein. Plenty of plants produce toxins, such as nicotine and mustard oils, that insects find obnoxious. Some toxins are medically important and a group known as the cardenolides particularly so because they inhibit an enzyme known as the "sodium–potassium pump" which is essential for the normal functioning of nerves and heart muscle (I am particularly fond of this pump because, years ago, the research project for my PhD was to work out its structure). The foxglove is but one of dozens of flowering species that synthesize one or more cardenolides (in this case digoxin) to protect themselves against marauding insects. Ingestion of foxglove can be lethal for humans, especially small children.

The investigation of interest here involved sequencing the genes that encode the major portion of the sodium–potassium pump from 18 cardenolide-resistant insect species that feed on flowers, selected from 15 different genera from 4 different orders (Dobler et al., 2012; Zhen et al., 2012).[34] The remarkable finding was that amino acids at positions 111 and/or 122 of the protein encoded by the sodium–potassium pump gene had been changed to a different amino acid in 14 insect species, coming from all four orders, that feed on plants containing cardenolides, whereas this amino acid remained unchanged in the insects that do not. In fact, in four of the species the amino acid substituted at position 122 was the same in each case (rather remarkable given that there are 20 amino acids in all). Further experiments in which the mutant forms of the pump were expressed in cell-lines in the laboratory showed that the variant forms of the pump did indeed display much greater resistance to cardenolides as compared to the versions of the protein with amino acid sequences characteristic of insects that do not feed on plants containing these toxins. Generation of variant forms of the sodium–potassium pump is not the only way that insects can become resistant to toxic cardenolides, but it certainly seems to be a common mechanism. As the writers of the News Report on these findings comment in the journal *Nature*: "The patterns identified by Dobler and colleagues in the insect sodium–potassium pump gene are likely to become a textbook example of convergent evolution at the molecular level – illuminating how a common selective agent can lead to a common set of evolutionary solutions" (Whiteman and Mooney, 2012).

Molecular constraints: the big picture

As the evolutionary biologist Franklin Shull remarked many decades ago: "It strains one's faith in the laws of chance to imagine that identical changes should crop out again and again if the possibilities are endless and the probabilities equal" (Shull, 1935). The point, of course, as we are now in a better position to see, based on a far greater wealth of data than that available to Shull in the 1930s, is that the probabilities are not equal. In some cases, this may involve mutational bias, as with the *Pitx*1 gene in which there is instability in a particular region of the chromosome where that gene is located. In other cases, as with the *TRIMCyp* fusion genes, the genome is bombarded with transpositional events involving a second gene present in multiple copies, increasing the possibility of a useful outcome. But in most cases, there is no intrinsic reason why a particular molecular solution to life's challenges emerges apart from the fact that it's so useful to the organism that, once generated, it's much the best strategy to hang on to it. As a reviewer of the field of convergence, David Stern, comments: "The abundance of parallel and collateral evolution... implies that genome evolution is not random, but rather that the origin or the selective consequences of genetic variants, or both, might be somewhat predictable" (Stern, 2013). The possibility that evolutionary processes might at some level be predictable would certainly have been deemed heretical had it been mentioned in a previous era, but now it's quite commonplace to find such claims in the literature. How times have changed.

More broadly, the observations on the sophisticated structure of the genetic code; the elegant selection of a limited repertoire of protein structures out of possible field of trillions; the "arrival of the frequent" due to the physical constraints on the structure of molecules such as RNA so that the material "presented" to natural selection is already heavily preselected and far from merely random; the way in which genomic systems are set up to facilitate evolvability; and the ubiquitous phenomena of convergence – all these facets of the molecules that make life possible point to a high degree of organization and constraint in which molecular mechanisms are "steered" along certain channels defined by the needs and challenges of being alive (and reproducing) on planet Earth. All this does render somewhat implausible the claim that the molecular systems involved, taken in their entirety, are necessarily Purposeless.

We now turn to consider in greater detail the role that "chance" and "randomness" play in these important processes.

4

Biology, Randomness, Chance, and Purpose

A picture held us captive. And we could not get outside it, for it lay in our language and language seemed to repeat it to us inexorably.

Ludwig Wittgenstein (1968, p. 48)

There is no doubt that soon after Charles Darwin published *On the Origin of Species* in 1859 there was a lot of huffing and puffing from critics about what they saw as the "random" element in his theory of natural selection. Critics did not like the role that chance played in the generation of the variation upon which, wrote Darwin, natural selection acted.

As outlined in Chapter 1, it was initially the more mathematical approach to Darwinian evolution of the 1920s and 1930s, later to be known as the neo-Darwinian synthesis, that began to challenge Herschel's concerns about "higgledy-piggledy", later followed up by all the kinds of observations that have been summarized in the previous two chapters, until today we find Richard Dawkins writing in the preface to his book *The Blind Watchmaker*:

Take, for instance, the issue of "chance", often dramatized as blind chance. The great majority of people that attack

Darwinism leap with almost unseemly eagerness to the mistaken idea that there is nothing other than random chance in it. Since living complexity embodies the very antithesis of chance, if you think that Darwinism is tantamount to chance you'll obviously find it easy to refute Darwinism! One of my tasks will be to destroy this eagerly believed myth that Darwinism is a theory of "chance". (Dawkins, 1986, p. xi)

Well, "Amen" to that, and the sections that follow begin to flesh out what that means in practice.

Some definitional issues

What do we mean by "random"?

In daily speech, the word "random" is often used to mean "without order" or "without cause" or "uncertain" or "without purpose". Clearly if one has this last definition in mind, and then proceeds to claim that "evolution is a random process", well it must be purposeless by definition, a circular argument if ever there was one. Here we will focus more on the mathematical and scientific understandings of "random".

In mathematics, randomness has a fairly clear meaning, although with some nuances and conditions. "Mathematicians typically use the word 'random' to describe processes in which multiple outcomes can occur and each is associated with a probability that gives the likelihood of that outcome" (Giberson, 2016, p. 66). This entails, for example, that if you take a string of numbers, let us say 1–100, if the numbers are randomly selected, then any single number in this series will have an equal probability of being selected. Such a series can be generated by random number generators of the kind that can be found on many computers. A traditional statistical approach then examines such a series of numbers to see whether they display the property of randomness (Bartholomew, 2008, p.

62). No single number can be "random", it is rather the process whereby the numbers have been generated that can be assessed as being random, and that process can only be assessed with a long list of numbers. For example, the number in a series should not depend on a number that has just gone before. If every time that we found a 57 it was preceded by a 23 in the series, we might worry that the series was not truly random, and indeed the series might then in part become predictable. If it were genuinely random, it could not be predictable. So no part of the series should provide any information about the properties of any other part of the series. However, we need to be careful at this point, because in a series of ten randomized numbers picked from 1–100 it is entirely feasible, if we continue to use our random number generator long enough, that we will come up with 23–23–23–23–23–23–23–23–23–23. This doesn't *look* random, but every one in the series 1–100 has an equal chance (1 in 100) of being chosen, so the series of 23s just shown is no more or less likely than any other series of ten numbers from 1–100. Furthermore, if we randomized that series to 11 numbers, then the eleventh number could be 72 – in other words, a random series of ten 23s provides no expectation that the eleventh number is going to be a 23: the series is non-predictive.

If you want to experience a computer as it randomizes several series, go to http://sunsite.univie.ac.at/Mozart/dice. There you can find a webpage dedicated to a piano piece by Mozart composed in 1787 consisting of 32 bars. Altogether Mozart composed 176 bars from which the 32 bars making up the piece could be selected randomly. He envisaged that the selection could be made by rolling the dice, but on the website you can choose a few variables and then click on a button to compose the randomized piece. For the minuet alone there are around 1.5×10^{15} compositions, a huge number, so the chances of all the possible minuets ever being played are rather remote (Bartholomew, 2008, p. 167). In any case, the pieces generated by this random process can be very pleasing because the components – the bars – have the appropriate initial internal components to be strung together.[35]

Random processes are all around us, although when averaged together, they lead to physical properties that are highly predictable and can be described by laws. One such random process was noticed by the Scottish botanist Robert Brown (1773–1858) in 1827 when he was examining some grains of plant pollen suspended in water under the microscope. As he watched, to his surprise the pollen ejected tiny particles which we now know to be particles made up of starch and lipids (fats). Even more surprising was the fact that the particles just wouldn't stay still however long he looked and kept jiggling about.

At first, Brown wondered whether he had found some basic unit of living matter that might lead to understanding the mystery of life's origin. But that theory went out of the window when he found that particles of chalk dust also jiggle around incessantly when suspended in water. We now call this phenomenon "Brownian motion". In Brown's time, the reason for the motion was not at all understood, but later investigators such as James Clerk Maxwell and Einstein discovered that the motion of the particles was due to the random motion of the movement of the water molecules surrounding them.[36] The water molecules had sufficient energy to push the larger particles around.

The same kind of random motion also applies to the atoms and molecules that comprise all liquids and gases. Boyle's gas law – the pressure of a gas increases as its volume decreases, which some may remember from school science class – depends on averaging out the random movements of trillions of gas molecules. Fortunately, there is no need to calculate the movement of each molecule separately – it is the average properties of very large numbers that counts. Today we have the laws of statistical mechanics that treat each molecule of liquids and gases as if they were moving randomly, but then calculate the probabilities of how they behave en masse. The laws are very precise, a case of randomness leading to order and regularity.

Somewhat confusingly, the main use of the word "random" in evolutionary biology is quite different from its use within mathematics and physics as just described. In evolution, it simply refers to the fact that genetic variation occurs in an organism without the well-being or otherwise of the organism in view. The primary meaning of "random mutations" is that their occurrence is not influenced in any way by the needs of the individual organism in which they occur.

That still leaves open the question as to whether mutations occur "randomly" in the genomes of organisms in the more technical mathematical sense. In other words, if we take the 3.2 billion nucleotides (genetic letters) in the sequence of the DNA in the human genome, is any single letter out of the 3.2 billion equally likely to undergo a mutation? The short answer, already briefly mentioned in the previous chapter, is "no", and the reasons for that answer will be discussed further below where we discuss the overall roles of randomness and chance in the evolutionary process.

What do we mean by "chance"?

The various meanings of the word "chance" are even more slippery than the word "random". Consider for example, the following sentences, with the meaning of "chance" in each case in brackets after the sentence: "Is there any chance you can come for dinner tomorrow?" (enquiring about someone's availability); "There is a chance that it might rain this afternoon and interrupt the match" (a possible event that depends on chaos theory); "I met William down at the shops today by chance" (an unexpected encounter); "I'm buying a ticket today for the National Lottery even though I know my chances of winning anything are really low" (statistically improbable); "My chances of getting a first in Finals are really low" (I haven't worked hard enough in my final year at university). One could go on, but you get the point – the word indeed does have many nuances.

Broadly speaking, we can say that there are three main meanings of "chance" relevant to our present topic, all being related to the question of uncertainty. The first is sometimes called *epistemological chance* because it refers to all those events that are perfectly lawlike in how they happen, but about which we have insufficient knowledge of their antecedents to make predictions. For example, coin-tossing is used as a fair and reasonable way to decide who will start off a football match or from which end. If we had the right machines, cameras, etc. in place, it would be possible, in principle, for a clever observer to predict whether the coin would fall as a heads or a tails. In fact, a group of mathematicians and others, mainly from Stanford University, have done just that.[37] They built a machine which did the coin-flipping for them, using a camera that can take up to 1,400 frames per second (seriously fast!) and, with some fine adjustments, found that if the coin was flipped heads up at the start, it would land heads up 100% of the time. Clearly such a system would be of little use to football referees as fairness would fly out of the window. More encouraging was their estimate that in a normal human flip of the coin, the chances of the coin landing heads up if it was flipped heads up was 0.51 (for why this might be, refer to their rather technical paper!). In other words, we might naturally assume that if we keep tossing a coin many hundreds of times and recording the results, eventually the heads:tails ratio should be 1:1, but other biased physical factors might be at play. For all practical purposes, however, a very small bias won't matter for a given match. Such is not the case for who wins the National Lottery. There we need many machine-generated randomly bouncing balls in order to generate the winning numbers and to be quite certain that there is no bias.

The point in all this, of course, is that if we want to be quite fair in delegating a decision to a process that has human consequences, we are best served by building a machine to do the job. But the process used to generate the chance result is entirely orderly, reflecting the known laws of physics. If we knew all the antecedents involved, an incredibly complex amount of complex information that we will never know, it would be possible, in principle, to predict the outcome. It is the fact of not knowing all this information that makes the chance process useful for us (in many circumstances).

The lawlike behaviour involved in epistemological chance is also useful because it allows precise predictions to be made about the properties of large numbers of chance events. Insurance premiums are calculated based on such assumptions. An individual car accident involving a non-drinking 70-year-old driver in a 5-year-old car who drives an average 2,300 miles per year in London may be difficult to predict, but if you have the data on thousands of car-drivers in this category, then working out the appropriate insurance premium for those in this cohort is relatively easy. Life insurance is based on similar types of consideration. We all know that we're going to die, but nobody knows when this particular individual is going to die, but it doesn't matter because the aggregate of the data allows some rather accurate probabilities to help the insurance-broker calculate the premium for any given individual. Many of the regularities of nature, not least death, are built on chance events. Many of the games we play, like Scrabble, are a pleasing mixture of chance and skill. (But if picking letters out of a well-shaken bag is supposed to be random, how come one ends up so often with just wretched low-scoring vowels or just as wretched high-scoring consonants for which you need vowels to be any use anyway?)

The second main type of chance we can call *ontological chance* because there are no antecedents that could possibly be known that could enable a prediction, even in principle. So in this case it's not a question of lack of knowledge – there is no knowledge that could be known. This is sometimes called "pure chance" because there is nothing that we can know which has predictive value. If I claimed that "It was pure chance that I met William down at the shops", I might be well understood in colloquial speech, but formally I would be wrong because there certainly were antecedents that could be cited to explain our unexpected meeting: for example, William always goes to the shops on a Saturday, like me; William always browses in a bookshop on Saturdays like me, and so forth. Our meeting was therefore a chance event epistemologically but not ontologically.

A classic example of ontological chance appears to be radioactive decay. We need to use the word "appears" because we can never be 100% sure that there isn't some hidden reason why a particular radioisotope (radioactive chemical) emits a particle of radiation energy at one moment rather than another. But to the best of our current knowledge, there are no such hidden reasons. In practice, this makes no difference in our use of radioisotopes for all kinds of purposes, not least in medical research. For example, I have spent much of my working life using the radioisotope phosphorus-32 in my experiments. The non-radioactive form of phosphorus found most commonly in our bodies is phosphorus-31 – it has just one less neutron than its radioactive counterpart. Phosphorus-32 is made in nuclear reactors and then decays by a half every 14.3 days. This means that it's generally only useful when used during the first month or so after its generation in the reactor, otherwise there is too little left. But the main point here is that its so-called "half-life" is known very precisely, because even though the timing of each emission of each radioactive particle of energy is unknown, averaging out trillions of these events very readily generates the precise value of 14.3 days for the half-life. The same point holds for all the other many radioisotopes that are known, ranging from a half-life of fractions of a second all the way to examples like potassium-40, which has a half-life of more than 1 billion years.

Ontological chance stems from quantum mechanics.[38] This is a well-established theory in physics which deals with the properties of the world of the very small, particles like electrons, neutrons, photons, that kind of thing. Perhaps the most famous experiment describing the quantum properties of electrons or photons of light is known as the "two-slit experiment" (Henson, 2016). We arrange a wall or other barrier with two slits in it. We bombard the wall with electrons or with photons (of light). Either the electron or the photon will go through one slit or the other in a way that is impossible to predict. Furthermore, the "particle-waves", to use the language of Richard Feynman, can go through both slits simultaneously without splitting into two separate particles. This is really very strange. If you were a bowler doing some cricket practice, and there were two sizeable holes in the wall of a gym, you would probably have no problem in throwing your ball through one of the two holes. But cricket is the world of "big physics" where things behave according to our common-sense understanding, whereas the quantum world of the very small is extremely peculiar and doesn't conform to any kind of common sense. And in our present context it is entirely unpredictable as to which slit the photon or the electron will go through: it is unpredictable in principle and not just in practice – an ontologically chance event in most people's understanding of the phenomenon.

When the electron goes through two different slits simultaneously, it interferes with itself, a phenomenon known as the "superposition principle". Basically, this principle states that the electron exists in every possible theoretical state simultaneously until it is measured. This collection of states is known as the "wave packet" since it represents a whole collection of options that interfere with each other like waves. Making the measurement causes the wave packet to "collapse" into just one of the options in the wave packet, that option happening by "pure chance". This idea is at the heart of quantum indeterminacy and Einstein didn't like the idea at all, claiming that "God doesn't play dice" – to which his fellow physicist Niels Bohr sagely responded, "Einstein, stop telling God what to do!" (Henson, 2016, p. 307). But once again, when all the quantum properties of all the trillions of fundamental particles of which matter is made are averaged out, you get the consistent properties of the objects familiar to us in everyday life – water, wood, metals, the texture of our own skin, and so forth.

If you understood the previous paragraph in terms of being able to conceptualize what is going on at the quantum level, you clearly didn't understand it. Those who teach quantum mechanics will often try and persuade their students in the very first lecture not to even try and understand it in terms of conceptualization, but just stick to the maths. For the maths works perfectly and the experiments work perfectly and can be repeated at any time with the same results, but meaningful conceptualization is out of the question. The quantum world is truly weird.

Is the ontological chance of quantum mechanics at all relevant to the mechanisms of evolutionary biology? Only indirectly, without playing any kind of central role, as will be discussed further below.

The third type of chance we might call *metaphysical chance*: chance that goes well beyond science. We might even call it *metaphysical Chance* where Chance is given a big "C". This is the idea that Chance somehow rules over everything, almost as if it were an agency or a metaphysical principle. Reading the book already mentioned – Monod's *Chance and Necessity* – one has the impression that for Monod Chance plays this type of role. With respect to genetic mutations, he wrote:

> *We say that these events are accidental, due to chance. And since they constitute the only possible source of modifications in the genetic text, itself the sole repository of the organism's hereditary structures, it necessarily follows that chance alone is at the source of every innovation, of all creation in the biosphere. Pure chance, absolutely free but blind, at the very root of the stupendous edifice of evolution: this central concept of modern biology is no longer*

one among other possible or even conceivable hypotheses. It is today the sole conceivable hypothesis, the only one compatible with observed and tested fact. And nothing warrants the supposition (or the hope) that conceptions about this should, or ever could, be revised. (Monod, 1997, p. 110)

Well of course the scientific conclusions on the role of chance have indeed been massively revised by more recent scientific advances as the discussion both above and below makes clear. But the interesting point here is how, based on the known science of his time (1970), Monod then goes on to make metaphysical inferences, as already noted. Monod was not the first scientist to extrapolate wildly from the currently understood properties of the world to conclusions that lie well beyond science. Here we have what sounds like *Tyche*, the Greek goddess of chance, together with *Fortuna* her Roman counterpart. Chance has become an agency, the "Lady Luck" so beloved by National Lottery winners.

Suffice it to say that Chance is not an agency and doesn't "do" anything. Chance is simply our way of describing our own position as observers in relation to various properties of matter, no more and no less. Despite this obvious fact, it is remarkable how often the language of "Chance as agent" creeps into otherwise sober scientific and philosophical texts.

What do we mean by "chaos"?

In daily speech "chaos" is used to mean "without order". "It was absolute chaos in London today due to the strike on the underground", or perhaps "Sarah, your room is really chaotic, tidy it up immediately!" The technical meaning of the word "chaos" is quite different. Chaos theory is particularly associated with the name of the American mathematician Edward Lorenz (1917–2008). It was his time serving in the US Army Air Corps from 1942 to 1946 that really got him thinking (Palmer, 2008). In the early days of desk computers (around 1960), Lorenz started using them to see if he could model weather systems mathematically and even make predictions about what the weather would be like in a week's time. Initially he used 12 different variables in generating his models. What was really puzzling for Lorenz was that when he undertook his analysis with what he thought were identical starting conditions, his computer generated quite different predictions about the weather. Was there something wrong with the computer? Probably not. In the end, Lorenz discovered that even changing the sixth decimal place in one of his variables (or similar) could dramatically change the outcome. In other words, tiny differences in the starting conditions could make a major difference to the weather pattern several weeks later, something that we all know from our personal experience. All those predictions about a barbecue summer and the like (in the British context at least) turn in to the "reality on the ground" – daily rain and thick mud just when you're going camping.

Lorenz's findings are commonly summarized as the "butterfly effect": if a butterfly flaps its wings in Brazil then it can impact on the weather pattern in Texas some weeks later. As it happens, it was the analogy not of a butterfly but of a seagull flapping its wings that Lorenz actually used (Palmer, 2008), but it is the slightly more evocative imagery of a butterfly that has come to dominate when making this point. Chaos theory is deterministic in the sense that if the starting conditions were really identical, then the outcome would be identical, but in reality for complex systems like the weather, the starting conditions never are identical, so in practice the weather some weeks ahead is never predictable.

Is chaos theory relevant to biology? As it turns out, it is, as shown by a previous President of the Royal Society no less, Robert May. Instead of modelling the weather, May was attempting to model animal populations (May, 1976). Using quite a simple calculation, May was attempting to see how a particular animal population would change in year 1, year 2, year 3, and so on. One of the factors in his equation, not surprisingly, was the growth rate. As long as the value for the growth rate was set fairly low, the population change would settle down quite predictably into one of two types of steady rhythm (either a fixed steady state or alternating years of high or low numbers). Furthermore, if the size of the starting population was varied a bit, one still obtained one of these two population patterns. But when higher values for growth rate were entered into the equation, something surprising happened: now the results year on year became quite erratic and non-predictable, going suddenly from high to low after some years of being stable, or even collapsing altogether for no apparent reason. The really interesting (and relevant) part of this story is that when May repeated a whole series of high growth-rate value entries again into the equation, the sequence of apparently random results was then exactly the same as before. In other words, chaos theory was relevant in the sense that very small changes in the starting conditions made large differences to the outcome, but the process was not really random in the technical mathematical sense discussed above, because it was reproducible. A genuinely random phenomenon would not be repeatable in this way.

Given that we now know that animal population dynamics can in many cases best be described using chaos theory, can we then also say that chaos theory is relevant to biological evolution? It turns out that there are other biological phenomena that are highly dependent on initial conditions, such as the spread of viral infections and the way that the immune system responds to infection (Shu et al., 2014). Such examples could be multiplied many times. In each case, we note that the phenomena being studied are essentially deterministic, but remain highly sensitive to the initial conditions.

Anything that affects population size, immune responses, the way that infections spread, and so forth is very likely to have an impact on evolutionary history. High sensitivity to initial conditions generally makes human predictions about the outcome difficult if not impossible, just like the weather. But for reasons discussed further below, our inability to make predictions about something should not be taken to mean that the process is random or operates by chance in any ultimate (ontological) sense.

Why Darwinian evolution is not a theory of chance

A few years ago, I was chatting with a bright second-year medical student at a well-known university (which will remain unnamed, given what I'm about to say next) after a lecture that I'd been giving on evolution and religion. How was it, she asked, given evolution, that the first anatomically modern human could be born out of an ape? How on earth would that poor first human find anyone to marry? At this moment, I realized that there were some significant gaps in her biological education – not at all surprising in those who choose other career paths, but a little depressing to find in a medical student (it wasn't Cambridge, just to be clear).[39]

A simple mantra (and, like all mantras, oversimplified) to summarize the basic idea of evolution that students learn in secondary school biology is:

GENETIC VARIATION HAPPENS

INDIVIDUALS ARE SELECTED

POPULATIONS EVOLVE

It is the third aspect of the process that tripped up the medical student. With a genes-eye view of evolution (not the only perspective), it occurs by the changing frequency of different genes within an interbreeding population. When two populations become isolated so that they can no longer physically interbreed due to such "reproductive isolation", speciation occurs when the accumulation of genetic variants in each separated population becomes so great that one population can no longer interbreed with the other population, even if they have the opportunity.

But in our present context it is the first and second aspects of the process that are most relevant if we are to address satisfactorily the claim that "evolution is not a theory of chance".

Genetic variation

Genetic variation provides the "raw material" of evolution. It generates much of the innovation involved in the process. Many people do not realize just how much genetic variation there is in different living organisms, not least within our own human species. We all vary from each other in around 0.5% of our total 3.2 billion genetic letters – that's around 16 million letters. Sometimes you'll read much lower estimates than this, but that's because a writer is counting only the single letter changes known as Single Nucleotide Polymorphisms (SNPs, pronounced "snips"). Since these occur in around 1 out of 1,000 nucleotides, or a bit more, estimates in the region of 3–4 million differences are common. But when all the various types of change (described further below) are included, the total variation estimate becomes considerably higher.

New mutations are coming into the human population at every new birth. This has been demonstrated most clearly in large family studies in which the whole genomes from individuals within families – father, mother, and child – were sequenced and compared. In one Dutch study, 250 families had their DNA sequenced in this way (Francioli et al., 2015). For each offspring in this study, there was an average of 38 mutations. Overall, 78% of the mutations came from the father and the rest from the mother, and studies on identical twins suggested that nearly all (97%) of the new mutations were in the germ line and only 3% had arisen in somatic (non germ-line) cells. On average, the offspring born to 40-year-old fathers had twice as many mutations as those born to 20-year-old fathers. In fact, it has been estimated that paternal age explains about 95% of the variation in the global mutation rate in the human population (Kong et al., 2012). The fact that more mutations come from the fathers than from the mothers is not unexpected because females are born with all the eggs they'll ever have, whereas sperm is constantly being produced in men right into old age by a series of development steps. By the age of 70, a male's sperm cells have undergone around 1,400 cell divisions. Each time a cell, along with its DNA, replicates (divides into two new cells), there is the possibility of errors creeping in, so many more mutations are due to replication errors than, for example, the perhaps better-known causes, such as radiation or nasty chemicals in the environment. Thirty-eight mutations in your precious newborn sounds like a lot, but don't worry too much about that number because in the vast majority of cases those mutations occur in regions of the DNA that are non-functional. In addition, for reasons discussed in the previous chapter, many mutations in protein-encoding genes won't make any difference anyway, because the changed codon will still encode for the same amino acid. Having said that, if you want to be a dad, from a geneticist's perspective it may be best to start your family earlier rather than later if circumstances allow you any choice in the matter.

It is worth considering how many ways there are for a genome to vary, because only then can we begin to address the question as to whether any given change that occurs is random or happens by chance. We have already mentioned the *point mutations*, changes in a single nucleotide (SNPs). Other mutations involve the insertion or deletion of a short section of DNA known as *indels* (abbreviation for insertion–deletion). For example, about 35 million SNPs separate us from our nearest living relatives, chimpanzees, representing about 1% of the genome. In addition, around 5 million indels make 3% of each genome different from the other based on this criterion. So the deletions and insertions win over the point mutations in terms of generating a different genome, and together they yield a 4% difference in total between us and the chimps.

In the previous chapter, we have already encountered "jumping genes" or *transposons* and the way in which they can bring new information into the genome. More than 3 million examples of transposons have been counted, so jumping genes are extremely abundant. "*Alu*" transposons, for example, consist of 300-nucleotide-long stretches of DNA and represent the most frequently repeated sequences in the whole human genome, with about 1 million copies accounting for roughly 10% of our entire genome.

Transposons have no known function at the time they are generated except to provide lots of padding for the rest of the genome. However, the insertion sites of transposons can certainly have an impact on the regulation of nearby genes, and occasionally they can change by mutation and acquire new functions. Incorporation of transposon sections of DNA back into the genome occurs more or less randomly, although for chemical reasons the molecular machinery prefers some spots rather than others. Transposons are added to the human gene pool at a frequency of one new insert every ten births (Cordaux et al., 2006). Usually the incorporation makes no difference to the functioning of the genome, although occasionally the results can be disastrous – for instance, if the transposon lands smack in the middle of a protein-coding gene, or sufficiently near it to interfere with its regulation. Indeed, more than 60 cases of newly inserted transposons causing disease in humans have been reported (Cordaux and Batzer, 2009). This may be one reason why protein-coding genes are scattered all over the genome and constitute only 1.5% of the genome. It's a bit like the strategy of spreading out airfields to make them a more difficult target during bombing raids.

Some new insertions have been generated so recently that they are found in only a single individual and are designated "private de novo" insertions. Around 600 million of these private germ-line insertions (insertions that occur in cells that make eggs or sperm) have been generated in human genomes throughout the world, generating a large amount of "extra" genetic diversity, some of it of functional significance (Mills et al., 2007; Cordaux and Batzer, 2009). Of course, if insertions did not happen in the germ cells (sperm and eggs) containing the information passed on to the offspring, they would be of no significance for evolution.

Gene duplication has played a big role in evolutionary history. Normally during DNA replication and cell division, the same number of genes in the parent cell are passed on to the daughter cells. Diploid cells contain pairs of chromosomes, so each cell contains just two copies of each gene, one on each chromosome. But occasionally a segment of a chromosome becomes duplicated and is passed on in the germ-line cells, and this segment may contain one or more genes. For example, a comparison of human, bonobo, chimp, gorilla, and orang-utan DNA revealed more than 1,000 gene duplications that were specific to one of these species (Fortna et al., 2004). Copy number expansions were particularly pronounced in humans (134 genes specifically duplicated in humans) and include a number of genes thought to be involved in the structure and function of the brain.

Structural mutations are another source of variation in the genome. These involve changes in larger segments of chromosomes than those involved in the smaller indels, and there are specialized techniques for detecting them. Chromosomal mutations can involve many genes – in some cases even hundreds of genes – and generally are more than 1,000 DNA nucleotides in length. They occur in some chromosomes more than others, for reasons not yet fully understood. For example, a preferential involvement of human chromosomes 22, 7, 21, 3, and 9 takes place in balanced chromosomal variation[40] of all types (Giardino et al., 2009), so talking about "random variation" leading to chromosomal mutations is not strictly accurate: their timing is random but not their distribution. Structural changes do not occur with equal probability in any one chromosome.

Variation can also enter the genome from outside an individual organism in at least five distinct ways. The first of these, and the most important, is *sexual reproduction*. During the formation of the germ cells (in the process known as meiosis), the paired diploid chromosomes are reduced to just one of each pair in each germ cell, randomly distributing any single chromosome from either the mother or the father to the germ cell in the process. Before separation occurs, the pair of chromosomes snuggle up to each other and exchange ("recombine") little stretches of DNA nucleotide sequences. So there are two different kinds of variation arising from this process: from the random assortment of chromosomes to the germ cells and from the exchange of genetic material between chromosomes, truly a fancy way of generating greater genetic diversity. Therefore, the set of single chromosomes (1 to 23 in the human) that end up in each germ cell of the individual is not quite the same as either one's mother's or father's. In biological terms, one of the reasons for the evolution of sexual reproduction might well have been to shake off parasites in the next generation. Parasites well adapted to life in or on the parents would have a much harder time infesting the offspring because their quite different genome would lead to the generation of a different set of defensive mechanisms.

Gene flow is the second mechanism for introducing genetic variation into an interbreeding population of animals or plants. This refers to the flow of new genetic variants that comes into a population when exposed to another population of the same species from which they have been separated for some time. Barriers to gene flow are usually but not always physical barriers, such as rivers or mountains. Even the Great Wall of China has been reported to hinder the gene flow of the surrounding plant populations (Su et al., 2003). Other types of barrier to gene flow may occur when, for example, male birds enter a new territory and their song is not recognized by the females of the same species. In this case, it is the lack of female response that prevents gene flow.

A different kind of gene flow, which deserves a separate category because it involves asexual reproduction, is known as *lateral gene transfer* (or horizontal gene transfer) (Keeling and Palmer, 2008). This involves the transfer of genes from one bacterium to another, and it dominated the first 2 billion years of evolution. Some people swap stamps or football cards. Other living organisms swap genes. Microbes are like gene-swapping collectives, to use the evocative phrase of the biologist Carl Woese. At least two-thirds of bacterial genes are thought to have originated or been modified by lateral transfer. In one extensive study of more than half a million genes from 181 different types of bacteria, 80% of them showed signs of lateral gene transfer (Dagan et al., 2008).

Retroviral insertion is another way of importing genetic variation from outside the organism, a mechanism that we have already encountered in the previous chapter. We normally associate viruses with catching the flu or other unwelcome diseases. But not all viruses are harmful to us, and they represent a huge pool of genetic information. Viruses consist of some DNA or RNA and a few proteins packaged together to infect host cells where they live as parasites, using the host cells' own molecular production machinery to churn out more copies of themselves.

Viruses are everywhere – 2,000 metres below the surface of the Earth, in the sands of the Sahara Desert, and in icy lakes. An estimated 10^{31} viral particles live on the planet (Hamilton, 2006), an astronomically huge number (especially considering that there are roughly 10^{22} stars in the universe). A kilogram of marine muck was found to contain up to a million genetically variant viruses. Our own guts may contain as many as 1,200 different viruses.

An estimated 10^{24} new viruses are created every *second* somewhere in the world. The vast majority of these die immediately as they are completely unsuccessful in infecting host cells (bacteria in most cases). But the number generated is so vast that fairly frequently their rapid mutation rates ensure that new genes are formed, which may eventually be incorporated into the genomes of other organisms. The huge number of viruses in the world may therefore be viewed as a giant gene production factory, generating a constant stream of new information, some of which other genomes take up and adapt for use.

Retroviruses, as outlined in the previous chapter, have the particular ability of incorporating their genetic information encoded in RNA into their host genomes as DNA, in most cases without any harm to the individual. In some cases, this infection occurs in germ-line cells, meaning that the inserted DNA becomes a permanent part of the genome of all the descendants of that single individual germ cell. In fact, roughly 8% of our own genomes comes from DNA copies of RNA-based viruses that have incorporated themselves into the primate germ line. Each of these long-resident DNA sequences was originally 8,000–11,000 base-pairs long, and they are known as human endogenous retroviruses. In other words, at some particular time in our evolutionary past, a particular retrovirus has incorporated its DNA message into the germ-line cells of our ancestors, and that sequence has been faithfully replicated over the intervening millions of years. This remarkable finding is useful for biologists because these retroviral "visiting cards" can be very informative in working out evolutionary lineages.

Retroviral insertions can also provide a valuable resource of new genetic information. Although such DNA sequences for the most part exist as non-coding regions and are initially neutral – neither deleterious nor beneficial for the recipient – with time they can vary due to mutation. In rare instances, the sequences can become functional genes, their heritage recognizable by their distinctive retroviral genetic fingerprint.

The *import of organelles* containing their own DNA represents a fifth and indeed rather dramatic way in which genetic variation has come into the genome at various critical moments in evolutionary history. This occurred when bacteria that had probably started living symbiotically inside cells (that is, they had found a lifestyle that gave some advantage to both partners), then became permanent residents and developed into the mitochondria and chloroplasts that we see in cells today. The mitochondria we now have are little organelles found in the cytoplasm (the region outside the nucleus) functioning as the "power-plants" of animal cells, using food to generate the energy that cells need to keep going. Chloroplasts are organelles found in plant cells responsible for photosynthesis, also "power-plants," but with a different energy source (the sun).

Mitochondria and chloroplasts both contain their own DNA, separate from the main storehouse of DNA found in the nucleus. Our own mitochondrial DNA contains only 37 genes, in comparison with the approximately 21,000 protein-coding genes found in our nuclear DNA. Mitochondrial DNA is inherited only from our mothers because it is the cytoplasm of the egg, with its contents, that is used to make more cells following fertilization. The mitochondria from the sperm are lost during this process. In the present context, the key point is the influx of extra genetic variation that came with the incorporation of microorganisms into cells, to later become permanent organelles. The process is a bit like acquisitions and mergers. If a big pharmaceutical company has too few drugs in development, the normal strategy is to buy up a smaller biotech company that has some new technology and promising drug leads – both parties benefiting in the process. Today mitochondrial DNA mutates at a rate about ten times faster than nuclear DNA, acting as a useful "genetic clock" which can be used to give approximate times to evolutionary events.

Given this extensive and rather bewildering array of different mechanisms for generating variant genomes, it might seem surprising that genetic variation between individuals of the same species is no more different than it is. For the moment, and with this background information in place, we are now in a better position to ask whether the generation of genetic variation is truly random or not.

Is the generation of genomic variation random?

It will be remembered that there are two quite distinct meanings of the word "random" in the context of biology. The most commonly used meaning simply refers to the fact that genetic variation comes into the genome without the good or the ill of the organism in view. When you think about it, this is a rather banal and obvious definition. How could it be otherwise?

The second and more interesting meaning involves the mathematical question as to whether each nucleotide in the genome, or each section of the genome, is equally likely to be mutated. This is what would need to be the case if mutations were truly random (in this second sense). The short answer is "no": that is clearly not the case. Hints that this is not so were already alluded to above in the context of the structural changes that are much more likely to occur in some chromosomes than in others, and in the observation that transposon insertions into the genome are more likely at some places than at others.[41] The most straightforward way of addressing the basic question as to whether genomes display random mutational variation is to sequence the complete genomes of a collection of individuals from the same species, look at all the differences between them, and then see if the new mutations (prior to any subsequent selection process) are randomly distributed or whether they cluster. As it happens, they cluster – they are not random.

This has been demonstrated in a number of studies, including the Dutch study mentioned above in which 250 family trios (father, mother, offspring) had their genomes completely sequenced

(Francioli et al., 2015). Given that an average 38 new mutations appeared in the newborn that were not there in the parents, if they were randomly distributed throughout the genome, then on average there should be some sizeable gaps between them. In fact, some simple maths (divide 38 into 3.2 billion) suggests that they should be separated by a median of around 84 million nucleotides. But they are not. For example, the researchers found that there were 78 instances in which there were clusters of 2–3 mutations found within 20,000 nucleotides of each other, which is a very much smaller number than 84 million. Several factors are likely to cause this clustering, although the phenomenon is not yet fully understood.

For example, it has long been known that mutations are more likely to occur where the sequence CpG is found in the DNA sequence. This means that the base cytosine has a guanine next to it, and the "p" refers to a phosphate group that links the two together in the long chain of nucleotides making up the DNA. Cytosines are more likely to be methylated where this sequence is found. This involves the transfer of a "methyl" chemical group on to the cytosine which is really important because if that region of the DNA encodes a gene, this has the effect of "silencing" the gene, which means inhibiting or even entirely switching off its functional use (its "expression" in the jargon of molecular biology). This is one of the key mechanisms involved in epigenetics. Epigenetics denotes all the various ways in which the DNA itself, or its surrounding proteins, are chemically modified in order to switch genes on or off. In mammals, 70–80% of CpG sequence units are methylated at any one time, whereas only 2–5% of all cytosines are methylated (remember that most cytosines don't have a G next door – they need a G next door to get methylated).

Methylcytosines are particularly prone to be mutated for chemical reasons that need not detain us here. Despite the fact that in human DNA only a few per cent of the nucleotides are methylcytosine, about 30% of all point mutations are found at these sites. So the epigenetic modifications that increase cytosine methylation also increase the chance of permanent DNA mutations occurring at those particular positions in the DNA sequence. Epigenetic modifications can "channel" mutations so that they are more likely to occur in one place than another. This explains the fascinating fact that we can cause the probability of more mutations appearing in our own cells by the choices we make, choices which in turn impact on the methylation of our genome. For example, smoking changes the methylation status of the DNA in cells in the lungs, which may contribute to the many mutations in lung cells caused by this toxic habit, eventually leading to cancer in many cases.

Coming back to the Dutch study, here paternal age is clearly a critical factor in the number of mutations appearing in the newborn. The methylation status of the genome of germ-line cells changes with the number of replication cycles that they have undergone during their generation (more in older men), and the CpG units that are methylated, and so more likely to mutate, are not evenly distributed throughout the genome. This could certainly be one reason for the non-random distribution of mutations in the newborn, but other factors are clearly at play as well.

Investigating the clustering of mutations in our own human offspring is clearly of great personal interest, but humans are not the easiest species in which to look at detailed mechanisms. It is much simpler to investigate the same question in rapidly dividing cells in the laboratory, such as yeast cells. Figure 19 shows the results from one study in which yeast cells were exposed to a nasty mutagen for a while and then had their genomes sequenced soon after to see where the mutations were found (Chan and Gordenin, 2015). As can be seen, the striking finding was that out of an average 45 new mutations, there was a cluster of 26 mutations in one particular region of chromosome 2, whereas only 19 mutations were found in the whole of the rest of the genome.

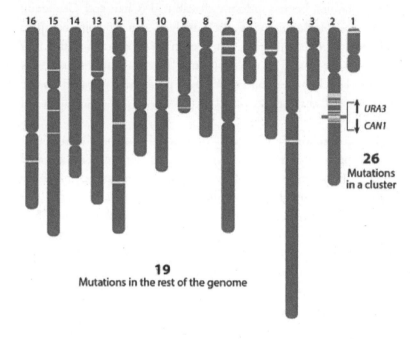

Figure 19. A mutation cluster caused by chronic damage to the DNA of proliferating yeast cells. The yeast has 16 pairs of chromosomes. Each chromosome consists of a molecule of DNA wrapped around with proteins. The yeast was exposed to a chemical that causes mutations. There is a cluster of 26 mutations in one particular region of chromosome 2, whereas only 19 mutations were found in the whole of the rest of the genome.

The unequal distribution of mutations in the genome have been demonstrated in numerous studies (Rogozin and Pavlov, 2003) and there has been much recent interest in why mutations are non-random. A recent review listed around eight different ways in which the molecular machinery involved in DNA replication can lead to a greater probability that mutation clusters occur rather than mutations being randomly distributed (Chan and Gordenin, 2015). The biochemistry of such analyses can be quite complex and need not detain us here, but in each case it's worth noting that mutations are caused by molecular mechanisms that in many cases are now largely understood and where predictability based on the knowledge of antecedents could be possible in principle, albeit not in practice.

The generation of genomic "mutational hot spots" is thought to have been critical in our own human evolution. This became apparent by a detailed comparison of the human and chimpanzee genome sequences. Based on the "genetic mutation clock", our last common ancestor with the chimp is estimated at around 5–6 million years ago. Not surprisingly, there has been a lot of interest in the genetic factors that contribute to us being so different from our chimp cousins, not least in the fact that we have brains that are more than three times larger. Several so-called "Human Accelerated Regions" have been found in the human genome that are quite different from the chimp genome (Burbano et al., 2014). These are regions of rapid mutation in which more mutations have accumulated during 10 million years of primate evolution than in all the previous 100 million years of mammalian evolution. Other studies have identified an enzyme, originally involved in providing protection against viral attack, now involved in introducing mutational clusters into hominid genome sequences (Pinto et al., 2016). The enzyme can even cause a "shower" of new mutations clustered together in one region of the genome in a single generation. As this enzyme became more "switched on" during the course of evolution so, it is thought, did hominin evolution speed up as new genetic information came into the genome.

With all this as background, we can now assess the processes involved in generating genetic variation according to the three different understandings of "chance" outlined above. Clearly there is plenty of epistemological chance going on here. The systems are generally far too complex to make any specific predictions as far as individual mutations are concerned. However, once we start averaging large numbers, well-justified generalizations can be made about such items as mutation rates, where mutations are more likely to occur in the genome, which chromosomes are more likely to undergo structural changes, and so on. Furthermore, in many cases we are improving our understanding of the molecular mechanisms underlying mutational changes and these mechanisms follow the normal rules of physics and chemistry. In some cases, we are able to link susceptibility of particular regions of the genome to mutational change with the evolution of the organisms involved. The "Human Accelerated Regions" could be an example of this. Another example already noted in the previous chapter is the *Pitx1* gene in sticklebacks, which is located in a particularly evolvable (mutational) region of the chromosome (Chan et al., 2010). Mutation rates have to be "set" just right in different parts of the genome to facilitate evolvability. If there were no mutations at all, life would be completely static and there would be no evolution, so no carbon-based life on Earth beyond, perhaps, some very early replicating life-forms. But if mutations were completely unrestrained, nothing would be alive either because all the information in the genome would end up as gibberish. In fact, it has been estimated that at least 10,000 DNA damage events occur every day in every cell of the human body (remembering that our bodies contain around 10^{13} cells).[42] So there has to be a "mutation thermostat" that controls the mutation rate. A key buffer that corresponds to the lowering of the thermostat is provided by the repair enzymes that recognize errors in the DNA sequence in its newly replicated strands and ensure that they are repaired back to the proper sequence. There are many different repair systems and they ensure the remarkable fidelity of replication of DNA. Without them, we would all be dead from cancer rather quickly.

What about ontological chance? The emission of radioactive particles, as noted, displays quantum uncertainty, so represents "pure chance", not something that could be predicted even in principle, at least not in its precise timing. Ionizing radiation causes mutations in DNA by directly breaking the chemical bonds that hold the nucleotides together. As discussed already, the radioactive properties of each radioisotope are known with some precision and their average outputs and consequent average effects on DNA can likewise be predicted. But it is impossible, even in principle, to predict the timing of individual mutational events. Could this then contribute to the idea that evolution is a theory of chance? Not really, because the natural selection considered in the next section acts as the stringent sieve that selects which mutations will be maintained in a population and which will be discarded. The sieve potentially operates on any kind of genetic variation, irrespective of how it was produced.

For the sake of completeness, we should also ask the question as to whether metaphysical chance, Lady Luck, could in some way be derived from the various ways in which genetic variation occurs in the genome. Jacques Monod thought the answer was "yes". But even based on the limited knowledge of molecular biology known at that time, it is hard to see how or why one might wish to extrapolate from the properties of cells to ultimate questions about the universe and its meaning. Furthermore, even if one thought that was possible and logical, half a century later the molecular biology looks very different. We now know that many types of mutation are not really random anyway in the mathematical sense in terms of their clustered distribution through the genome, as we have just been discussing (although systematic studies of the type described have not yet been carried out on *every* type of mutation). The lack of randomness in the origins of genetic variation highlights the risk of hitching one's philosophy to scientific theories or understandings. Science moves on very fast and so the philosophy in question can be very quickly widowed.

Natural selection

We now come to the second main phase of the evolutionary process. Darwin used the phrase "natural selection" in order to distinguish the process from the human selection involved in domestic breeding of animals such as pigeons (Darwin spent a lot of time investigating pigeon-breeding). In contemporary evolutionary theory,

> *Natural selection is the differential reproduction of alternative genetic variations, determined by the fact that some variations are beneficial because they increase the probability that the organisms having them will live longer or be more fertile than organisms having alternative variations. Over the generations beneficial variations will be preserved and multiplied; injurious or less beneficial variations will be eliminated. (Ayala, 2007, p. 51)*

Notice that the term "natural selection" is often used (albeit not in this definition) as the subject of a sentence as if it "does something". Of course, natural selection doesn't "do" anything, any more than chance "does" anything – in both cases they are short-hand for describing or referring to particular complex processes – but it seems a bit pedantic not to allow such linguistic short-cuts on occasion.

In practice, much variation in genomes is selectively neutral. In other words, this is the kind of variation that really makes no difference to the organism in question. If we have one amino acid rather than another at the 816th position in the string of amino acids that make up a particular protein, it really makes no difference either way. So the variant amino acids at that particular position will drift around quite happily in a population (through breeding) without any effects, beneficial or otherwise, on the carrier. But as neutral mutations accumulate in the genome of an individual, there may come a day when a new functionality comes into being as these genes interact in some way, either via their protein products and/or as a consequence of regulatory sequences, and in that case natural selection may begin to operate.

When genetic variation does make a difference to the organism, for good or for ill, the organism will tend to leave, over many generations, greater or fewer numbers of offspring: "reproductive success". The term "survival of the fittest"[43] has sometimes been used to describe natural selection, but is not very accurate because survival is not really the main point in this process. Of course, if an animal does not survive then it won't reproduce, but the key point about natural selection is the successful reproduction which ensures that an individual's genes are passed on to the next generation.

Natural selection therefore acts as a rigorous filter to reduce the amount of genetic variation in a population. It is a very conservative mechanism. The reason for this is that the great majority of genetic changes, if not neutral, are likely to be deleterious for the organism, and it is these that will be removed from the population after some generations – or even immediately if lethal – since they lower reproductive success. On the other hand, the few beneficial changes that will readily pass through the filter of natural selection will quickly spread throughout an interbreeding population as they bestow reproductive benefits on their recipients. The term "selective sweep" is used to describe the rapid spread of a beneficial genetic variant through such a population.

Just how conservative natural selection is in its operation may be illustrated by the conservation of the amino acid sequence of many proteins that are essential to biological life as we know it. For example, cytochrome c plays a crucial role in the energy production of cells required to keep them alive in the presence of oxygen and is found in virtually all animals and plants. It is a small protein, generally around 105 amino acids in length. Change a single amino acid at certain critical positions in the protein and it loses all functionality, in which case you're a dead mouse, or a dead bat, or a dead human for that matter. This explains why the amino acid sequence of this protein is incredibly conserved across species. For example, humans share 97% sequence identity of cytochrome c with the rhesus monkey, 87% with the dog, 82% with the bat, 67% with the fruit fly, 64% with the moth, and 44% with yeast with which we last shared a common ancestor about a billion years ago (Keya and Priya, 2016). Natural selection is a *really* conservative process.

The conservative nature of natural selection may also be seen in the types of convergent evolution that were surveyed in the previous two chapters. The same or similar adaptations keep popping up in evolutionary history in independent lineages for the simple reason that these happen to be the best that you can get under a given set of circumstances. When similar ecological niches occur again with similar environmental properties, natural selection ensures that similar adaptive solutions will be found to life's challenges.

As already mentioned, not all genetic variation will be "seen" by natural selection because it makes no difference to the fitness of the organism. "Genetic drift" is also relevant to this point. This refers to the variation in the relative frequency of different genotypes in a small population, owing to the chance disappearance of particular genes as individuals die or do not reproduce. "Chance" here is epistemological chance: there are very good reasons why an animal might die young before getting the chance to reproduce. For example, it might get eaten by a lion. So "genetic drift" can involve useful genes that natural selection would operate on had it been given half a chance, but the opportunity never came. Genetic drift, like natural selection, is therefore a mechanism for reducing the amount of genetic variation in a population.

It should by now be clear why it doesn't really matter whether variation comes into the genome via the pathway of epistemological chance (most of it) or ontological chance (as in radiation effects), as in both cases the winnowing effects of natural selection are what have the upper hand in bringing about certain constrained outcomes. Natural selection is like the potter moulding the clay – over a long period of time the consequences of genetic variation are moulded by the potter of natural selection to shape an interbreeding population into a slightly different collection of phenotypes.

Genetic variation plus natural selection are the central mechanisms in Darwinian evolution. But clearly there are many other events that impinge on the process. Around 65 million years ago a huge asteroid struck the Earth, estimated to be up to nine miles in diameter, which left a massive crater (called the Chicxulub crater) about 112 miles in diameter and 30 miles deep buried beneath the sediments off the Yucatan coast in the Gulf of Mexico. It was this catastrophe that probably contributed to the demise of the dinosaurs, along with increased volcanic activity around this time. But as the Earth recovered from the shock and climates were restored, so new opportunities were created for adaptive radiation, the process whereby rapid diversification of species occurs in order to fill up a collection of empty ecological niches. This is how primates began to get a real foothold on the planet, becoming more common about 50 million years ago. The 200 primate species alive today, including us, represent the remains of an adaptive radiation that probably gave rise to about 6,000 species altogether.

So do such "chance events" as the hitting of the Earth by a large asteroid, thus altering the history of evolution during the past 65 million years, not suggest that evolution taken as a whole is a "chance process"? Well, not really. Clearly there is plenty of epistemological chance here, given that there is no way that we could describe all the antecedents of these processes. However, it is worth noting that the orbits of asteroids, at least large ones, are now well known, which is good because NASA and other space agencies can track any big ones that might hit planet Earth. Unlike the situation 65 million years ago, we can at least try deflecting an asteroid on a collision course with Earth into a slightly different orbit. Asteroid orbits are, in principle, as predictable as planetary orbits. In any event, had the asteroid not hit Earth 65 million years ago, the dinosaurs would have eventually gone extinct anyway, perhaps for climatic reasons, as all species eventually do, especially species comprising large animals. Darwinian processes end up with replenishing the Earth once again in the end, even though there may be some big knocks along the way.

None of the above should be interpreted as if genetic variation plus natural selection were the *only* two phases of the evolutionary process. There are plenty of other candidates jockeying for position in order to play important roles also in the overall process although, as already mentioned, evolutionary biologists are somewhat divided on their relevance. Some candidates have already been mentioned above: cooperation; the role of evo-devo in "channelling" the paths that evolution takes; and so forth. But the important point here is that none of these ideas or factors introduces the idea that evolution is a chance process; instead they tend in the other direction, highlighting constraint and convergence.

So is evolution a chance process taken overall? Dawkins is right, it doesn't look like it. Mutations are indeed random in the trivial sense that they happen without the organism in mind, but this is hardly relevant to the main question. More significant is the fact that the generation of genetic diversity is not random in the mathematical sense, because mutations are not evenly distributed across the genome. And in any event the winnowing necessity of natural selection generally plays the trump card in the end. Certainly there are plenty of chance events involved of the epistemological variety (asteroids hitting the Earth, and so forth). Furthermore, initial conditions are vital in many contexts, rendering chaos theory relevant. But the system as a whole is incredibly fine-tuned to bring about a carefully orchestrated balance between stasis and change. We are the fortunate beneficiaries of this history of fine-tuning.

Is evolution Laplacean?

Pierre Simon de Laplace (1749–1827) became one of France's most influential scholars of his era. Mathematician and astronomer, Laplace was a deist and so eager to exclude the miraculous from any accounts of the world. With this in mind, and in the period when Newtonian mechanics ruled over all, Laplace insisted on the ordered and predictable properties of the universe. He is perhaps best remembered today for his assertion that if one knew the laws of nature perfectly, then:

> *An intellect which at a certain moment would know all forces*
> *that set nature in motion, and all positions of all items of*
> *which nature is composed, if this intellect were also vast enough*
> *to submit these data to analysis, it would embrace in a single*
> *formula the movements of the greatest bodies of the universe and*
> *those of the tiniest atom; for such an intellect nothing would be*
> *uncertain and the future just like the past would be present before*
> *its eyes. (Laplace, 1951, p. 4)*

In other words, if one knew all the causal chains that led to the present state of the universe, its present state would be predictable in principle and indeed in practice could be no other that what it is. So Laplace's view represents a strong assertion of determinism. Understandably, many did not like Laplace's view because it appears to threaten human free will,[44] but in any case it went completely out of fashion in the twentieth century with the advent of quantum mechanics and, later on, chaos theory.

But what happens if we now just consider evolutionary biology, leaving aside the properties of the rest of the universe – could that be Laplacean? Ultimately, we can only address that question by thought experiments, albeit informed by the kind of data and ideas that we have been considering in these last three chapters. We have already noted the claim by Simon Conway Morris that the extent of evolutionary convergence is so great that it seems likely that if one replayed the tape of life again, biological diversity would look rather similar (not identical, no one is claiming that, just similar). But with a thought experiment we can take things much further. Imagine the lifeless planet 4 billion years ago with no life. However life began, a process that still remains little understood, it must have happened by long causal chains whereby one thing led to another (Alexander, 2014). Once life got going around 3.5 billion years ago, then long causal chains, however complex and interactive, consistent with the laws of physics and chemistry, must have been in operation. It doesn't make any difference, for our thought experiment, whether we include random events, in either of the senses discussed above, or epistemological chance, or indeed chaos theory (which, remember, is deterministic). The trillions of causal chains are of course mind-boggling, but then this is a thought experiment, so no worries. If Newtonian mechanics[45] were still the only game in town, and assuming no breaking of the laws of physics and chemistry, then what there is in the way of biological diversity, and what there has been in the way of evolutionary history, must be the case – how could it be otherwise? Asteroids must have struck the Earth at certain times, a mutation due to an error in DNA replication must have happened when it did, and Lion A must have eaten Antelope B at a specific time. So within that Newtonian framework, we are at least close to a Laplacian biology.

But of course if we assume that ontological chance is a reality, this seriously scuppers any chance of complete adherence to Laplace. Both background radiation levels and oxygen levels in the atmosphere have changed dramatically during the history of the Earth (Karam et al., 2001). The mutation rate caused by radiation has fluctuated between 1.5 times and 2.5 times its current levels through most of the history of this planet, perhaps partly linked to changing concentrations in oxygen. As we have already noted, the precise timing of the emission of radioactive particles is unknowable in principle and not just in practice. So an ionizing radiation particle might cause the death of Lion A from cancer at one moment when that wouldn't have happened had the particle been emitted at another moment (the lion had just entered a cave so was protected from radiation). Because of that event, Lion A was no longer around to eat Antelope B, which went on to have a large and successful family of baby antelopes. Remembering the importance of initial conditions in chaos theory, we can now see how the precise trajectory of future evolution might be affected once this particular "mutational butterfly" had flapped its wings. But note the proviso "precise trajectory". As already indicated, given natural selection, it doesn't really matter how variation comes into the genome, be it by radiation, chemical mutagens, or replication errors – any and all variation is (potentially) grist to the mill as the variant genomes are tested out in the workshop of life.

One final point on this topic of quantum involvement: in the vast majority of biological processes (including, to the best of our current knowledge, the brain), specific single events at the quantum level make no difference. This is because the processes involve the interactions of molecules, each one of which has properties that represent the "average" of trillions of quantum events. One single quantum event is neither here nor there. But in photosynthesis, the process whereby the sun's energy is converted into chemical energy in plants and some bacteria, that is not the case. One single and particular quantum event in photosynthesis involves capturing the energy of a single photon of light from the sun and is really important. Of course, when this event occurs many times, cumulatively this results in plant growth, but the process depends on individual quantum events. Other quantum events are also involved in vision, in the actions of various enzymes, and in the mechanisms whereby animals navigate using the Earth's magnetic field. But in all cases the quantum events are playing roles in overall systems which are highly organized and orderly with consistent functions and outputs (such as photosynthesis) – they are not some hidden source of "pure chance" coming into biology.

Narratives of chance and of purpose

It is a common assumption that a chance process cannot at the same time be one with a purpose. This chapter highlights the implausibility of that suggestion. Two out of the three kinds of chance discussed above have clearly been critical in the evolutionary process. Yet individual animals and plants exist for the purpose of being alive, of feeding, and of procreation. Their existence is teleological, purpose with a small "p". The giraffe has a long neck for the purpose of reaching food on high branches; the whale rises to the surface for the purpose of breathing; the polar bear has white fur for the purpose of camouflage; and so on. You cannot avoid *telos* in biology.

Yet Purpose with a big "P" is not something that can be derived from biology. We have already had cause to critique Monod with his attempt to extrapolate metaphysical lack-of-purpose out of molecular biology. But by the same token, we cannot infer Purpose simply from the fact that the evolutionary process is highly organized, constrained and, to a limited extent, predictable. Biology is simply not up to the herculean task of providing some overall Purpose and meaning in life that everyone can agree on. It is beyond evolution's pay-grade to play that kind of role. On the other hand, the evolutionary process is perfectly compatible with having some overall Purpose as we shall consider further in the following chapter. A detailed mechanistic description of a process may be seen as complementary to a narrative describing the Purpose of the process taken as whole.

Consider, for example, the National Lottery. All those little balls with numbers on bouncing around in the machine are fulfilling their Purpose, designed by the government, to take money from the poor,[46] make a few people rich, give out money to lots of good causes (which often benefit the rich), and in the process (in the UK context) generate a handy 12% tax for the government. A chance process is used to generate outcomes that are absolutely certain. If someone does not win the jackpot this week, they certainly will next week or the week after. Many charities will definitely benefit, and the government will definitely receive its 12%. Chance processes are by no means incompatible with determined outcomes.

What should equally be clear from this and the previous two chapters is that the claim that evolution is *necessarily* Purposeless is now looking simply irrational.

5

The Christian Matrix Within Which Biology Flourishes

Science takes things apart to see how they work. Religion puts them together to see what they mean.

Rabbi Jonathan Sacks (2014)[47]

Everyone needs some purpose in life if they wish to flourish and maintain good mental health. This is equally valid for those who believe that life and the universe has no ultimate Purpose, such as those from whom we quoted in the Introduction. When Dawkins observes rather gloomily that "The universe we observe has precisely the properties we should expect if there is, at bottom, no design, no purpose, no evil and no good, nothing but blind pitiless indifference" – given his worldview it is difficult to conclude otherwise. From the perspective of atheism, everything is ultimately going to be swallowed up in the second law of thermodynamics and that's that.[48] Yet it is quite clear that Dawkins has imposed his own purposes upon his own life which are highly fulfilling: writing bestselling books, giving highly paid lectures all round the world, marrying a well-known film actress, organizing his own foundation, and so forth. And in one way or another that is what everyone does who holds to the view that there is no ultimate Purpose in the universe, nor indeed in their own lives. Some find purpose in their career, others pursue an enjoyable hobby, or campaign for some great social or political cause, or do charity work, or find fulfilment in their family life, or go on frequent world cruises – or all of the above. These are all good and worthy pursuits, but there is just one problem: if the universe is really as Dawkins describes, then all these activities will soon be forgotten, swallowed up in the march of time and death, totally forgotten after the passage of a few decades or a few centuries. If there is no ultimate Purpose, the activities of life are mere Elastoplast, patching over the brutal reality that however good they might be at providing immediate feelings of purpose, not only are those feelings transient, but they also highlight a profound mismatch between the logic of the ultimate meaninglessness of life and the various futile attempts to deny that logic by means of an increasing whirl of activities.

Please don't get me wrong – we all have pastoral responsibilities to encourage people to behave irrationally for their own flourishing and well-being. If people firmly believe that there is no ultimate Purpose for the universe, nor for their own lives, then we should encourage them to have goals for their own lives and to engage in meaningful activities – for the simple reason that the metaphysical logic of the situation can engender despair, or even, in the worst-case scenarios, suicidal behaviour. Fortunately, most people don't see the profound irrationality of living a life without any ultimate meaning and yet acting as if it did have precisely that. For the sake of mental health, this is a topic we need to approach gently.

Just as people who disbelieve in ultimate Purpose still proceed to impose purpose upon their own biographical narratives, so evolutionary biologists will often impose purposes of various kinds upon the evolutionary narrative.[49] They are aware in doing so that such narratives of purpose are not intrinsic to evolutionary history itself, but are happy to introduce purpose from outside, as it were. Some see the evolution of the human mind as providing the central purpose of evolution. But more often the conclusion is the opposite: man the destroyer has been bad for biological diversity, and it is the beauty and wonder of diversity that provides the purpose of biology. Others see the evolution of altruism or the evolution of morality as providing purposes for the evolutionary process. One of the key founders of the field of sociobiology, Bill Hamilton, whose ideas Richard Dawkins popularized in his book *The Selfish Gene*, once stated in an interview that "I'm also quite open to the view that there is some kind of ultimate good which is of a religious nature – that we just have to look beyond what the evolutionary theory tells us and accept promptings of what ultimate good is, coming from some other source."[50] When pressed by the interviewer as to what that "other source" might be, Hamilton went on to suggest that planet Earth was a kind of experiment by extraterrestrial beings who occasionally interfered with the experiment ("miracles"), going on to affirm that "it's a kind of hypothesis that's very, very hard to dismiss". In each of these cases purpose – or Purpose in the case of Hamilton – is imposed on the process from outside by human reflection and interpretation: the purpose or Purpose is consistent (to varying degrees) with the evolutionary story but cannot be derived directly from it.

This chapter is about the same approach – imposing Purpose from outside, but in this case baptizing evolution (if that is the right expression) into a much broader overall Purpose, that provided by Christian faith. That is by no means the only metaphysical system into which evolution can be incorporated, but there are reasons to believe that it is a particularly appropriate one, hopefully for reasons that will become apparent as we go along.

In the first instance, we may note that Christian faith was Darwin's own worldview as he puzzled over the vast amount of observations and data that came out from his famous voyages on the *Beagle*. Indeed, we may go further than that and say that, in its roots, the theory of evolution has a particular affinity with

Christianity via its nurturing within natural theology, a point already highlighted in Chapter 1. As noted there, many of Darwin's Christian contemporaries were quick to incorporate evolution into Christian faith. The Scottish evangelical Henry Drummond (1851– 97) maintained that natural selection was "a real and beautiful acquisition to natural theology" and that the *Origin* was "perhaps the most important contribution to the literature of apologetics" to have appeared during the nineteenth century (Alexander, 2001, p. 200). Indeed, Drummond built Darwin's theory into his own apologetics for Christian faith in his highly popular writings. Another great Victorian clerical enthusiast for Darwinism was the Anglo-Catholic Aubrey Moore, already cited in Chapter 1. Moore maintained that Darwinism had done the church a great service in helping to get rid of the more extreme forms of natural theology and claimed that there was a special affinity between Darwinism and Christian theology. The reason for this affinity, claimed Moore, was based on the intimate involvement of God in his creation as revealed in Christian theology, for

There are not, and cannot be, any Divine interpositions in nature, for God cannot interfere with Himself. His creative activity is present everywhere. There is no division of labour between God and nature, or God and law... For the Christian theologian the facts of nature are the acts of God. (Alexander, 2001, p. 177)

It should not be thought that such theologians were merely seeking to hook their theological wagon on to a newly successful theory in order to gain some prestige from the theory, for the same era saw other scientists and theologians being critical of "Mr Darwin's new theory", and in any case there were plenty of robustly independent theological thinkers around in the late Victorian era. We should also note that the very first theological response we have on evolution is dated six days *before* the official publication date of the *Origin*, so no opportunity for hooking theology on to a successful new scientific theory there. Thanking Darwin for his kind gift of an advance copy, in a letter written on 18 November 1859, Revd Charles Kingsley wrote that: "All I have seen of it awes me", going on to comment that it is "just as noble a conception of Deity, to believe that He created primal forms capable of self-development... as to believe that He required a fresh act of intervention to supply the lacunas [gaps] which He Himself had made." Darwin was so impressed with this response that he quoted these lines in the second edition of the *Origin*. The historian James Moore writes that "with but few exceptions the leading Christian thinkers in Great Britain and America came to terms quite readily with Darwinism and evolution" (Moore, 1981, p. 79), and the American historian George Marsden reports that "... with the exception of Harvard's Louis Agassiz, virtually every American Protestant zoologist and botanist accepted some form of evolution by the early 1870s" (Marsden, 1984, p. 101).

So baptizing evolution into Christian theology is nothing new and Darwin's *Origin of Species* has even been dubbed "the last great work of Victorian natural theology" (Durant, 1985, p. 16). The present chapter is no anomaly in the context of the history of ideas but simply continues in that tradition. The only difference is that with the more contemporary form of evolutionary theory than that espoused by Darwin, the task is made even easier.

The meaning of creation

As we noted in the previous chapter in our discussions about chance and randomness, understanding the meanings of words really does make a difference, especially as we apply those words to biology. As in science, so in theology, the word "creation" has some clear meanings, but unfortunately the waters can readily be muddied by its different uses in daily speech. For example, the word "creationist" is often used to refer to someone who denies evolution and believes that everything was made in six days of 24 hours about 10,000 years ago. It should by now be apparent that this is not the use of the word "creation" that we have in mind here. But more subtle confusions come from the ways in which we use the words "create" or "creation" in our daily speech. We speak of painters "creating" great works of art; we talk of politicians "creating mayhem" as they unsuccessfully try and sort out some world crisis; and cooks "create" incredible chocolate cakes. These and many other similar usages all have one aspect in common: when human beings make things, they work with already existing material to produce something new.

But God as creator is nothing like that, and here the communication problem begins. The human act of creating is not the complete cause of what is produced; but God's creative act *is* the complete cause of what is produced. As the theologian Bill Carroll expresses the point, drawing on the writings of Thomas Aquinas:

> *God's causality is so different from the causality of creatures that there is no competition between the two, that is, we do not need to limit, as it were, God's causality to make room for the causality of creatures. God causes creatures to be causes… Creation is not essentially some distant event; rather, it is the on-going complete causing of the existence of all that is. At this very moment, were God not causing all that is to exist, there would be nothing at all. (Carroll, 2012)*

So creation is about ontology, the existence of things and the meanings of their existence.

As Carroll also points out: "Creation concerns first of all the origin of the universe, not its temporal beginning" (Carroll, 2012). This highlights a further problem with our daily use of the word "creation" to refer to human activities. In Christian theology, the "origin" of the universe refers to its complete and utter dependence on God's ongoing creative activity for its very existence. Whatever is created has its origin in God. The universe may also well have had a temporal beginning when time and space were brought into being at the Big Bang. But this is not (primarily) what creation is about: creation is about the utterly contingent dependence of all that exists upon God's say-so. Of course, creation includes temporal beginnings, just as it includes everything else, but to focus merely on how things begin, be that in cosmology or biology, as if that was mainly what creation was about, is to miss the point.

Although metaphors are invariably limited in what they can convey, thinking of God as the author of all that exists has some merit. A published book's relation to the author is one of complete and radical dependence (depending, of course, on how much the publisher edits, but let's not push the metaphor too far). From a Christian perspective, if you want to know what a creation is like, just look around: you're living in one and you're part of one, because that's what existence entails. You're living in a book and the author is not within the pages of the book but intimately involved in its ongoing and dynamic existing.

With such an understanding of the created order in mind, it now becomes clear why the Bible contains no concept of "nature" as referring to the natural world – the word is nowhere to be found. This was felt to be such an important point by Robert Boyle, one of the founders of modern chemistry and a founding member of the Royal Society, that he wrote a whole book about it entitled *Free Inquiry into the Vulgarly Received Notion of Nature* (1685). For Boyle, the "vulgar notion" was the idea that "nature" had any kind of autonomous existence, or that it acted as a mediator between God and his works. He attacked the expression, popular since the time of Aristotle, that "God and nature do nothing in vain", since this implied the old Greek idea of divine nature, rather than the relationship of "Creator and creature". God has not appointed a "vicegerent called nature" wrote Boyle; and if there were such a "Lieutenant she must be said to act too blindly and impotently to discharge well the part she is said to be trusted with" (Boyle, 1685, IV, p. 363). In the hands of Boyle, and indeed of the biblical text, the idea of nature as a quasi-independent entity has been demythologized.

This understanding of creation is continually highlighted in a book of the Old Testament known as the Psalms by the phrase "the Lord the maker of heaven and earth". The object of worship is "the Maker of heaven and earth, the sea, and everything in them – the Lord, who remains faithful forever" (Psalm 146:6). The reference to "heaven and earth" simply means "all that exists". The reference to the sea here is also of particular significance because in the polytheistic worldview of the nations that surrounded the Jewish people in the ancient Near East, the sea with its creatures were seen as an arena of threat and chaos. In biblical thought, by contrast, all that exists is seen as being part of God's good created order. When the very early church community was facing opposition as they preached the message of the risen Christ, they prayed to the "Sovereign Lord," who "made the heaven and the earth and the sea, and everything in them" (Acts 4:24).

Since our great creator God is not encompassed or constrained in any way by the present created order in which we find ourselves, that means that we as human creatures are in no position at all to guess how God might wish to do creation, nor to tell him how he should be doing it. As God says, speaking through the prophet Isaiah: "For my thoughts are not your thoughts, neither are your ways my ways... As the heavens are higher than the earth, so are my ways higher than your ways and my thoughts than your thoughts" (Isaiah 55.8–9). "Our God is in heaven", says the psalmist, "he does whatever pleases him" (Psalm 115:3). Historians of science have often pointed to this sense of the transcendence of God and the consequent radical contingency of the created order as one of the great motivations for empiricism, for the experimental method. For no one could simply guess how the created order might work starting from common sense or simple human logic. The only way to find out how it works is to do experiments. Quantum mechanics is weird, as we have already noted, and mental representations should not be attempted, otherwise one ends up with a headache. No one could have guessed starting from first principles that the world of the very small would have such strange properties. It is the actual properties of the world around us that force certain conclusions upon us.

The radical contingency of the created order upon God's say-so was very much in mind when Cotes wrote his preface to the second edition of Isaac Newton's great work the *Principia Mathematica* in words clearly approved by Newton himself:

> *Without all doubt this world… could arise from nothing but the perfectly free will of God…. These (laws of nature) therefore we must not seek from uncertain conjectures, but learn them from observations and experiments.*

The idea of scientific laws first start appearing in the writings of Newton, Boyle, and Descartes, who all make the point that it is precisely because God is the free Agent who creates an orderly and intelligible universe, that the cosmos can be described by means of laws. But we cannot second-guess God ahead of time to infer what those laws might be: we can only find out by making observations and doing experiments. René Descartes, writing in 1644, makes the point in these words:

> *Since there are countless different configurations which God might have instituted here, experience alone must teach us which configurations he actually selected in preference to the rest. We are thus free to make any assumption on these matters with the sole*

proviso that all the consequences of our assumption must agree
with experience. (Descartes, 1983, p. 100)

The idea of the transcendence of God and of the radical contingency of the intelligible created order upon his say-so, needs to be complemented by a further helpful insight from Aquinas, who popularized the view that God is the primary cause of all that exists, whereas the means whereby they exist are known as secondary causes. By these terms Aquinas did not imply any temporal relationship. It is not a question of God at one moment bringing something into being that then continues upon its merry way in independence of the primary cause, but more the idea of a "package deal" in which the primary and secondary causes are in an ongoing and continually contingent relationship. The former idea leads to deism, the latter idea to theism. In the deistic idea, God creates by establishing the "laws of nature" and then withdraws from the scene. In theism, God is actively involved in creating and upholding all that exists at every moment.

This idea of primary and secondary causes is useful in drawing attention to the functional integrity of the created order: "God causes creatures to be causes." From what has been said so far, one could imagine a deterministic universe in which God is the divine puppet-master micromanaging every event, actively intending that A rather than B should occur in the created order. But that is no necessary consequence of the creation theology that has been outlined so far. For by faithfully guaranteeing order and nomic regularity in the properties of matter in the created order – the secondary causes – by the same token God, the primary cause, bestows upon the created order its own functional integrity. We find some hint of this idea in Genesis 1 where God uses the language of gracious allowance in saying "Let the land produce vegetation…" (verse 11) and "Let the water teem with living creatures…" (verse 20) and "Let the land produce living creatures according to their kinds…" (verse 24). Matter does what matter does and if it didn't we wouldn't know where we were, with "all coherence gone".[51]

It is remarkable how in the literature of both atheists and believers, God is tacitly or explicitly demoted to the role of secondary cause, as if God were merely another force within the created order acting on various parts of it. In Dawkins's book *The God Delusion* the "god" that Dawkins doesn't believe in is portrayed as a kind of superman, like us only a lot more powerful, pushed out as an explanatory device for things because science does a much better job at explaining things. But Christians are atheists also like Dawkins with respect to the god that he doesn't believe in. As Rupert Shortt so aptly puts it in the title of his helpful book: "God is No Thing" (Shortt, 2016). Tilting at windmills is a "new atheist" speciality. Equally, though, do Christian writers sometimes portray an understanding of God that is not dissimilar to Dawkins's understanding, so he cannot be blamed for getting the wrong idea. God is sometimes portrayed by Christians as the engineer who occasionally designs bits of living things that evolution, it is fallaciously assumed, is unable to explain. God is brought in as a last resort to explain those "mysteries" that currently baffle science, leading to the infamous god-of-the-gaps argument for God's existence. Not surprisingly, as science extends its explanatory domain to ever-increasing corners of the world around us, the need to call in God's services as an "explanation" declines in parallel. This is why the arguments for God based on biological "designs" so loved by the natural theologians of previous centuries represented such hostages to fortune – once the idea of adaptation by natural selection came along, what need was there for God as an explanation? Aubrey Moore, from whom we have already quoted, summarizes this point well (in 1889) when he writes that:

> *The one absolutely impossible conception of God, in the present day, is that which represents him as an occasional visitor. Science has pushed the deist's God further and further away, and at the*

moment when it seemed as if He would be thrust out all together,
Darwinism appeared, and, under the guise of a foe, did the work
of a friend... Either God is everywhere present in nature, or He
is nowhere. (Moore, 1891, p. 73)

If only other theological commentators on Darwin had taken this
insight more to heart.

It is the intelligibility of the created order that renders science
feasible. Without its nomic regularity, not only would science be
impossible, but also our very existence as rational moral agents.
Within the creation theology that we have sketched so far, the
scientific enterprise simply represents the investigation of the
created order. Whatever exists – "laws of nature", trees, bacteria,
planets, stars, Higgs bosons, quantum phenomena, love, radiation,
humans, or whatever – if it exists, then within the framework
suggested here, it is part of the created order and therefore open
to scientific investigation in principle. The phrase "in principle"
is worth adding here because science is very good at investigating
entities to do with matter and energy, not so relevant for things
like ethics ("how ought we apply the latest scientific discoveries?"),
aesthetics ("the film I just watched was really inspiring"), or personal
relationships ("I love you"). Within the Christian worldview, all
scientific investigation must be, by definition, an attempt to further
understand the properties and workings of the created order. So
our present state of scientific knowledge about a particular aspect
of the created order is irrelevant to its theological status as creation.
It is a very odd argument, made by some, that the present gaps in
our scientific knowledge in the year 2018 (or whatever it is), a tiny
speck of time in the vastness of the age of this planet (4.6 billion
years), let alone the universe (13.8 billion years), has some kind of
theological relevance. The claim that human ignorance should be
relevant to the existence of God as creator is a bit like the reviewer
of a book reporting that they had found Chapter 3 a little difficult

to follow, therefore the author must have written it. Ignorance of the created order is irrelevant to its divine authorship in the way that failure to comprehend Chapter 3 is likewise irrelevant to the question of its human authorship.

In thinking about the created order, there is a further red herring that we need to head off, a claim known as "occasionalism" that in some respects is diametrically opposite to the god-of-the-gaps idea. This is the view that God is the only true cause of events and therefore, in its strongest version, that God's creation is actually a series of trillions of individual acts of creation joined together. The view was widespread in the Islamic theology of the tenth and eleventh centuries, popularized by al-Ghazali (c.1055–1111) in his influential work *The Incoherence of the Philosophers*. The best-known occasionalist in the Western philosophical tradition is Nicolas Malebranche (1638–1715), who claimed that "there is only one true cause because there is only one true God;... the nature or power of each thing is nothing but the will of God;... all natural causes are not *true* causes but only *occasional* causes".[52] For Malebranche, since God is the true cause, all "natural causes" are merely "occasions" of divine will. But the view being presented here is not like that. Instead it represents a seamless cloth of God's authorship in which the cloth has its own functional and causal integrity. God causes creatures to be causes that are truly "true causes". That's what functional integrity entails.

We find overtones of occasionalism in Darwin's query to the Professor of Botany at Harvard, Asa Gray, a Christian, in a letter dated 3 July 1860: "Do you believe", wrote Darwin "that when a swallow snaps up a gnat that God designed that that particular swallow should snap up that particular gnat at that particular instant?" Gray's reply is not available, but it was a question clearly on Darwin's mind, who repeats his question in a letter to his brother-in-law Hensleigh Wedgwood and then reports Hensleigh's wise answer to Asa Gray in a letter written on 10 September 1860:

Hensleigh Wedgwood… is a very strong Theist, & I put it to him, whether he thought that each time a fly was snapped up by a swallow, its death was designed; & he admitted he did not believe so, only that God ordered general laws & left the result to what may be so far called chance, that there was no design in the death of each individual Fly.

It is the understanding of the immanence of God in the created order that subverts occasionalism and also provides some clues as to how God interacts with the world of biology, so it is to that topic that we should now turn.

The immanence of the Trinitarian God in the created order

Many people are puzzled by the Christian insistence that God is a Trinity of God the Father, God the Son, and God the Holy Spirit. It is therefore worth pointing out that although the doctrine was formalized in creedal form many years after the first century AD, it all began with the personal experience of Jesus of Nazareth by his first disciples. When they first started following Jesus they were all Jewish monotheists. They knew about God as Father because that was a familiar idea from the Hebrew Bible (such as Isaiah 63:16; 64:8) and they believed in God the Father as creator of heavens and earth. Then gradually, very gradually, they came to realize that Jesus was who he claimed to be, the Son of God, one not just to follow as a wandering rabbi, but one to worship. For some it was when Jesus stilled the storm, demonstrating his power over the created order, when the penny dropped: "Then those who were in the boat worshipped him, saying, 'Truly you are the Son of God'" (Matthew 14:33). For a woman called Martha it was after Jesus had raised her brother from the dead that she realized Jesus' true identity, as he said to her: "I am the resurrection and the life. He who believes in me will live, even though he dies; and whoever lives and believes in me will never die. Do you believe this?" "Yes, Lord," she told him, "I believe that you are the Christ, the Son of God, who was to come into the world" (John 11:25–27). It was because Jesus made the direct claim to be the Son of God that he was crucified (Luke 22:70). As the onlookers saw Jesus hanging on the cross, they jeered: "He trusts in God. Let God rescue him now if he wants him, for he said, 'I am the Son of God'" (Matthew 27:43).

Throughout his teaching period leading up to his crucifixion, Jesus drew attention to his role as the one whose coming was intimately linked with the gift of the Holy Spirit (Luke 11:13; John 14:26), but it was only after Christ's resurrection that the disciples had personal and dramatic experience of the Holy Spirit on the first day of Pentecost (Acts 2). Only then could they really understand the deeper meaning of Jesus' Trinitarian command given at the end of his life on earth to "go and make disciples of all nations, baptizing them in the name of the Father and of the Son and of the Holy Spirit" (Matthew 28:19). The New Testament book of Acts, which records the growth of the early church, has rightly been dubbed the "Acts of the Holy Spirit" because it was the Holy Spirit who was so intimately involved in the spread of the gospel (the good news about Jesus) across the area surrounding the Mediterranean.

The Trinitarian concept of God was not therefore some dry academic doctrine cooked up by a group of professional theologians, but arose out of the transforming personal experience of God as Father, Son, and Spirit, in the lives of the early followers of Jesus of Nazareth. And if we find it difficult to get our heads around the idea of three persons in one God, perhaps we should not be that surprised. A God whom we could easily describe and grasp with our (relatively) puny minds, more like the pathetic superman god of Dawkins than the creator and sustainer of all that exists, runs the risk of being an entity that humans make up for their own convenience, rather than the God who has graciously chosen to reveal something of his character to us in Christ.

The historical emergence of the doctrine of the Trinity is not dissimilar in one respect, and one respect only, with the emergence of quantum theory. Quantum mechanics was not dreamed up by a group of clever scientists sitting around thinking that it would be rather fun to have a really mysterious theory. As we have already noted, Einstein and others protested that because it was so mysterious, therefore it was unlikely to be true. But the theory was forced upon physicists because of the weird behaviour of very small physical particles. It was their experience of the world that forced the theory upon them in an attempt to describe the properties of the world accurately, not the other way round. So with the Trinity – it was their own personal experience of what happened in the world that forced this understanding of God upon those first disciples. After all that they had seen, heard, and experienced, how could they believe otherwise? Explanatory models in theology, as in science, have to fit the facts, even if on occasion we find the models in both contexts hard to conceptualize.

The Trinitarian concept of God as creator is important because in Christian theology all three persons of the Trinity are seen as being intimately involved in creation. Charles Raven, once Master of Christ's College, Cambridge, Charles Darwin's old College, and an influential voice in the science–faith dialogue in Britain in the first half of the twentieth century, put it like this: "God as Father was like an artist deciding to create a picture; God the Son was the design on which the work was modelled; and the Holy Spirit was the creative energy in the artist that created the picture" (Randall, 2015). This expresses well the *immanence* of God in the created order, that moment by moment involvement in upholding and sustaining the created order, God's faithfulness being displayed in the nomic regularity, the lawlike behaviour of energy and matter, which renders the world coherent and makes the scientific enterprise possible. This is a Trinitarian immanence. Right at the beginning of the Bible in Genesis 1:3 the Spirit of God hovers over the waters ready to bring order out of the formless and empty earth. Or in Hiebert's memorable translation, far from being the hovering of a bird, the *ruach* becomes the wind sweeping in on a storm from the Mediterranean: "God's *ruach* swept over the surface of the water" (Hiebert, 2008, p. 15). As the theologian Jürgen Moltmann expresses the point: "the divine Spirit (*ruach*) is the creative power and the presence of God in his creation. The whole creation is a fabric woven by the Spirit, and is therefore a reality to which the Spirit gives form" (Moltmann, 1985, p. 99). Calvin put it this way in his *Institutes*:

> *For it is the Spirit who, everywhere diffused, sustains all things, causes them to grow, and quickens them in heaven and on earth... In transfusing into all things his energy, and breathing into them essence, life and movement, he is indeed plainly divine. (Calvin, 1986, 1.13.14–15)*

The New Testament insists that we live in a Christological creation. Using one of the most powerful metaphors in the whole of the New Testament, John tells us in the Prologue to his Gospel that "Through him [the Logos] all things were made; without him nothing was made that has been made." In Colossians 1, Paul writes that by the Son of God "all things were created: things in heaven and on earth, visible and invisible... all things were created by him and for him. He is before all things, *and in him all things hold together*" (verses 16–17, my italics). In other words, the complete created order, in all its breadth and diversity, goes on existing by the same divine Word, the Lord Jesus, who was intimately involved in the bringing into being of everything in the first place. The point is further underlined by the writer to the Hebrews when he writes that "The Son is the radiance of God's glory and the exact representation of his being, *sustaining all things by his powerful word*" (Hebrews 1:3, my italics). God is the one "for whom and through whom everything exists" (Hebrews 2:10). Here is no absentee landlord but rather the key to the whole of existence. Trinitarian creation entails an active "holding in existence" of the complete created order.

The Apostle Paul made the immanence of God in creation a central point of his speech on Mars Hill in Athens, reminding his listeners that God "gives all people life and breath and everything else" (Acts 17:25). Those who are pictured as worshipping God faithfully in the apocalyptic visions described by John in the book of Revelation, express their worship to God as the one "who created all things, and by your will they were created and *have their being*" (Revelation 4:11, my italics). Later in Revelation God is portrayed as the one "who created the heavens and *all* that is in them, the earth and *all* that is in it, and the sea and *all* that is in it" (Revelation 10:6, my italics). This is what creation is about: existence and being held in being. So if someone asks the Christian biologist what difference it makes to her biology if there were no God, the first answer has to be: "Well, if there were no God, there wouldn't be anything, neither the universe, nor biology, so no us." In the Christian way of thinking, all that exists is radically contingent upon the Trinitarian God's say-so: it is the ultimate cause of how things "have their being".

And it is this Spirit-energized Christological created order that the Old Testament insists is a biologically fruitful created order. As the theologian, the late Colin Gunton, wrote:

> *the only satisfactory account of the relation between creator and creation is a Trinitarian one… It is because God the Father creates through the Son and the Spirit… that we can conceive a world that is both real in itself, and yet only itself in relation to its creator. (Gunton, 2005, p. 75)*

This message comes through loud and clear in many Old Testament passages such as Psalm 104 and Job 38–39 where God is portrayed as the one who sustains every aspect of the living world.

As we consider the immanence of God in the created order, a further striking observation emerges from the biblical narratives, and that is the three tenses of creation: past, present, and future. There is a definite biblical sense of looking back at creation – at all that God has done in the past in bringing this world of rich biological diversity into being. We also read of a God who is actively involved in the created order in the present tense as we have just been thinking. God the Father, God the Son, and God the Holy Spirit are all intimately involved in *creatio continua*, the ongoing work of creation. As Jesus remarked in John 5 after healing the man on the Sabbath: "My Father is always at his work to this very day, and I, too, am working" (John 5:17). And then as far as future creation is concerned, God tells us through the prophet Isaiah: "Behold, I will create new heavens and a new earth..." (Isaiah 65:17). So the biblical doctrine of creation tells us about a dynamic process in which God is the author of the narrative, and Jesus is "the Alpha and the Omega, the First and the Last, the Beginning and the End" (Revelation 22:13). God's creation encompasses past, present, and future. That's the matrix.

All analogies are limited, but God's continuing creative activity has been likened to the continual flow of digital signals without which there would be no picture on our TV screen. Our favourite TV drama is a self-contained drama, and talk of digitally encoded signals will add nothing to it, yet without the continuous signals the drama would cease to be conveyed to your living-room.

To use a different analogy, God is both the musical composer and conductor in relation to the symphony of creation, the one who is immanent in the whole creative process as the beautiful harmony emerges from the coordinated output of the many different musical components. And maybe if you like jazz there is plenty of improvisation along the way to produce basically the same tune.

A highly significant fact about the Trinitarian character of God is that God is intrinsically relational. This is spelled out in John's Gospel (chapters 14–17) where the relational character of God's being as Father and Son leads to a theology of imaging and corresponding: as the Father loves the Son and the Son loves the Father, so the Son loves his disciples, so the disciples should love each other, so are they called to express that love to the world in community. More than that, it is the very existence of the Father that defines the meaning of Sonhood and vice versa. This whole dynamic is summarized in the concluding verse of Jesus' high priestly prayer (John 17:26). The biblical proclamation that "God is love" (1 John 4:8, 16) should therefore be seen not as a claim about some Platonic "essence" that is a property of God's being, but rather as reference to a dynamic ongoing relationship of love between Father, Son, and Holy Spirit. This is what Christians mean when they refer to God as Person – not that God has any resemblance to a physical person, but rather that the language we use to describe human persons has some traction, at least, when in metaphorical language we seek to understand something of the personhood of God.

For those who believe in a personal God who is immanent in the created order, we may therefore claim that it is not "unexpected" (as it were) that personhood has emerged through the creative evolutionary process. God's intentions and purposes for the biological world certainly seem to have included personhood. This is not the claim that we can somehow "read off" God's character and purposes by an inspection of the living world described to us by biology. That would indeed be a very strong form of natural theology, well beyond any kind of claim being made here. Yet as outlined in Chapter 2, the emergence of mind and, with it, personhood, so rapidly and within a few seconds before midnight on the time-scale of evolution (were it compressed into a 24-hour scheme), is at least consistent with the Trinitarian God who creates persons with whom he wishes relationship, not out of any need to do so on God's part, but because it is intrinsic within the creative relational being of God to create personhood.

How does God act in the world?

Many conferences have been held and many books written on the topic of divine action, so all this brief section will attempt to do is to frame the discussion in order to "set the scene" a little in preparation for the discussion on biology that follows.

It seems reasonable to suppose that theological questions demand theological answers. My starting assumption is that addressing theological questions primarily by science is likely to produce headaches, if not out-and-out red herrings. There have been a number of commentators over the past few decades who have sought to locate the nexus of divine action in particular scientific properties of the world, be this in quantum uncertainty, chaos theory, or some other particular feature of the created order. Worthy as such efforts have been, I think it is difficult to avoid the impression that God in such scenarios ends up looking more like a tinkerer with the world rather than the author and sustainer of the whole created order. Once again it is Aubrey Moore who hits the nail on the head:

> The scientific evidence in favour of evolution, as a theory is infinitely more Christian than the theory of "special creation". For it implies the immanence of God in nature, and the omnipresence of His creative power. Those who oppose the doctrine of evolution in defence of a "continued intervention" of God, seem to have failed to notice that a theory of occasional intervention implies as its correlative a theory of ordinary absence. (Moore, 1891, p. 184)

It is difficult to avoid the impression in providing answers from science, wherever the nexus of divine action is supposed to reside, that a "god-of-the-nexus-gaps" is hovering somewhere in the background, however much the proponents of such scenarios might seek to distance themselves from such conclusions.

So instead I would like to highlight the language of top-down causation used by the Bible when it refers to the activity of God in creation, and that is the theological language of God speaking. The dramatic introduction to such language is of course in Genesis 1 where God speaks on every one of the six days to bring order and beauty into the world that is formless and empty. The idea of God speaking to create is all over the place in the Bible once we start looking for it, especially in the Psalms. "By the word of the Lord the heavens were made, their starry host by the breath of his mouth" writes the psalmist (33:6). "Let all the earth fear the Lord; let all the people of the world revere him. For he spoke, and it came to be; he commanded, and it stood firm" (Psalm 33:8–9). The whole of Psalm 29 is about the voice of the Lord: "The voice of the Lord is over the waters; the God of glory thunders, the Lord thunders over the mighty waters" (Psalm 29:3). In the Gospels, we find Jesus rebuking the wind and the raging waters on Lake Galilee so that the astonished disciples exclaim "Who is this? He commands even the winds and the water, and they obey him" (Luke 8:25). The writer to the Hebrews tells us that "By faith we understand that the universe was formed at God's command, so that what is seen was not made out of what was visible" (Hebrews 11:3). And so we could go on – these examples are but the tip of a very large iceberg.

Speaking expresses power, mind, intelligence, and will. Through top-down causation we ourselves exert dramatic influence through language over the behaviour of those around us or far away. "Please would you pass the salt?" we say to someone at the dinner table and our invisible words are causally effective in bringing about the desired result, with no breaking of scientific laws in the process. A preacher exhorts his congregation to consider the great needs of the world in light of the words of Jesus in Luke 12:48 that more is expected from those who have been given much, and a young person listening finds themselves serving God in the slums of a great city overseas soon afterwards. Human words are incredibly powerful. How much more so divine words that bring *creatio ex nihilo* and that guarantee the properties of matter. As Isaac Barrow, who was the first to be appointed to the new Lucasian Chair of Mathematics at Cambridge in 1663, expressed it: "God uses no other means, instruments or applications in these productions, than his bare word or command" (Harrison, 2002), where "productions" are referring here to both the usual and the more unusual works of God in creation.

One should not imagine for a moment that such reflections somehow "explain" divine action. Indeed, given that we humans can only see an incredibly tiny part of the totality of the created order in both time and space, claims to understand processes of divine action can appear somewhat hubristic. But by emphasizing the biblical notion of God creating and sustaining the created order by speaking, a process of top-down causation, we can at least steer our images away from God the heavenly engineer who occasionally tinkers with the machinery of creation, or God the heavenly designer who enjoys making the occasional eye or who has fun designing the genetic code. With all due respect to engineers, I am personally relieved that I do not worship a heavenly version of this species. As it happens, the notion of God as "designer" is not one found in the Bible. There are many other metaphors used for describing the character of God, but "designer" is not one of them. Of course, all who believe in God as creator see the intelligibility of the created order in some overall sense as being "designed" to be that way by God, so that we can speak sensibly of the intentions and purposes of God being fulfilled in creation, but that is a very different concept from the idea that God is actively designing some particular aspect of a living organism, for example.

We should not therefore expect the science generated and published by a scientist who believes in God as creator to be any different from that of his atheist colleague. From the perspective of the Christian worldview, both are investigating the properties of the created order. The Christian recognizes that it *is* a created order, the atheist doesn't, but in any case it doesn't change what they do in the lab as they work together, nor how they seek to understand the workings of the created order (although with the benefits of hindsight, historians have pointed to some ways in which concepts of God have impacted on the actual content of scientific theories – but that is a story for another time…).

The term "theistic evolution" has a long history and is used with various nuances. For Darwin's friend Asa Gray at Harvard, it entailed that God "guided" or "directed" evolution along certain beneficial paths. In the language of contemporary evolutionary biology, the philosopher Elliot Sober has proposed that it is not irrational to maintain that God could "engineer" mutations in such a way that they help to bring about his purposes (Sober, 2014, p. 32). Maybe, but this is not the kind of understanding of God as creator being presented here. Top-down causation entails that all secondary causes without exception reflect the functional integrity of the created order. It is the system as a whole, operating as a system, which reflects God's intentions and purposes. In the way the term is used here, the "theistic" in "theistic evolution" simply acts as a reminder that evolution is as much an aspect of the created as anything else. The biological theory itself doesn't differ between Christians and others, any more than do other scientific theories. So what's the point of using the term "theistic evolution" anyway? Why not also have "theistic cosmology", "theistic accountancy", or maybe "theistic football", for example? The reason is simple. It so happens that attempts have been made for a long time now to capture the language and concepts of evolution in the cause of atheism, as if evolution were somehow inherently atheistic. The term "theistic evolution" acts as a reminder that that ain't necessarily so. If atheists would stop trying to pump their ideology into the theory, then there wouldn't remain any need, either, to label evolution with this "theistic" tag in such discussions.

At this point in the conversation, someone will usually raise the question of deism, the idea that God established scientific laws at the beginning, but then withdrew from the creation without any further interaction. It seems likely that Darwin held to a somewhat deistic view of creation at the time when he was writing *On the Origin of Species*, although some of his statements on the matter are somewhat ambiguous. In any event, if the science described by the atheist is the same (in principle) as that described by the theist, is this not deism? Hopefully sufficient biblical insights have been provided by this stage to see that this cannot be the case for Christian theists. The metaphor of authorship (not perfect, but then all metaphors are inadequate) has already been used and will serve our purpose again here. The author is completely immanent in her novel, the text being radically contingent upon the will and creativity of the novelist. Applied to God, this is theism not deism.

Where the metaphor of authorship can perhaps lead us astray is in its implication that the people involved are mere puppets in the hands of the author. In the case of novels written by human authors this is clearly the case, although every author will point out that the characters that they create need to "have a life of their own" if they are to come across to the reader as authentic characters. Some authors have little idea as to where the novel is going to lead them when they set out on their creative voyage: it is the characters and the basic starting plot that pull them onwards.

In the real world of freely choosing human actors, it is worth highlighting that within the Christian worldview it is precisely because of divine action that we have genuine free will. For the creative order is one characterized by nomic regularity and it is this that enables the emergent properties of human personhood, which includes free will, as a consequence of a long process of hominin evolution. As a biologist, I see "free will" as a Darwinian trait which all adult humans in good health display in the same kind of way that they are typically characterized by having two arms and two legs. A free will worth having can be defined as the "the ability to intentionally choose between courses of action in ways that make us responsible for what we do", which is why nomic regularity is crucial because it is a properly working brain that allows this ability to prosper. A proper discussion of free will is way beyond the scope of this book,[53] but is mentioned here simply to reiterate the point that a created order constantly sustained by the creator God is precisely one in which genuine free will is possible. Free will is one of God's great gifts to humanity without which genuine love and genuine morality would equally be impossible. It is a consequence, not a casualty, of the kind of nomic regularity that is guaranteed in God's created order.

Before turning to look more closely at biology as part of this created order, it is also worth addressing the concern of some Christians that if atheist scientists and Christians who are scientists end up with mutual commitments to the very same theories, then is this not some covert form of naturalism? Naturalism is the philosophy that maintains that everything arises from natural causes and processes, denying the involvement of supernatural entities of any kind. A move that Christians often make at this stage is to distinguish between so-called "methodological naturalism" and "ontological naturalism". "Methodological naturalism" is presented as the benign form of naturalism in which scientists simply agree to keep theological explanations out of their scientific discourse, whereas "ontological naturalism" is the claim that in any case supernatural agency does not exist and the scientific explanation is all that really counts. But while recognizing that there is clear water between these two types of description, my own view is that the language is not particularly helpful. As a scientist who is a Christian I do not leave behind my Christian worldview when I enter my laboratory to do experiments. Far from it; exploring and seeking to understand God's world is a holy enterprise, part of a Christian's worship. A labbratory is a sacred space where the aim is to understand further the properties of God's created order. So naturalism may exist as a philosophy in the heads of individual scientists, but as far as Christians doing science are concerned, they are certainly not engaged in any kind of naturalism, neither methodological nor ontological.

There is therefore only one main answer to the subheading posed for this section: God interacts in the universe continuously and unfailingly, at all times and in every place, top-down and bottom-up, and everything in between. That is why the universe exists and is the way it is. That is what authorship entails.

God and biology

We have managed so far in this chapter to avoid any discussion of Purpose in biology in the light of the Christian understanding of creation. It is now high time to address that deficit.

We started the chapter by pointing out that many of Darwin's Christian contemporaries, not least the leading voices in the Anglican church, were happy and willing to baptize the theory of natural selection into the Christian doctrine of creation. By the mid-1860s, just a few years following the publication of the *Origin* in 1859, questions were already beginning to appear in Cambridge University science papers requesting students to discuss various aspects of "Mr Darwin's theory". In this context, it is good to remember that all science teaching at the time was carried out by Anglican clerics.

Hopefully it will now be clearer why such a baptism was not only possible but actually welcomed by some Christians, as already mentioned. If the created order is equivalent to everything that exists, then the more that science can uncover of the mechanisms involved in such existence, the better. One of Darwin's critical moves in developing his theory was to bring history into biology. The system that evolution replaced was a series of static steps, each one created separately by God, which formed a great "chain of being" in which each step represented an increase in complexity. But evolution in Darwin's hands was, and is, a dynamic system in which everything has a joined-up history, linked together in the great tree of life. Theologians of Darwin's time were very familiar with the providential working of God in the salvation history of the people of Israel as described in the Old Testament. If God could fulfil his intentions and purposes through such a complex human history, why could it not be the case that God equally fulfilled his purposes through a complex historical biological process? Indeed, it was Reformed Christians with a strong belief in God's providential working in history and in the world who most readily embraced Darwinian evolution in the late nineteenth century (Moore, 1981; Livingstone, 1987).

The biological descriptions of Chapters 2 and 3 counteract the assumption that evolution is necessarily Purposeless. However, this in itself does not force upon us the inference that biological processes must therefore be part of God's Trinitarian created order in the sense in which we have been describing the concept in this chapter – although biology can provide some pretty big hints about certain aspects of this framework. Generally, those who believe in this kind of theological matrix for framing the world do so based on the biblical witness to God's salvation history as interpreted through the church community down the centuries, not because of their study of biology. On the other hand, biological evolution is certainly consistent with such a theological matrix. In the discussion sections of our scientific papers, we scientists often make the claim that the new data presented in the publication are "consistent with" our favourite model or theory, whatever that might be at the time. Biologists don't go in for "proving things", but they are very concerned with concepts like consistency and plausibility. Their theories need to be coherent and consistent with the data, otherwise they won't be believed. Evolutionary theory is consistent with a creator God who has intentions and purposes for the world.

Is there any problem, then, with chance and randomness being part and parcel of the created order? As suggested in Chapter 4, when looked at carefully, these concepts cease to be the bogeymen as often portrayed in the literature hostile to evolution. Most forms of both chance and randomness, as was noted in that chapter, refer to the human inability to predict due to the complexity of the system or to small differences in the starting conditions. In the evolutionary process, multiple epistemological and ontological chance processes work to bring about variation in the genome which turn out not to be random in any strict mathematical sense of the word; in any case, natural selection ensures that necessity wins in the end. Chance and randomness in all these senses are all part of God's good creation, and without such processes we wouldn't be here because life would, as it were, get stuck in the rut without scope for variation and creativity. Furthermore, ontological chance is as much an aspect of the created order as any other aspect. Of course, something that is "pure chance" as far as we are concerned does not entail that it's "pure chance" as far as God is concerned. If we take the concept of the immanence of God in the created order seriously, energized by the Spirit, existing in Christ, and providentially ruled over by the Father, it is hard to know what ontological chance might mean from a heavenly perspective.

Reading the theological reflections of some mathematicians and philosophers on this issue, one rather gains the impression that "pure chance" is either a bit of a problem for God, because even poor God cannot then predict the future or, more positively, that "pure chance", as in quantum events, provides God with a "useful opportunity" to interact with the world. Both suggestions, it seems to me, imply a very impoverished view of the omnipotence of God, portraying a God who seems more like Dawkins's superman god rather than the God portrayed in the biblical text. It is we humanity who are made in God's image and we need to be careful about not trying to create God in our image, with our human limitations applied to God in the process. The stance being critiqued here is often justified by appeals to *kenosis*, the Greek word meaning "emptying" used to describe the emptying of Christ's heavenly power and glory entailed in his incarnation, described so powerfully in Philippians 2:5–11. *Kenosis* seems a very appropriate word to use in the context of the incarnation. The problem comes, however, when it is applied to the supposed relationship between God and the created order, a suggestion further discussed in the following chapter. The idea is that God "allows the creation" to be itself expressing its "own freedom". The problem with this suggestion is that, first, it is hard to know what it means for the creation to be "free". Matter does what matter does. People are free, but matter is not. Second, there is nowhere in the biblical literature which suggests that God in any way denies his power in bestowing functional integrity upon the created order. As we have already noted, God speaks and it is so, as in Genesis 1. The nomic regularity of the world depends upon the continued exertion of God's power in upholding and sustaining the created order. The intelligibility and coherence of the material world are not due to God withholding himself in any way from the universe, but rather infusing the world with his Spirit so that in Christ all things hold together. That is not *kenosis*, but it is a sign of God's faithfulness.

It should also be noted that when the Bible does refer to chance events, which is not often, it has no hesitation in seeing those events as part and parcel of God's normal activity in creation (1 Kings 22:15–28; Psalms 33:6–11; 148:8; Proverbs 16:33). There is never a hint in the Bible that certain types of event in creation are any more or any less the activity of God than other events.

What we describe in our scientific descriptions is our human attempts to describe and understand the properties of the created order. But we evolutionary biologists who believe in God as creator do not bring theological language into our scientific discourse, because that would represent a simple category error. It could even be heretical, from a Christian perspective, if our theological discourse implies that God is reduced to the level of one force among many, on a par with scientific forces. Our biological discourse is complementary to our theological discourse. We need both levels of discourse to do justice to biological realities. Theological discourse presents no kind of rival narrative to biological discourse. It is just that when biology is placed within the kind of theological matrix described here, it gains a broader overall interpretive coherence as an academic discipline than it would otherwise possess.

If our understanding of evolutionary biology is consistent with a God who has intentions and Purposes for the world, then we should now consider what those Purposes might be, and here we will highlight just three.

The first Purpose of biology that we note as we start reading the Bible is the intrinsic value of the great riot of biological diversity that we see all over the planet. One problem with the natural theology of previous centuries is that it portrayed a very anthropocentric view of humanity. In contrast, a careful reading of the biblical text reveals God as creator revelling in the living diversity of his own created order, not because it had some utilitarian purposes for human use, but simply because it was there. We may gain some very limited understanding of what that entails from the way a human artist (most of the time) enjoys looking at their own paintings or an author occasionally sneaks an enjoyable read of a book they wrote years ago (but doesn't tell anyone they did it).

Having filled the earth with a great array of living creatures "God saw *everything* that he had made, and it was very good" (Genesis 1:31, my italics). "The earth is the Lord's, and *everything* in it" (Psalm 24:1, my italics). In Psalm 104:24 the psalmist speaks of the earth as being full of "God's creatures". These are creatures that look to God "to give them their food at the proper time" including the "beasts of the field" and "the donkeys" (verse 11). The writer of Proverbs visualizes Wisdom personified as being the first of God's creations, who was "the craftsman at his side. I was filled with delight day after day, rejoicing always in his presence, rejoicing in his whole world and delighting in humankind" (Proverbs 8:30). We note that it was the "whole world" that brought Wisdom joy, not just humankind. It is not therefore surprising that the "great sea creatures" together with "fruit trees and all cedars, wild animals and all cattle, small creatures and flying birds" are involved in praising the Lord "from the earth" (Psalm 148:7–10), and all the trees of the field "clap their hands" (Isaiah 55:12). "Let everything that breathes praise the Lord!" (Psalm 150:6).

These wonderful poetic passages highlight an important insight relevant to the contemporary challenge of biodiversity loss. Those who campaign against biodiversity loss starting from a purely utilitarian position often find themselves flummoxed as to exactly *why* it should matter that we might lose ten more species of beetle, or whatever the cause of the moment might be. The theological framing outlined here suggests that it is the intrinsic value of the created order in all its wonderful diversity that matters to God. It reflects God's creativity, a created order that has been in existence for 3.5 billion years before humanity ever came on the scene to enjoy it, during which period God was *really* enjoying it. Yes, there have been many mass extinctions during the history of life on Earth and yes more than 99% of species that ever lived have gone extinct. But this does not subvert the fact that every species has its own intrinsic value, its own special way of being. Lions are characterized by their lion-ness, their own particular way of being, just as a species of beetle or tree are characterized by their beetle-ness or their tree-ness, not as some "Platonic essence", but as a set of properties unique to that particular species. Diversity reflects creativity and that in turn is rooted in God's own Trinitarian being and the way in which God places great value upon materiality. Such a narrative gives a powerful motivation and rationale for caring for the created order. As the well-known environmental campaigner and US advisor on climate change, James (Gus) Speth comments:

> *I used to think that the top environmental problems were biodiversity loss, ecosystem collapse and climate change. I thought that 30 years of good science could address these problems. I was wrong. The top environmental problems are selfishness, greed, and apathy, and to deal with these we need a cultural and spiritual transformation. And we scientists don't know how to do that.*[54]

Recognizing the living world as a contingent created order can, together with a profound recognition of the mess that we humans have made of the world, be the first step towards experiencing that "spiritual transformation".

Such a reflection becomes all the more relevant when we come to the second main Purpose of biology, which is equally clearly written all over the Bible, namely, that God's intentions and Purposes for biology are that creatures like ourselves should emerge that have the capacity for free will, and so moral choice, creatures with complex minds that enable the use of language, the appreciation and investigation of the properties of the created order, reflection on the meaning of life, and engagement in loving relationships. It is all this that opens up the possibility of a relationship of love with the God who is love. In the biblical framework, it is humankind who are made in the image of God and delegated by God as his "earth-keepers" (Genesis 1:26–28; Psalm 8). We have certainly made a big mess of it due to our own selfish, sinful behaviour, coupled to lots of ignorance. But the good news is that Christ through his death and resurrection has opened up a new way to experience Purpose in biology in which we can become once again the good carers for creation that God originally intended us to be. In Romans 8:19–23, the Apostle Paul pictures a "groaning creation" as waiting "in eager expectation for the sons of

God to be revealed". In the context of this passage, Paul is clearly referring in his phrase "sons of God" to those who have repented of their sin and put their trust in Christ for their salvation, thereby experiencing the kind of spiritual transformation to which Gus Speth refers (cf. verses 12–14). One implication of this passage (the whole of Romans 8 needs to be read in the context of the book as a whole) is that the creation is waiting, as it were, to be looked after properly again as God originally envisaged. Those who have turned their back on selfish behaviours that will destroy the Earth, and biological diversity with it, become better motivated and equipped to help reverse the "groaning" of creation.

In the context of biology, this second Purpose – that God's intention is to bring humanity into existence – can easily open up a big discussion. We can ask Stephen Jay Gould's question once again: if we replayed the tape of life again, would we end up with *Homo sapiens*? From the biological perspective, taking on board all the data from Chapters 2–4, the answer seems to be "not necessarily the same as the *H. sapiens* we know, but similar", eventually. In other words, a being with high intelligence, a mind sufficient to engage in language and personal relationships, and so forth. In any case, the arguments about "what might have been?" are invariably defeated by the facts about what has actually happened: "Yesterday bacteria, today New York".[55] The fact is: we are here, and we do have these particular properties, and we have a pretty good idea as to the evolutionary mechanisms whereby we came into being. Furthermore, our discussion on Laplacean biology suggests that the laws of physics and chemistry were not broken in any way on the long and winding path until we came on the scene. Yes, quantum events would prevent an actual Laplacean interpretation, but once carbon-based life came on the scene, it seems that the rest of evolutionary history was bound to follow, if not in this particular way, then in another similar way with very similar outputs.

From a theological perspective, if God wanted humans on this planet, humans there would be. Remember top-down causation and immanence. This excludes God's "occasional interference" in the fabric of creation, for there is no need for that. The point is that as a matter of fact God has brought about his will on planet Earth by bringing humanity into being, for indeed here we are. On many other life-bearing planets it is very likely that such a conversation is not going on, because there may be plenty of biological diversity but no intelligent minds on those particular planets, at least not with the capacity to ponder on the meaning of their existence. On yet other planets other intelligent minds like our own are very likely to exist. There are an estimated 10^{11} galaxies, each one with an average 10^{11} stars, and most of the stars in our own galaxy have planets, so the likelihood of life of some kind on other planets is very high. God is a creative God who clearly loves diversity, and carbon-based life seems to be the best way (that we know about) for life to occur, with complex carbon compounds everywhere we look in outer space, so the existence of biological diversity based on carbon-based life in many parts of the universe seems a reasonable guess.

It is a fair question to ask as to what role miracles play in the kind of creation theology that we have been outlining. If the created order has its own functional integrity, what room is there for miracles? Miracles in the Bible are seen as special signs of God's grace to God's people in particular historical circumstances. Often, not always, they involve the unusual working of God in the created order. But the usual properties of the created order, involving the consistency in the properties of matter that are guaranteed by God's faithfulness, are not seen by the biblical writers as miraculous, though without doubt equally reflecting God's power and actions as much as in the miraculous. Instead it is the orderliness and predictability of the created order to which Scripture draws attention. We have already noted Proverbs 8, with Wisdom there at the beginning, "when God established the clouds above and fixed securely the fountains of the deep, when he gave the sea its boundary so the waters would not overstep his command, and when he marked out the foundations of the earth" (Proverbs 8:28–29). "The moon marks off the seasons, and the sun knows when to go down", writes the psalmist (Psalm 104:19). This is the order of creation, God's normal pattern of activity, and it is against such an orderly background that miracles then stand out as the unusual working of God. In some cases, the biblical writer provides an explanation as to how the miracle took place, so in these cases it may be a miracle of timing (Exodus 14:21; Joshua 3:16). With many of the miracles of Jesus there is clearly no physical explanation as to how the miracle occurred (John 2:9; 11:43), the resurrection itself perhaps providing the supreme example (Luke 24). Given the immanence of the Trinitarian God in the created order, the language of "intervention" or "interference" to refer to the orderly and reproducible properties of matter seems inappropriate for, as we have already quoted Aubrey Moore: "God cannot interfere with Himself." On the other hand, the language of "intervention" seems perfectly appropriate when speaking of God's particular answer to prayer in the life of a believer today, or bringing about some special act of grace or performing a miracle. "God intervened in John's life in a remarkable way to prevent him proceeding further on a life of alcoholic addiction." That certainly seems a reasonable use of the language of intervention.

The third Purpose of God for biology that is expressed in different ways in many parts of the Bible is that the end of our own planet does not entail the end of life as we presently know it. This is probably the aspect of Purpose that those not within the Christian community find most difficult to get their heads round. Nevertheless, it is integral to the biblical message from beginning to end (literally), and without it any other kind of Purpose for biology doesn't really make much sense. It is the conviction that there will be a "new heavens and a new earth" following on from this one.

The idea is first found explicitly in the book of Isaiah, where God, speaking through the prophet declares that one day "I will create new heavens and a new earth…" (Isaiah 65:17). "Heaven" in biblical thought is envisaged as the place where God dwells. Of course, it is not a place in the physical way in which we understand "place", but metaphorical language is the only language we have when speaking of God. As we have already noted, God as the "maker of heaven and earth" is a commonly used biblical trope to refer to creation in all its completeness. So here in Isaiah is the startling claim that the complete created order will eventually be renewed and transformed by God, re-created, into a totally different entity where perfect harmony will exist, free of predation. This is something that God will make just as he makes the present created order (Isaiah 66:22).

Central to the preaching of Jesus in the New Testament is the coming of the kingdom which starts right now as his reign begins in the hearts and lives of all those who follow him (Matthew 9:35), but also continues onwards as a future fulfilled kingdom where God's reign will be complete (Matthew 25). Christ came to die for the whole cosmos: "For God so loved the *cosmos* [world] that he gave his one and only Son, that whoever believes in him shall not perish but have eternal life" (John 3:16). Yes, individuals enter the kingdom as they put their trust in Christ, but his redemption extends to the whole created order, one in which the "groaning" is finally brought to an end. As the Apostle Peter writes in his second letter: "in keeping with his promise we are looking forward to a new heaven and a new earth, the home of righteousness" (2 Peter 3:13). In the book of Revelation, the fulfilled kingdom is pictured as the one in which there will be no more suffering, no more death (Revelation 21:1–4). This is no ethereal existence, but rather far more real than our present existence, with people with resurrected bodies, and biological organisms with resurrected bodies, in intimate continuity with the present created order, yet now transformed into a totally new kind of created order with different properties, clearly no longer carbon-based life, but another type of materiality altogether. For those who believe in God as the source of the present created order, believing in God as the source of a further created order, towards which we are heading, is really not such a stretch.

The "continuity yet transformed" part of the story is critical for ideas of Purpose in biology. For this entails that everything that ever lived will be caught up into this new creation. One can speculate as to whether this involves literally every creature (somewhat mind-boggling for the imagination) or whether there is a repertoire of every species that ever lived on this planet; the main point here is that there will be continuity with present biological life. The best of every aspect of human creativity will be brought into the fulfilled kingdom (Revelation 21:24) and, one imagines, the best of every aspect of evolutionary diversity in terms of living organisms. This is important for our present struggle to care for the environment, for we can see now that the promise of redemption shows us the true value of all living things. What we do now for biodiversity *really* counts, not only because that biodiversity in itself brings glory to God as creator in the present age but also, one might speculate by analogy with the human situation, because that diversity will be represented in a transformed state in the age which is to come.

We started this chapter by pointing out that everyone imposes their own metaphysical narrative of Purpose upon biology because biology in itself is unable to tell us what that Purpose is, any more than the rest of science can, and pragmatically it is the only way we can maintain our sanity while living our short lives on this planet. The Christian narrative of Purpose goes well beyond mere stoic acceptance in order to celebrate the three Purposes that we have just outlined: the intrinsic value of biological diversity in the here and now; the emergence of humankind, made in God's image, to play a critical role in God's created order; and the guarantee of eternal Purpose in the new heavens and the new earth.

But there is a fly in the ointment. How can such a Christian narrative of Purpose possibly fit with the observation that the evolutionary process is marked by such a huge amount of pain, suffering, and death?

6

Death, Pain, Suffering, and the God of Love

*When the perishable has been clothed with the imperishable, and
the mortal with immortality, then the saying that is written will
come true: "Death has been swallowed up in victory." "Where, O
death, is your victory? Where, O death, is your sting?"*

1 Corinthians 15:54–55

Dozens of books and book chapters are available on the
challenging subject of evil and suffering, including the death and
apparent waste involved in the evolutionary process. Here we will
focus on the kind of biological and theological narratives that have
been introduced in the previous chapters, so the focus will not
be on the evil that arises from human free will, a huge topic in
itself, but on the pain and death involved in biological processes.
If we believe in a God of love who is immanent in upholding and
sustaining the created order, then how come evolution works the
way it does, entailing competition, food-chains, and lives which
can end abruptly in the animal's first few days of life in the mouth
of some hungry predator?

Clearly these are not "evils" in the way we normally use the
word since no moral decision-making is entailed. We don't seek

punishment for animals that eat each other, and when a dangerous dog kills a child it is the owner who is held responsible. But I think theologically we are justified in calling certain aspects of the biological world "evil" in the rather specialized sense that they do not belong to the ultimate fulfilled kingdom of God in which God's reign will be finally vindicated. When Jesus came teaching and preaching the kingdom of God, he clearly saw sickness as an evil to be confronted on the grounds that it had no place in God's fulfilled kingdom, as we will consider further below. So "natural evil" is ultimately "unnatural evil" because it does not belong in the age which is to come, even though it is very much part of our experience now in the present evil age. And even if we do not wish to attach the word "evil" to such characteristics of the created order at all, we can at least all agree that they represent facets of creation that we would rather do without.

What about our own load of human disease and suffering, much of it arising from the same kind of genetic variation that acts as the raw material for the evolutionary process? The onset of cancer, followed by surgery, followed by 12 rounds of chemotherapy, as I experienced a couple of years ago, helps to focus the mind on this topic. One out of three of us will experience cancer before our lives come to an end, so that in itself is nothing very unusual. I happen to find the place where this chapter ends up rather encouraging under such circumstances, but then I'm a biologist, so perhaps that is not surprising. Others will find other approaches more helpful, and there are many good books on the topic, more pastoral than this chapter is likely to prove for many (Carson, 2006; Tinker, 2012; T. Keller, 2013; White, 2014). There are also some very good books on animal suffering (Murray, 2008; Southgate, 2008). It is good to read a range of books on this subject because different people will find one approach more helpful than another and there are certainly no simple answers. The kind of theological and philosophical issues addressed in this chapter are unlikely to be of great help for someone currently in the midst of suffering, though, as I say, everyone is different in this regard. The philosopher Laura Ekstrom has some wise advice in her essay in the *Blackwell Companion to the Problem of Evil*, writing that

> *I still do think that the best way for a Christian, and indeed any person, to respond to those who suffer is with compassion, which can both prompt actions that bring practical relief and bring comfort to the psyche. Alleged divine justifications, on the other hand, are often the last thing a suffering person needs to hear. With respect to offering theodicies to those enduring pain and loss, 'Just shut up' remains, to my mind, decent advice. (Ekstrom, 2013, pp. 266–67)*

Wise words indeed. And yet to tackle these issues when we are not in the midst of some period of suffering is also wise.

The term "theodicy" (from the Greek words *theos*, God, and *dikaioun*, to justify) derives from the famous book of that name written by the great philosopher and mathematician Gottfried Leibniz (1646–1716) and published in 1710. Traditionally it has been taken to refer to arguments justifying the ways of a good, omniscient, and all-powerful creator God in a world where evil and suffering are obviously rife (van Woudenberg, 2013). In recent years, and especially since the work of Alvin Plantinga (Plantinga, 1974), it has been customary to define a theodicy as an argument that purports to offer God's *actual* reasons for permitting evil, while a defence merely offers *possible* reasons. However, it is fair to say that even professional philosophers in this field do not agree on the precise definition of the word "theodicy", and in any case the suggestions below represent a mix of the *actual* and the *possible*.

One point in this discussion is clear: it is possible to predict the kind of stance that a theologian or philosopher will take on this topic depending on their understanding of what is meant by

God's omniscience ("having total knowledge about everything") and by his omnipotence ("having total power to do anything"). We can illustrate this by giving a brief overview of the various stances taken by different commentators on the theodicy question.

God's omnipotence, omniscience, and theodicy

Start reading the voluminous literature on this topic and you soon find that there is a spectrum of opinion, ranging from the "hands-off" God who basically lets the world run itself, all the way to the "total control" God who determines everything that happens at the other extreme, and in between there are various shades of view on the spectrum. I am going to imagine the extreme pole of the "hands-off" God as if it were at the "left" of the spectrum, whereas the "total control" proponents are up the other end on the "right" of the spectrum (with no political connotations intended).

Up the "left end" we find commentators like the Jewish philosopher Hans Jonas who suggests in his posthumous collection of essays *Mortality and Morality* (Jonas, 1996) that God self-empties himself of mind and power in giving the creation its existence and then allows the interplay of chance and natural law to take its course. God's only further involvement is to hold a memory of the experience of the creation, which in the end is in a sense given back to God "transfigured or possibly disfigured by the chance harvest of unforeseeable temporal experience" (p. 125). So in this view, the universe is almost like a giant experiment on the part of God and the outcome is not really under his control at all.

A little further to the right from Hans Jonas we find the process theologians, who suggest that the evils of the world are explained by God's non-omnipotence, often defended by its proponents on the grounds that it does a better job at theodicy than traditional theism. So James Keller writes that "Because I believe that none of the responses by traditional Christian theists… are adequate, I propose process theism as a better way to respond to the problems of evil" (J. Keller, 2013, p. 344). Within the process philosophy of A.N. Whitehead, God cannot unilaterally bring about any particular state of affairs in the universe, but instead can, using Whitehead's term, "lure" the universe to behave in ways that he might wish. In fact, God has the maximum power of any actual being, but he is unable to guarantee that his "lure" will be followed, and indeed in many cases it isn't, hence explaining the evils in the world. In process philosophy, and the theology derived from it, God becomes but one component among many in influencing the future course of the universe.

So representatives "on the left" seek to solve the problem of evil by denying God's omniscience and omnipotence altogether. If God is not really in charge, how can he be blamed for the bad things that happen? Yet that seems to be a very high price to pay if the main reason, for some at least, is to "find a better way to respond to the problems of evil". The "high price" in this case entails the loss of any traditional understanding of God as creator, certainly of the kind outlined in the previous chapter.

We now move further towards the "middle" area of the spectrum and here we find a range of views very commonly found within the science–religion field of discussion. These commentators insist on God's omnipotence but also suggest that God has deliberately chosen to restrict his omnipotence in order to allow the created order to be itself and in a sense express its own "freedom". The theologian Jack Haught, for example focuses particularly on the theological notion of *kenosis*, of God letting the creation be itself out of love "willing to risk the disorder and deviation that actually occur in the evolution of cosmic beauty" (Haught, 2008, p. 158). Many other writers represent this middle

DEATH, PAIN, SUFFERING, AND THE GOD OF LOVE

range of the spectrum with various nuanced positions, including Arthur Peacocke, John Polkinghorne, Keith Ward, and Holmes Rolston among others. W.H. Vanstone speaks of God's activity in creation "in which each step is a precarious step into the unknown". The perceived advantage for constructing a coherent theodicy is of course that now God is no longer directly responsible for the ills of the created order, but instead its "disorder and deviation" to use Jack Haught's evocative phrase is a consequence of giving creation its freedom to develop.

In her book *Ask the Beasts: Darwin and the God of Love* (Johnson, 2014), Elizabeth Johnson adopts a similar line: just as God bestows free will upon humans, so he also bestows "free-process" upon the natural world (p. 158). The world, writes Johnson, is "gifted with its own freedom in and through which the Creator Spirit's gracious purpose is accomplished" (p. 179). Evolutionary biology is therefore an "unscripted adventure" in which the "natural world freely participates in its own creation" (p. 173) and "free process in nature works in ways not necessarily always according to divine design" (p. 191).

In a variant of this perspective, the focus is placed less on *kenosis*, more on the autonomy of the evolutionary process itself, so that it is not really God's fault that the process involves so much death and suffering, it's evolution's fault. This idea is found very soon after Darwin first expounded his great theory. In his book *Evolution and Religion* published in 1885, Henry Ward Beecher wrote that:

> *If single acts would evince design, how much more a vast universe, that by inherent laws gradually builded itself and then created its own plants and animals, a universe so adjusted that it left by the way the poorest things, and steadily wrought toward more complex, ingenious, and beautiful results! Who designed this mighty machine, created matter, gave it its laws, and impressed upon it that tendency which has brought forth almost infinite*

results on the globe, and wrought them into a perfect system?
Design by wholesale is grander than design by retail. (Mathisen,
2006, p. 386)

More recently, the evolutionary biologist Francisco Ayala writes
along similar lines that "A major burden was removed from the
shoulders of believers when convincing evidence was advanced
that the design of organisms need not be attributed to the
immediate agency of the Creator, but rather is an outcome of
natural processes" (Stewart, 2010, p. 763). Here we have a view
that tends more towards deism in which God creates the laws that
define the properties of the world and then basically the world
proceeds according to those laws. Indeed, as already mentioned,
this seems to have been Darwin's own theological position at the
time when he was writing *On the Origin of Species*. Clearly not all the
representatives of this middle part of the spectrum move in such
a deistic direction – far from it – but the problems inherent in all
these varied "middle of the spectrum" type of positions turn out
to be rather similar.

Three particular problems come to mind. The first problem has
already been raised in another context in the previous chapter. The
material world is not really "free" to do anything. Matter does what
matter does, it is not free even in the metaphorical sense intended by
these commentators. Heisenberg's uncertainty principle might make
the behaviour of matter indeterminate from a human perspective,
but it does not thereby become "free". "Freedom" makes sense as
a term applied to human decision-making, but it makes no sense
as a way of describing the material world around us. Now if one
wishes to emphasize that the created order has its own functional
integrity, then that is a different matter. We have earlier emphasized
the very real causal efficacy of secondary causes that operate in
clear distinction to God as primary cause. But especially when we
consider the reproducibility and to some extent even predictability

of the evolutionary process, as outlined in Chapters 2 and 3, then "free process" does not seem to be the most appropriate description of the biological realities that we actually observe.

The second problem comes with the use of the word *kenosis* to describe God's supposed self-imposed restriction on his own omnipotence in allowing creation to be itself, a point already mentioned in the previous chapter. As also mentioned there, *kenosis* has a well-established theological meaning based on Philippians 2 in which the incarnation entails Christ leaving the glories of heaven and making "himself nothing, taking the very nature of a servant, being made in human likeness" (verse 7). But that is not at all like the way in which the Bible describes God's actions in creation. As already noted, it is the metaphor of God "speaking" that the Bible uses most often when describing God's creative work. God speaks in Genesis 1 and things happen. Jesus speaks to the waves and the storm is stilled. There is never a hint in such passages that these words of command entail any self-emptying on God's part. Rather the opposite, creation for God doesn't seem to entail any effort at all as far as Scripture is concerned. I am reminded of the late Colin Gunton's comment in his book *The Triune Creator* that "there is no suggestion in the Bible that the act of creation is anything but the joyful giving of reality to the other" (Gunton, 1998, p. 141).

The third and most important problem with these "mid-spectrum" positions is that a hands-off God who allows the "free process" of his creation to have an "unscripted adventure" in which the outcomes are uncertain is still just as responsible for the evil and suffering in the world as a God who determined the created order down to its smallest detail. If I take my hands off the steering-wheel as my car goes down a hill and it then proceeds to crash into the pavement killing a child, I am just as culpable as if I had killed the child with my hands still firmly on the steering-wheel. The hands-off, free-process God provides no real answer to the problem of the evil and suffering entailed by evolutionary history.

So now let's move to the various positions expressed towards the right of our spectrum. These represent the more robust expression of God's omnipotence, highlighting God's faithfulness in both creating and sustaining the properties of matter, properties which as a matter of fact do perfectly fulfil his intentions and purposes. I suspect that there may be some theologians and philosophers who have moved away from this kind of traditional creation theology precisely because it appears to them that too much blame thereby attaches to God, the author of creation, and such a scenario should somehow be avoided. If you find something you don't like in a book, then you only have the author to blame. I think that inference is exactly right, but if I might say so without sounding disrespectful, I think God is well able to look after himself in this respect.

In the views on the right of the spectrum, there is no room for *kenosis* in the context of God's creative work, because God is in no sense denying his own nature or emptying himself in the creative process. At the same time, God is not the puppet-master, micromanaging the created order, but the God who operates via secondary causes that have their own causal efficacy. This is a robust Trinitarian theism which takes the problem of natural evil right on the chin, fair and square. There is no ducking the issue. God really is responsible for God's created order. How could it be otherwise? From the previous chapter, it will already be clear that my own sympathies lie up this end of the spectrum, mainly because this is the kind of God as creator that I read about in the biblical literature, but also because I think it is difficult to give coherent meaning to the term "omnipotence" unless one adopts this kind of position.

From a pragmatic perspective, it should be noted that some of the positions (not all) in the mid-range of our imaginary spectrum of ideas end up with the same consequences as the positions more to the right. If you hold more to the "hands-off" concept of God as creator, the created order is "graciously given the freedom that it needs to operate independently of God's control". If you adopt the emphasis presented here that God is immanent in the created order, it has consistent properties with their own functional integrity utterly contingent upon God's ongoing faithfulness. Either way, you end up with an intelligible universe accessible to scientific investigation. So on the face of it you might wonder whether it's important to adopt one theological framing of the discussion rather than another.

Those who take the biblical literature as their starting point for theological understanding need to delve into that literature to see how God is portrayed as creator in that literature. As one drills down into the "mid-spectrum" positions, various theological problems begin to emerge. If it is uncertain as to whether God's intentions and purposes can indeed be fulfilled in the created order, how can one be sure (in the Old Testament context) that God's promises concerning the coming Messiah would indeed be fulfilled? How, in the present, can one be sure that God's kingdom will be fulfilled in the way that Christ promised? Come to that, how can a Christian be sure that their own salvation is secure? Even master chess-players sometimes lose their matches. Now a possible response to all these questions is to try and isolate the way God works in creation well away from the way God works in redemption. But then one ends up with all kinds of problems, not least that the triune God then appears to be mighty inconsistent, operating in one way in one sphere and in quite a different way in another sphere. Clearly a full discussion of such points would take us well beyond our present scope. They are mentioned here simply to underline the fact that adopting a position simply because it appears to give some good arguments on the theodicy question may turn out to have hidden costs and create more downstream problems than are worth the move.

If the position presented here is maintained, that God really is omnipotent and God really is omniscient, and therefore that God's intentions and purposes really are being fulfilled in the created order, and that therefore God really is ultimately responsible for all the "biological evils" of the world (but not the moral evils arising from human free will), then the discussion can really begin.

Biology and morality

One common objection to the idea that the created order is contingent upon God's continuous creative activity is based on the assumption that the creation is there to tell us something about God's character. This comes back to the idea discussed in the previous chapter that the human word "create" is so inadequate when speaking of the relationship between God and his creation. When we humans create things, then it is often the case that our "creations" reflect something of who we are. But clearly that is not always the case. A novelist might portray her hero as a mass-murderer, but in her own personality might be mild-mannered and wouldn't hurt a fly. I have often been surprised to meet authors, or read their biographies, and find them to be so different from the person that I had imagined from their created works. So human analogies can only get you so far on this topic.

Given many centuries of natural theology of the kind described in Chapter 1, one cannot really blame people who think that God's character can somehow be "read off" from God's creation.[56] In this respect, it is interesting to read the words of the Apostle Paul that "since the creation of the world God's invisible qualities – his eternal power and divine nature – have been clearly seen, being understood from what has been made" (Romans 1:20). This echoes the psalmist:

> *The heavens declare the glory of God; the skies proclaim the work of his hands. Day after day they pour forth speech; night after night they display knowledge. There is no speech or language where their voice is not heard. Their voice goes out into all the earth, their words to the ends of the world. (Psalm 19:1–4)*

Yet such passages still only provide a fairly minimalist list: the fact that God exists and that he's powerful and full of glory – nothing here about other aspects of God's character.

To that rather short list might be added other aspects of God's character based not on natural theology but on a "theology of nature" in which certain aspects of the created order are appreciated more, or seen in a new light, when viewed through a theistic lens. The psalmist remembers the love of the God who "gives food to every creature" (Psalm 136:25); Psalm 136 as a whole reflecting both on God's faithfulness in upholding the orderly properties of creation as well as on physical deliverance from enemies. The Bible frequently draws attention to the wisdom of God in creation: "How many are your works, O Lord! In wisdom you made them all; the earth is full of your creatures" (Psalm 104:24). But such aspects of God's character are not built from the "ground up" as it were, but are derived from God's saving work in history. As the actions of God to humans in particular historical circumstances reveal his love to them, so the care and provision by God for daily needs is seen in a new light.

Once it is appreciated that the main Purpose of the created order is not to reveal to us the *character* of God, then much of the huffing and puffing on this matter down the ages may be seen to be somewhat wide of the mark. We have to appreciate Darwin's own immersion in Paleyan style natural theology if we are to understand his comment in a letter to his friend, the botanist Joseph Hooker: "What a book a Devil's Chaplain might write on the clumsy, wasteful, blundering low and horridly cruel works of nature!"[57] As it happens, the immediate context of this much-quoted reflection was a comment on pollen as a way of fertilizing flowers, a topic that might not immediately strike one as particularly inefficient, considered overall. Perhaps nearer the point were Darwin's comments in a letter to his good friend, the committed Christian Professor of Natural History at Harvard, Asa Gray:

*But I own that I cannot see, as plainly as others do, & as I
shd wish to do, evidence of design & beneficence on all sides of
us. There seems to me too much misery in the world. I cannot
persuade myself that a beneficent & omnipotent God would have
designedly created the Ichneumonidae with the express intention
of their feeding within the living bodies of caterpillars, or that a
cat should play with mice.*[58]

The *Ichneumonidae*, it should be explained, are a parasitic wasp
family that burrow into various invertebrate hosts and their larvae
in order to feed off them. Given Darwin's misconception that such
animals had been specifically "designed" by God, it is perhaps good
that Darwin did not have access to the full repertoire of (often
stomach-churning) parasitic behaviours that we now know about.
What about, for example, the experience of Jess Greaney, a 19-year-
old undergraduate from Nottingham University, who went to the
doctor in 2015 complaining of an eye infection, only to find that
there was a parasite called *Acanthamoeba* feasting on her eyeball, a
parasite that can cause permanent visual impairment or blindness?[59]
In this case, the infection was traced to contaminated tap water
used to clean contact lenses. Fortunately, the student's eyesight was
saved after a tricky operation, although others are not so fortunate.

Hopefully it will already be clear from our discussion so far
that there is nothing in the biblical view of creation that suggests
that God "designs" particular living organisms in order to do nasty
things to other living things. As already intimated, God is not like
some heavenly engineer who goes around "designing" things.
Neither is there any evidence (thankfully) that we are supposed to
infer God's character from the behaviour of parasites. Only those
deeply imbued with certain forms of early nineteenth-century
natural theology are likely to think otherwise. If there is any
"moral" to come out of Jess Greaney's unfortunate experience, it
is that it's best to wash contact lenses in really clean water. And as

far as cats playing with mice are concerned, play is a very common animal pastime, often involving practice and training in how to hunt, and once the movement of things becomes embedded within the cattish psyche as a trigger to "respond now", the object for attack might equally well be a piece of string, an old sock, or your finger (ouch!).

We have given the floor here initially to what we might deem the "nasty" aspects of the biological world. More will follow on that more negative theme below. But to provide a balanced perspective, we also need to highlight what we can look on as the more "positive" fruits of the evolutionary process: cooperation, care for offspring, creativity (as in tool use, making bowers, weaving nests, etc.), communication (language in the case of humans), and minds that can perceive the wonderful world that God has made. The created order is not there to teach us about the character of the creator – we learn that through revelation – but many of its properties are perfectly consistent with the God who has Purposes for the world, and we can enjoy and appreciate those properties when viewed through such a theistic lens, in some cases also arguing that such properties can act as "signs" pointing to the fuller revelation that we have in Christ (Nowak and Coakley, 2013).

Biology and the cost of existence

So what is the overriding good that is generated by a world with these particular properties in which death, pain, and predation are part and parcel? I would like to suggest that it is coherent existence itself which is the overriding good, including the existence of living things, and most especially the existence of creatures like ourselves with the capacity to respond freely to God's love. The existence of anything of any interest is only feasible within the framework of nomic regularity, that is, the lawlike behaviour of the properties of matter that reflects the faithfulness of God in sustaining the created order moment by moment. Without that nomic regularity, there would be no universe. There would be no life. There would be no reproducibility of the properties of matter. There would be no science. There would be no ethics or moral decision-making, because the outcome of the decision would be random. There would be no relationships and certainly no coherent worship of the living God. In other words, without nomic regularity there would be no coherent existence at all.

But coherent meaningful existence of living things in particular comes at a cost, and to see what that cost looks like, we only have to look at the world of biology. Of course, there is nothing new in making that suggestion – already in the nineteenth century we find Asa Gray writing to Darwin from Harvard and arguing that animal and human pain are not features of nature to be deplored but rather necessary concomitants of the creative process. After more than a century of further biological research, we are now in a far stronger position to appreciate just how prescient were such insights. Imagine, for example, a giant diagram in the form of a table, in which all the positive aspects of the biology of living things are lined up on one side of the table – positive, that is, in the sense that they contribute to the life and well-being of the organism. We could pick eating, or the mutations that are required for our individuality and for the proper functioning of our immune systems; or we could pick apoptosis, the programmed cell death that is essential for normal development and for protecting our bodies against cancer; or we could pick the fact that our own bodies contain as many bacteria as the number of our own cells, contributing significantly to our health and well-being. Whatever we pick, we find that there is a debit side also to the very same item. So eating results in an increased production of the free oxygen radicals that can lead to mutations and cancer; the mutations that are essential for our very existence because evolution depends on them can also cause genetic diseases that can kill us; the programmed cell death that is so essential for normal brain development can also be a root cause of cancer when its regulation goes wrong; and, yes, good bacteria are good for us, but bad bacteria can also kill us.

So being alive, at least as far as carbon-based life is concerned, is a package deal. Whatever plus you might pick in the table will also have a minus in the big scheme of things. If we eventually find life on other planets, which seems rather likely, will it also be carbon-based life? All we know of the chemistry and biochemistry of the universe at present suggests that this will indeed be the case. Whichever way we look in the universe, it's full of carbon compounds, some of them quite complex. Around 200 different compounds, mostly organic, have been identified in the so-called "dense molecular clouds" of outer space. These include large molecules such as the polycyclic aromatic hydrocarbons anthracene and naphthalene and two types of fullerene: C_{60} and C_{70}. A fullerene is any molecule composed entirely of carbon, and the terms C_{60} and C_{70} simply mean that these represent structures containing 60 and 70 atoms of carbon, respectively. Because space is huge, the actual amounts of these organic compounds in space are likewise huge, so that the mass of polycyclic aromatic hydrocarbons detectable in space has been estimated to be much higher than the total mass of biological material here on Earth.

Since the carbon-based chemistry of the universe does look so dominant everywhere we look, and since the combining power of carbon in comparison with elements such as silicon, does seem to give it some clear advantages in generating the building-blocks of life, it seems very likely that if and when we find life on other planets, it will be carbon-based life. The elements that are essential for life – carbon, nitrogen, oxygen, phosphorus, and others – are all synthesized in exploding stars, supernovae, in which the temperatures attained provide sufficient energy to drive their synthesis. And as these stars become exploding supernovae, so their components are scattered through space, there eventually to undergo the accretion necessary to form the next solar systems that will be rich with anthropic possibilities.

In our giant table, life on one side of the table entails death on the other, both on this planet and, most likely, on any other life-bearing planet. Carbon-based life is impossible without carbon-based death. No multicellular animal can live by deriving all its energy needs from chemical elements, all are completely dependent on the food-chain whereby organic molecules synthesized in other organisms are passed on to them. Plants can of course derive at least some of their nutritional needs from the sun by photosynthesis. But that comes at the cost of not being able to move around. And it comes at the cost of not having a brain, because brains are very costly in energetic terms: 25% of our own energy as adults is consumed by our brains. Large trees can generate huge amounts of energy by means of their photosynthesizing leaf area, around 2,000 square feet of leaf for a 33-foot Californian oak tree, but the tree is stationary and has no brain, so no conscious relationships. If you want to generate organisms with language, mobility, consciousness, relationships, and social organization, you need a complex nervous system and a big brain. Energetically that doesn't come cheap – it requires a food-chain in which complex carbon molecules are synthesized in other organisms and then consumed by the bearer of the brain by eating.

Death is also part of the carbon-based life package deal because it is death that makes space for the next generation. It is easy to forget the massive scale of biological death on our planet. There are around 4×10^{13} bacteria in our bodies, called the "microbiota", roughly equivalent to the number of our own cells (Sender et al., 2016), bacteria which taken together contain around 100 microbial genes for each human gene. One gram of human gut contains 60 billion bacteria, around tenfold higher in number than the human population of this planet. Yet these huge numbers are as nothing compared to the estimated 5×10^{30} bacteria in the world, more than 92% living underground and weighing roughly equivalent to all the plants in the world. That's certainly a lot more than the 10^{22} stars in the universe and it involves a huge amount of daily death. And if you don't care very much about bacterial death, think of the roughly 155,000 human deaths every day or nearly 108 every minute. The dead are constantly making space for the living on planet Earth. If it were not so, the planet would run out of space and resources in a very short space of time. Death is written into the package deal. In the very early microseconds after the Big Bang, the physical laws were emerging that define the properties of the chemical elements that comprise the periodic table, which in turn define the properties of life. Carbon-based life and carbon-based death are written into the anthropic script of God's created order right from the beginning.

Along with that script comes the inevitability of pain. Pain is an essential property of biological life, especially as nervous systems become more developed. All organisms, even single-celled organisms like bacteria and yeast, have mechanisms for sensing their environment. With higher organisms, the awareness of pain becomes greater as sentience increases. Feeling pain is an inevitable consequence of sentience. Therefore, brain complexity, awareness of the environment, and experience of pain appear to increase in parallel.

Occasionally humans are born who can feel no pain due to various mutations in their pain receptors, a condition known as congenital insensitivity to pain.[60] It is a very dangerous condition and historically children suffering from it have often not survived their teenage years. It might seem strange to talk about "suffering" as a consequence of having no pain, but the description is correct. It is only when pain is absent in their children that parents realize how much extra care they need. For example, children with this condition are provided with helmets to prevent damage to their head of which they might be quite unaware. One patient describes how he used to enjoy banging his head against a wall as a child because he liked the vibrations. A helmet sounds like a good idea under such circumstances.

Cases of congenital insensitivity to pain are often caused by mutations in the SCN9A gene which encodes a sodium channel required for the perception of neuronal pain signals (Sawal et al., 2016). This mutation was first characterized in individuals from three different Pakistani families with a complete inability to feel pain due to SCN9A mutations (Cox et al., 2006). The index case was a child who performed "street theatre". He placed knives through his arms and walked on burning coals to earn money for his family, but experienced no pain. He died before his fourteenth birthday by jumping off a house roof – all because of a single point mutation in the gene encoding one of his ten different types of sodium channel.

But do we really need so *much* pain to ensure our survival? The biological answer is almost certainly "yes". Our nervous system has been shaped by millions of years of evolution to generate precisely the types of pain that will be most likely to ensure our survival. The mammals whose nervous systems worked inefficiently and failed to pass urgent "action" messages back to the brain are presumably among the species which became extinct and failed to pass their genes on to us. The pain levels that we experience, however much we might dislike the idea, have played a critical role in our evolutionary past and continue to be essential for ensuring our survival in the present. Without pain, we would be walking around on broken legs, happily going to school with meningitis, merrily ignoring fatal tumours, and munching on broken glass with rotting teeth. In short, our lives would be considerably briefer than they are at present. One reason why cancerous tumours can be so difficult to detect in their early stages is because they have no pain receptors. Only when they start pressing on surrounding tissues that do have pain receptors are "danger signals" passed on to the brain, but by that stage they may be much more difficult to treat.

Much was learned about the importance of pain from the work of Dr Paul Brand who went to work among those with Hansen's disease (leprosy) in India during the late 1940s. His amazing story has been told with Philip Yancey in a book called *Pain: The Gift Nobody Wants* (Brand and Yancey, 1993). What Dr Brand found was that the failure to heal among Hansen's patients was so often due to their loss of pain receptors. Pain is indeed a gift that we cannot do without, even though we may not want it.

Death and pain are all essential aspects of a carbon-based living world that displays nomic regularity. The cost of existence is huge. We all bear that cost, and by "we" in this context I mean every living creature that has ever lived. We do not share pain and suffering equally – it is a communal experience in which the burden falls more on one than another. Very understandably there is an instinctive reaction to cry "why me?" when hit by some medical condition out of the blue or, worse, seeing one's child suffer or even die from some terrible disease. Yet from a biological perspective the playing field is the same for everybody: the biological answer to "Why me?" is "Why not you? It had to be somebody." The genetic variation of the human population, together with all the varied challenges from pathogens around the world, entails that the human community will suffer a certain disease load which is not born equally. This is all part and parcel of the cost of existence.

We tend to value items that are costly in their production. Precious diamonds are formed under huge pressure in the depths of the Earth. The ceiling of the Sistine Chapel in Rome took Michelangelo years of painstaking work to complete. Some famous novels took their authors decades to write. Cost and value tend to go together. We should value all life because it is costly life, but especially those costly human lives that bear the image of God.

Yet at this stage of the discussion we might still feel like Ivan in Dostoyevsky's *The Brothers Karamazov*, who objects to his brother Alyosha:

> *I don't accept this world God has made. It's not that I reject God Himself, but this world of His I cannot and will not accept. Let me explain a bit better: like a child I am convinced that pain will heal and balance itself out... But still I do not and will not accept this state of things! Too high a price is asked for harmony! My purse does not allow me to pay such an entry-charge. So I am in a hurry to give back my ticket. (Dostoyevsky, 1992, Part II, Book V, Chapter 4)*

Ivan is the super-rational character in Dostoyevsky's novel who always wants an explanation for everything. Fair enough, though oddly enough it is perhaps evolutionary biology that might have helped Ivan towards a different perspective, because now we are in a much better position to see how everything is joined up. Pain and suffering are not gratuitous evils but part and parcel of being alive, the price of existence. Without billions of years of death, we would have no possibility of being alive. Take one component from the system away and the drama as a whole collapses. But that fact by itself, though revealing, is not the end of the story.

The kingdom of God, present and future

When Jesus came preaching and teaching the kingdom of God, it was very often associated with healing. "Jesus went throughout Galilee, teaching in their synagogues, preaching the good news of the kingdom, and healing every disease and sickness among the people" (Matthew 4:23). The kingdom refers not to a place but to God's reign. When Jesus told the parable about "A certain nobleman" who "went into a far country to receive for himself a kingdom, and to return" (Luke 19:12, King James Version), more modern translations correctly interpret this as "to have himself appointed king". The nobleman was not going off with the intention of bringing back a piece of real-estate, but rather seeking the authority to reign. Every time Christians pray the Lord's prayer, they pray "your kingdom come, your will be done on earth as it is in heaven" (Matthew 6:10), and in the same breath they are defining what the present kingdom is all about: God's will being done on earth. God's kingdom, said Jesus, starts now. When the disciples were sent out to preach the good news in the towns and villages of Palestine, they were instructed to "heal the sick who are there and tell them, 'The kingdom of God is near you'" (Luke 10:9). As Jesus told his disciples: "The kingdom of God is within you" (Luke 17:21).

So for the Christian, having the kingdom, God's reign, "within us" entails practising its values and priorities. This includes the command to "subdue" the earth (Genesis 1:28), and it entails the healing of the sick along with the preaching of the kingdom. We can rail against the evils of the world all we like, but maybe much better to save all that emotional energy for the practical task of caring for the poor and the needy. This explains why there has been such a strong Christian tradition of being involved in medical care. In the many years previously spent in research on cancer and on genetic diseases more broadly, many is the time that I have felt the deep offence of cancer, or of a genetic disease, killing children before they have had the chance to have much of a life at all. Why "offence"? Because we humanity should have got this sorted years ago. For me "subduing the earth" includes the healing of cancer, and lethal genetic diseases, especially in kids. Thankfully the outlook for many children's cancers has grown far more positive than it was a few decades ago, but there is still a long way to go with no room for complacency. So how come we humanity didn't get there quicker? Of course, there are many answers to that complex question, but I hope you can share with me the deep sense of offence that we humanity have failed to subdue the earth in this context – and, of course, many other contexts besides. The healing process is like a pilot plant in relation to the final factory. As far as we can tell, the need for healing will always be with us, but as an activity it acts as a signpost pointing forwards to the new heavens and the new earth in which the "healing of the nations" will finally be complete (Revelation 22:2).

By now those who have been tracking the main arguments of this book so far will be spotting an apparent dilemma. If the created order that we observe and investigate all around us every day is precisely the one God intended to bring into existence, how come Jesus in his incarnation made a central part of his ministry the healing of diseases for which he, within the Trinitarian Godhead, was ultimately responsible? One answer sometimes given by Christians is that all the "natural evils" of the world, including the genetic variation that causes cancer, and all other human illnesses, are the result of human sin. But I think this is a cop-out, which in any case finds little or no biblical support. In the context of an individual's medical condition suffered since infancy, Jesus made it perfectly plain that it wasn't due to his own sin nor that of his parents. When Jesus saw a blind man, his disciples asked him: "Rabbi, who sinned, this man or his parents, that he was born blind?" Jesus responded: "Neither this man nor his parents sinned, but this happened so that the work of God might be displayed in his life" (John 9:2–3) and then proceeded to give the man back his sight. The first part of this account helps to head off the misconception that medical conditions are a result of sin, but it is what happens next, the man's healing, that actually begins to answer our query.

With the healing ministry of Jesus, the future fulfilled kingdom begins to break into the present evil age. The door to the future is pushed open and a beautiful healing breeze blows through, giving a taste of what is still to come. Jesus confronts sickness because it doesn't belong to the fulfilled kingdom and his mission is to inaugurate the kingdom. In a US presidential inauguration there's a lot of fanfare, promises are made about plans to help the country, and there is a general feel-good factor as people (at least those who voted for the new president) look towards the future. Of course, within a very short space of time, disillusionment creeps in, promises are broken, and many voters wish they had voted for someone else. By contrast, with the inauguration of the kingdom of God, Jesus ushered in a kingdom "that will never be destroyed" (Daniel 7:14), a kingdom that "cannot be shaken" (Hebrews 12:28) that will "last for ever" (Luke 1:33), and in which all God's promises are fulfilled. Jesus confronted sickness because it forms no part of the new heavens and the new earth, the fulfilled future kingdom. Jesus in his incarnation comes into the midst of Phase One and inaugurates Phase Two.

With the power and proclamation of the future kingdom breaking in with the life and ministry of Jesus, physical death likewise is shown to have no place in God's ultimate purposes. "The last enemy to be destroyed is death", writes Paul (in 1 Corinthians 15:26). Death is an enemy like illness because it's not part of Phase Two – it has no part there at all. The Apostle Paul explains that we can either belong to Adam, the prototype of the "dusty man", the man made from dust (*adamah* in Hebrew), or we can identify with the risen Christ, the "man from heaven", and share with him our future resurrection in the new heavens and the new earth (1 Corinthians 15:42–58). At that time "He will wipe every tear from their eyes. There will be no more death or mourning or crying or pain, for the old order of things has passed away" (Revelation 21:4). And through the death and resurrection of Christ the whole cosmos will ultimately be redeemed, including all those who are part of the family of God, and including the whole created order, "so that God may be all in all" (1 Corinthians 15:28).

Does that mean that every single creature that ever lived will be raised from death and find a place in the new heavens and the new earth? Every bear, every kangaroo, every fish, every beetle, and every mosquito that ever lived? Every extinct species? Irenaeus, Basil and the late Augustine thought "yes", though of course they were not in a position then to know the huge scale of what they were suggesting. Aquinas said "no", no resurrection for plants and animals, only humans. Today a number of contemporary theologians, such as Christopher Southgate and Elizabeth Johnson, say "yes". The answer, of course, is that we really don't know. But surely much of the richness and creativity of the biodiversity of the present world will be brought into the fulfilled kingdom of God, and for myself I am happy to leave it to God to surprise us with the details when the time comes.

But for the present, let us be quite sure that without nomic regularity there would be no world, no us, and certainly no free will, no moral responsibility, and no possibility of participating in God's new creation, for God only wishes people there who have freely chosen his way of love, no room for puppets. And the only way to get there is through the portal of death when the mortal will be swallowed up by immortality. As already indicated, incredibly valuable outcomes sometimes demand incredibly costly ways of achieving them and carbon-based life represents one such costly way.

Carbon-based existence is also wrapped up in the cost of the incarnation. As the late Ernan McMullin from Notre Dame University expresses the point so memorably:

> *When Christ took on human nature, the DNA that made him the son of Mary may have linked him to a more ancient heritage stretching far beyond Adam to the shallows of unimaginably ancient seas. And so, in the Incarnation, it would not have been just human nature that was joined to the Divine, but in a less direct but no less real sense all those myriad organisms that had unknowingly over the eons shaped the way for the coming of the human.*[61]

Without the physical properties of the world we in fact observe, there would be no life, no evolution, so no free will, no moral responsibility, therefore no sin, no incarnation, no redemptive work of Christ upon the cross for sin, so no resurrection and no possibility of entering into Phase Two, the fulfilled kingdom of God. The path that God has chosen for us is a tough path, more boot camp than holiday camp, but with huge potential for the enjoyment of life both now and, even more so, in the age yet to come.

Could it have been otherwise?

But is Phase One really necessary in order for people, with the rest of creation, to become part of Phase Two? From a Christian perspective, we know that there is this other realm of existence in which existence is by means of resurrection bodies that will never die. So as a God of love, why doesn't God just create that existence with us within it immediately? Why this long and sometimes tortuous pathway to get there by living first on planet Earth? Here it is obvious that we move into the realm of speculation. But one obvious answer to the question might be: "Because carbon-based life really is the only way in which creatures can come into being with genuine free will and moral responsibility, equipped to enter into a saving relationship with God as a result of the atoning death and resurrection of Christ." Now that really does provide a Purpose for biology. There is absolutely no way that we can know whether carbon-based existence really is the only way. But we can do thought experiments and certainly when we start on these, it's hard to think of other options.

One idea frequently mooted is: why cannot it be that God creates beings who always choose the good? But then any possibility of love flies out the window. The God of love will never force people into his kingdom, and love is predicated on genuine freedom. If God wishes only those who really want to be there to be part of his fulfilled kingdom, the messy pathway involving the generation of genuine free will seems to be the only way. And a genuine free choice to follow God's way also entails the partial hiddenness of God. I have had atheists tell me that if God wrote in big letters across the sky "God loves John" (or whoever it might be), they would believe in him. But that childish idea sounds very much like *force majeure*. It doesn't take much to subvert free will. A genuine free choice to follow the way of Jesus involves a reflective search in which there is an opportunity to weigh up the pros and cons. God working through the created order, as described by biology, delivers the opportunity to do just that. Considering the huge cost involved in bringing humanity to this point in time, and the huge cost involved in God, through Christ, reconciling the world to himself in order to make our transition into the new heavens and the new earth possible, that choice is something to be treated with respect.

A personal story

For those who might be used to thinking biologically, but not at all used to thinking theologically, this chapter may have proved somewhat heavy going (assuming you made it this far!). So a more personal story might help as we finish.

I gave the Herrmann lecture on which this chapter is based, the third and last of the series, on 7 November 2014. Colorectal (bowel) cancer had been diagnosed just 11 days prior to flying over to Boston to give the lectures. I was recommended not to undertake long-haul flights due to the possibility that the tumour might block the gut altogether, which would necessitate an emergency operation – not good. But I decided to go to Boston anyway as I didn't want to let my hosts down just before the lectures were due and the extra travel insurance premium wasn't as much as feared. Plus, to show that I wasn't completely irresponsible, I cancelled the second leg of my journey to Nassau where I was due for some meetings. Nobody knew at the Herrmann Lectures (apart from the organizer) that I had a medical challenge on board and neither did I want them to know – very distracting for the listener. But the situation did give an added *frisson* to the speaker, at least, when speaking about genetic diseases, cancer, death, and other cheery topics.

Just over five weeks later, I was due to have my tumour removed. It was a grey cool December morning and I had to get to the hospital just 15 minutes' walk away. I set out with a small backpack to reach the 7.00 a.m. appointment, very hungry (you have to starve before the operation) but also very exhilarated. Final exams day had finally come, or that's what it felt like. I sang hymns of praise all the way, under my breath or out loud depending on whether there was anyone around. I had complete faith in my surgeon, one of the top surgeons in the country for this kind of operation. Nevertheless, it is well known that surgery, particularly in slightly older folk (ahem), is not without some risk, and therefore the chances of dying during surgery were not zero. That made me even more excited. Fancy going to heaven under anaesthetic – what better way to go! I didn't think that was going to happen, but you never know.

The waiting room at the hospital was a bit like a dentist's waiting room only more so: nervous chatter, a sense of anticipation, and underlying everything the deep hope that the operations that day weren't going to be postponed to another day through lack of beds (the previous day everyone in the same waiting room had been told to go home at the last minute for that very reason). Finally, my name was called, phew, no cancellations today – into the green surgical gown, a friendly visit from a Christian medic who goes to my church, a chilly trip in a wheelchair down long corridors (but why can't I walk? I walked a mile to get here… Not allowed, sir, sorry), a meeting with a big *baboushka* anaesthetist, surely a Russian, and then finally allowed to walk myself the last few steps to lie on the slab under bright lights. The surgery team bustle around and I watch fascinated and feel a strange sense of calm. I also know that a lot of people are praying for me this day – that certainly helps. The theatre nurse is chatty, exactly what they're supposed to be, calming the patient by small talk. "So what would you normally be doing today if you weren't here today?" she asks cheerily, inserting a cannula in my left arm to inject various medications. "Finishing off my book *Genes, Determinism and God* for CUP I reply." Oh, says she, "tell me what that's about" and at the same moment injects the first dose of pre-anaesthetic opiate and I go out like a stone. Clearly there were more important things to be getting on with (and just when I was gearing up to give a really interesting little summary!). A few hours later I wake up groggy – no heaven this time then, but very happy to spend a bit longer on planet Earth, and post-op chemotherapy here we come.

What's the point of telling you all that? Only that for the Christian who sees God's Purposes being worked out in all the nitty-gritty of a long history of biological evolution, it is all part and parcel of the same theology to know that God is working out his purposes in the history of our own individual lives. Just as I trusted my surgeon during the operation, based on good evidence that he had a good success rate in his job, how much more can we depend for our lives, present and future, on the God of the whole universe who is sovereign over the whole created order. It's very unlikely that we'll know in this life the Purposes that God has for our own particular experience of pain and suffering, though sometimes this can be the case. Even more so, we can never be sure about the ultimate reason for the "natural evils" of the world, though we have perhaps made a very small start on the problem in this chapter, helped massively, of course, by the reflections of many others. All we can be sure of is that the high cost of the existence of the created order is a price worth paying for the privilege of existence. And for that we can be thankful.

If we look at the biology, we see the sheer power and wisdom of God in bringing into being and sustaining the beauty and complexity of the living world. But if we look *only* at the biology, all we see is that life eventually ends in death – and indeed with the eventual energy death of our sun, all life on this planet will eventually become extinct. But if we lift up our eyes and also look to the cross, we see the doorway into a new creation that God is preparing for all those who put their faith in him through Christ. And we realize that life is going somewhere very good indeed – albeit via a tough and rocky road for us at present – when ultimately the whole present cosmos for which Christ died will finally be fully expressed and fully realized in the new heavens and the new earth. And that is the eschatological perspective we need if we are to make any sense of the ultimate Purpose of biology in this present world.

Postscript

This book only has one main argument – the claim that biology is not necessarily purposeless as is often assumed. It took us three chapters (Chapters 2–4) to critique that assumption, by pointing out that evolution doesn't look as if it's necessarily purposeless if you examine the process objectively. That might seem like using a steamroller to crack a nut, but in this author's opinion, the effort was worthwhile. This ground-clearing exercise, I hope, then helped us to be more open to the realization that we all impose our own narrative of Purpose upon biology, at the least as a minimal strategy for providing some sense of direction for our own lives, essential for mental health and human flourishing. But we need to be crystal clear that all such strategies, whether they draw on religious beliefs or not, cannot be derived from science itself. Scientific descriptions, however sophisticated, are unable to generate Purpose for us. For that we have to look to metaphysics, worldviews that lie beyond science.

It is not the claim of this book that biological evolution can only rationally be baptized into a Christian matrix and not into other metaphysical worldviews. That would indeed be a hubristic claim. However, it is my claim that evolution fits particularly well within the Christian narrative, complete with a traditional understanding of God as creator. This is partly for historical reasons: the theory was born within a framework of natural theology. But the theological reasons are even more compelling, as we have noted: the data of Chapters 2–4 are rather consistent with a God who has intentions and Purposes for the world, with special Purposes for those made in God's image. The work of the triune God is reflected in the outcomes of the evolutionary process. And the suffering of Christ that has brought our own redemption at great cost is only possible in a world in which physical suffering and death are present realities.

We started this book by saying that its title was nothing to do with the pursuit of a career in biology. On second thoughts, maybe it is. For the Christian in particular, the study of God's created order is both an honour and a fascination, part of the Christian's worship. If you are a Christian and, in addition, at the stage in life when you're thinking about your future employment, then do consider pursuing a career in one of the biological sciences. Spending your life in understanding and appreciating a little more of God's created order and, for some, applying that understanding to help others, is a great privilege.

Notes

1. The word "teleology" refers to statements that describe things in terms of their goal or purpose.

2. The word "metaphysical" refers to those ideas or philosophies that lie "beyond science", that are not part of science itself.

3. While staying in Samarkand some years ago at a very traditional guest house my wife succumbed to the same condition. Our host then produced a dark, evil-looking, brown liquid which she proclaimed as "Avicenna's mixture" which would solve the problem. My wife took the potion and it worked wonderfully.

4. The authorship of *Chance or Creation? God's Design in the Universe* is not completely sure, but the work is generally attributed to al-Jahiz. A discussion by the translator, M.A.S. Abdel Haleem, may be found in Al-Jahiz, 1995.

5. The account may not be entirely without an observational basis. There would be blood on the pelican's chest feathers from the fish it would kill, and this may have been misunderstood as the pelican's own blood with which it would nurture its young (hence the analogy to Christ).

6. http://wp.blessedearth.org/wp-content/uploads/2010/08/KruegerCreationCareQuotes.pdf (accessed 5 August 2017).

7. The Medieval Bestiary. See http://bestiary.ca/beasts/beast149.htm (accessed 4 August 2017).

8. The Medieval Bestiary. See http://bestiary.ca/beasts/beast267.htm (accessed 4 August 2017).

9. The biological writings of Aristotle were translated from the Arabic into Latin during the second decade of the thirteenth century.

10. The word "hermeneutics" refers to the various methods and approaches used for interpreting texts.

11. "Natural theology" refers to attempts to infer the existence of God, and in some cases certain aspects of the character of God, based on observations of the natural world. Such arguments are often mingled with a "theology of nature" in which the properties of nature are appreciated and assessed within a theological worldview. With a few exceptions, the Boyle Lectures then ceased until they were restarted in 2004, continuing annually to the present day.

12. The arguments are well summarized in an article by Paul Russell in the online Stanford Encyclopedia of Philosophy, http://plato.stanford.edu/entries/hume-religion/ (accessed 23 November 2016).

13. https://plato.stanford.edu/entries/teleological-arguments/ (accessed 4 August 2017).

14. For example, see the Stanford Encyclopedia of Philosophy article by Del Ratzsch and Jeffrey Koperski at http://plato.stanford.edu/entries/teleological-arguments/ (accessed 23 November 2016).

15. http://charles-darwin.classic-literature.co.uk/the-autobiography-of-charles-darwin/ebook-page-08.asp, Page 8 (accessed 4 August 2017).

16. In letter written 10 December 1859. www.darwinproject.ac.uk/letter/?docId=letters/DCP-LETT-2575.xml;query=higgledy-piggledy;brand=default (accessed 8 November 2016).

17. This means 1 followed by 11 noughts, which is 100 billion.

18. "Genera" is the plural of "genus" and represents a category referring to a collection of species, both terms referring to one of the seven major taxonomic ranks, which classify animals from the most basic category – the species – all the way up to the most general category of all, the kingdom.

19. A taxon (plural taxa) refers to a taxonomic group of any class in the sevenfold classification hierarchy explained in the previous footnote, be it a family, a class, or other.

20. A mutation simply means a change in one or more of the genetic letters in the DNA of the bacteria. The term "genome" refers to the total complement of genetic information in an organism as encoded in its DNA. This consists of long strings of nucleotide base-pairs, the genetic "letters" that comprise the genetic "alphabet".

21. "Reproductive fitness" refers to the numbers of progeny resulting from each reproductive generation, be that generation in self-replicating bacteria or in sexually reproducing animals.

22. Those interested in new ideas and results contributing to changing views of evolutionary theory may be interested in the Third Way website: www.thethirdwayofevolution.com (accessed 18 November 2016).

23. www.mapoflife.org.

24. More extensive accounts describing the convergence of eye evolution can be found in Richard Dawkins, *Climbing Mount Improbable* (1996) and *The Ancestor's Tale: A Pilgrimage to the Dawn of Life* (2016); and Simon Conway Morris, *Life's Solution: Inevitable Humans in a Lonely Universe* (2003) and *The Runes of Evolution: How the Universe Became Self-Aware* (2015).

25. Dingos are not marsupials but real dogs probably introduced by aboriginals. It is possible that it was the proliferation of dingos that drove the Tasmanian wolves to extinction. Dingos never reached Tasmania, which may be why the Tasmanian wolves survived longer there.

26. Richard Owen's philosophical trajectory is not always clear and is well discussed in Rupke (2009, pp. 125ff.). Rupke maintains that Owen Platonized his archetype in order to avoid any accusation of pantheism – on which the Cambridge professor of geology, Adam Sedgwick, who taught Darwin geology, once proclaimed: "May God for ever save the University of Cambridge from this base, degrading, demoralizing creed"!

27. Exemplar crows can be watched on Youtube: www.youtube.com/watch?v=flInOjXqW-A (accessed 7 November 2016). It is not agreed if crows have any causal understanding of this process.

28. Watch "crowboarding" at www.youtube.com/

watch?v=3dWw9GLcOeA (accessed 7 November 2016).

29. Watch black swans surfing at www.youtube.com/ watch?v=TcmDN9BJLY4 (accessed 7 November 2016).

30. The word "hominin" is used to refer to all those intermediate species between anatomically modern humans and our last common ancestor with the chimpanzee.

31. www.templeton.org/evolution/Essays/Nowak.pdf (accessed 7 November 2016).

32. www.astrobio.net/news-exclusive/mapping-amino-acids-to-understand-lifes-origins/ (accessed 13 November 2016).

33. "Crickets in two places fall silent to survive", BBC News, 29 May 2014, www.bbc.co.uk/news/science-environment-27592656 (accessed 4 August 2017).

34. See Note 18 for definitions of genera, etc.

35. See www.youtube.com/watch?v=fK2MCXpDWB4 for an example of how this works by throwing dice, the original method that Mozart envisaged (accessed 13 November 2016).

36. A simulation of the process can be found at https://en.wikipedia. org/wiki/Brownian_motion (accessed 13 November 2016).

37. http://statweb.stanford.edu/~susan/papers/headswithJ.pdf (accessed 14 November 2016).

38. There remains much discussion in the physics literature as to whether our observations of chance quantum phenomena reflect the intrinsic behaviour of basic particles – in other words, whether "chance" at this level is an objective reality, the so-called Copenhagen interpretation maintained by Walter Heisenberg – or whether there are "hidden variables" that determine the behaviour of the particles, a minority view supported by physicists such as David Bohm (Byl, 2003). The Copenhagen interpretation is the one assumed here. If the "hidden variables" view were correct, quantum mechanics would join the epistemological chance club, in that while we couldn't know what was

going on, at least we would know that there were causal chains involved. As a matter of fact, we do not know that those causal chains exist.

39. For those who might be tempted to ask the same question, may I direct you to Denis Alexander, *Creation or Evolution – Do We Have to Choose?* (2014).

40. "Balanced" variation occurs when a stretch of one chromosome is exchanged with a stretch of equivalent length from another chromosome.

41. It should also be noted that when genetic variation comes into the offspring due to sexual reproduction, this is not initially by chance since it depends on the choice of mate, but the final composition of the offspring's genome depends on the chance assortment of the parent's chromosomes.

42. https://news.vanderbilt.edu/2015/10/29/new-class-of-dna-repair-enzyme-discovered/ (accessed 17 November 2016).

43. "Fittest" in evolutionary biology has a technical meaning which refers not to the strength or agility of a particular organism, but rather to its ability to generate most progeny for the next generation in comparison with other individuals within an interbreeding population.

44. There are many reasons to think that assumption to be incorrect, but to discuss that point would take us way beyond the scope of this book. In the context of genetic determinism, see the discussion of free will in Denis Alexander, *Genes, Determinism and God* (2017), where many more references to source materials on free will may be found.

45. Newtonian mechanics refers to the theories that describe the motion of matter in relation to the forces causing motion. The theory of relativity and quantum mechanics now do a better job at describing the properties of very small and very big things.

46. http://journalistsresource.org/studies/economics/personal-finance/research-review-lotteries-demographics; www.theosthinktank.co.uk/files/files/Reports/NationalLotteryreport.pdf (accessed 18 November 2016).

47. www.salon.com/2014/09/27/jonathan_sacks_on_richard_dawkins_new_atheists_lack_a_sense_of_humor/.

48. The second law of thermodynamics states that entropy, the degree of disorganization of an open system, is always increasing. The implication is that our universe will therefore finally end in a "heat death" in which no life is feasible.

49. It is difficult to be entirely consistent about the use of the small p for "purpose" as compared to Purpose. However, in the Introduction it was stated that Purpose with a big "P" would be used to refer to the claim that there is some ultimate metaphysical reason for the existence of a biological process such as evolution. In the paragraph that follows, small "p" purpose has been used because the various suggested purposes go well beyond evolution itself, yet without metaphysical entailments intrinsic to the chosen definition of Purpose.

50. www.nytimes.com/2016/12/12/opinion/can-evolution-have-a-higher-purpose.html?mwrsm=Email&_r=0 (accessed 17 December 2016).

51. From a poem entitled "The Anatomy of the World" by John Donne (1572–1631).

52. Stanford Encyclopedia of Philosophy, http://plato.stanford.edu/entries/occasionalism/#NicMal (accessed 30 November 2016).

53. There is a huge literature on the topic of free will. Books that are in general support of the assertions made all too briefly here, albeit written from contrasting perspectives, include: D.R. Alexander, *Genes, Determinism and God* (2017); P.G.H. Clarke, *All in the Mind? Challenges of Neuroscience to Faith and Ethics* (2015); J. Baggini, *Freedom Regained: The Possibility of Free Will* (2015); A.R. Mele, *Surrounding Free Will: Philosophy, Psychology, Neuroscience* (2015). There are hundreds more!

54. http://winewaterwatch.org/2016/05/we-scientists-dont-know-how-to-do-that-what-a-commentary/ (accessed 28 November 2016).

55. Quote from Simon Conway Morris: www.youtube.com/watch?v=uBrsHMxDOXk (accessed 24 December 2016).

56. A helpful summary of the main current discussion points in natural theology may be found in Faraday Paper No 19 by Revd Dr Rodney Holder entitled "Natural Theology" available for free download at www.faraday-institute.org.

57. Letter to Joseph Hooker, 13 July 1856. See Darwin Correspondence Project at www.darwinproject.ac.uk.

58. Letter from Charles Darwin to Asa Gray dated 22 May 1860. Professor Asa Gray was the good friend of Darwin who had arranged for the publication of *On the Origin of Species* in the USA, and Darwin is writing to Gray firstly to thank him for the £22 royalties arising from the initial sales of the American edition. Darwin writes: "I am in simple truth astonished at all the kind trouble you have taken for me."

59. www.cnet.com/uk/news/meet-the-parasite-that-can-burrow-its-way-into-the-human-eye/ (accessed 5 December 2016).

60. There is rather a good Wikipedia entry on this topic at https://en.wikipedia.org/wiki/Congenital_insensitivity_to_pain where a short video can be viewed of interviews of people who suffer from this disorder (accessed 5 December 2016).

61. www.asa3.org/ASA/topics/Evolution/CRS9–91McMullin.html (accessed 5 August 2017).

Bibliography

Adamowicz, S.J., Purvis, A. and Wills, M.A. 2008. Increasing Morphological Complexity in Multiple Parallel Lineages of the Crustacea. *Proceedings of the National Academy of Sciences USA*, 105: 4786–91.

Aftab, M. 2000. Groundwork in Islamic Philosophy. *Meteorite*, 2: 26–42.

Ai, W.M., Chen, S.B., Chen, X., et al. 2014. Parallel Evolution of IDH2 Gene in Cetaceans, Primates and Bats. *FEBS Letters*, 588: 450–54.

Al-Jahiz. 1995. *Chance or Creation? God's Design in the Universe*, transl. M.A. Abdel Haleem. Reading: Garnet.

Alexander, D.R. 2001. *Rebuilding the Matrix: Science and Faith in the 21st Century*. Oxford: Lion.

Alexander, D.R. 2011. *The Language of Genetics: An Introduction*. Philadelphia: Templeton Foundation Press.

Alexander, D.R. 2014. *Creation or Evolution: Do We Have to Choose?* 2nd edn. Oxford: Monarch.

Alexander, D.R. 2017. *Genes, Determinism and God*. Cambridge: Cambridge University Press.

Alexander, D.R. and Numbers, R.L. 2010. *Biology and Ideology from Descartes to Dawkins*. Chicago, IL: University of Chicago Press.

Allen, C., Bekoff, M. and Lauder, G.V. 1998. *Nature's Purposes: Analyses of Function and Design in Biology*, Cambridge, MA: MIT Press.

Alroy, J. 1998. Cope's Rule and the Dynamics of Body Mass Evolution in North American Fossil Mammals. *Science*, 280: 731–34.

Aristotle. 2001. *On the Parts of Animals*, transl. J.G. Lennox. Oxford: Clarendon Press.

Ayala, F.J. 2007. *Darwin's Gift to Science and Religion*. Washington, DC: Joseph Henry Press.

Baggini, J. 2015. *Freedom Regained: The Possibility of Free Will*. London: Granta.

Banavar, J.R., Cooke, T.J., Rinaldo, A., et al. 2014. Form, Function, and Evolution of Living Organisms. *Proceedings of the National Academy of Sciences USA*, 111: 3332–37.

Bartholomew, D.J. 2008. *God, Chance and Purpose: Can God Have It Both Ways?*. Cambridge: Cambridge University Press.

Bentlage, B., Cartwright, P., Yanagihara, A.A., et al. 2010. Evolution of Box Jellyfish (Cnidaria: Cubozoa), a Group of Highly Toxic Invertebrates. *Proceedings of the Royal Society B: Biological Sciences*, 277: 493–501.

Besnard, G., Muasya, A.M., Russier, F., et al. 2009. Phylogenomics of C(4) Photosynthesis in Sedges (Cyperaceae): Multiple Appearances and Genetic Convergence. *Molecular Biology and Evolution*, 26: 1909–19.

Boyle, R. 1688. *A Disquisition About the Final Causes of Natural Things*. London.

Boyle, R., Taylor, J. and Clark, H. 1685. *A Free Enquiry into the Vulgarly Receiv'd Notion of Nature; Made in an Essay, Address'd to a Friend*. London: Printed by H. Clark, for John Taylor at the Globe in St Paul's Church-yard.

Brand, P.W. and Yancey, P. 1993. *Pain: The Gift Nobody Wants*. New York: HarperCollins Publishers.

Bruns, G.L. 1992. *Hermeneutics, Ancient and Modern*. New Haven, CT: Yale University Press.

Burbano, H.A., Green, R.E., Maricic, T., et al. 2014. Analysis of Human Accelerated DNA Regions Using Archaic Hominin Genomes. *PLoS One*, 7: e32877.

Byl, J. 2003. Indeterminacy, Divine Action and Human Freedom. *Science and Christian Belief*, 15: 101–16.

Calvin, J. 1986. *The Institutes of Christian Religion*, ed. A.N.S. Lane and H. Osborne. London: Hodder and Stoughton.

Carey, T.V. 2004. John Herschel. *Philosophy Now*, October/November.

Carroll, S.B. 2001. Chance and Necessity: The Evolution of Morphological Complexity and Diversity. *Nature*, 409: 1102–9.

Carroll, S.B. 2005. *Endless Forms Most Beautiful: The New Science of Evo Devo and the Making of the Animal Kingdom*. New York: Norton.

Carroll, W.E. 2012. Aquinas and Contemporary Cosmology: Creation and Beginnings. *Science and Christian Belief*, 24: 5–18.

Carson, D.A. 2006. *How Long, O Lord? Reflections on Suffering and Evil.* Grand Rapids, MI: Baker Academic.

Chan, K. and Gordenin, D.A. 2015. Clusters of Multiple Mutations: Incidence and Molecular Mechanisms. *Annual Review of Genetics,* 49: 243–67.

Chan, Y.F., Marks, M.E., Jones, F.C., et al. 2010. Adaptive Evolution of Pelvic Reduction in Sticklebacks by Recurrent Deletion of a Pitx1 Enhancer. *Science,* 327: 302–5.

Christin, P.A., Edwards, E.J., Besnard, G., et al. 2012. Adaptive Evolution of C(4) Photosynthesis through Recurrent Lateral Gene Transfer. *Current Biology,* 22: 445–49.

Clarke, P.G.H. 2015. *All in the Mind? Challenges of Neuroscience to Faith and Ethics.* Oxford: Lion.

Conway Morris, S. 2003. *Life's Solution: Inevitable Humans in a Lonely Universe.* Cambridge: Cambridge University Press.

Conway Morris, S. 2015. *The Runes of Evolution: How the Universe Became Self-Aware.* West Conshohocken, PA: Templeton Press.

Copleston, F.C. *A History of Philosophy, Vol. 6: The Enlightenment: Voltaire to Kant.* London: Bloomsbury Continuum, 2003.

Cordaux, R. and Batzer, M.A. 2009. The Impact of Retrotransposons on Human Genome Evolution. *Nature Reviews Genetics,* 10: 691–703.

Cordaux, R., Hedges, D.J., Herke, S.W., et al. 2006. Estimating the Retrotransposition Rate of Human Alu Elements. *Gene,* 373: 134–37.

Cox, J.J., Reimann, F., Nicholas, A.K., et al. 2006. An SCN9A Channelopathy Causes Congenital Inability to Experience Pain. *Nature,* 444: 894–98.

Dagan, T., Artzy-Randrup, Y. and Martin, W. 2008. Modular Networks and Cumulative Impact of Lateral Transfer in Prokaryote Genome Evolution. *Proceedings of the National Academy of Sciences USA,* 105: 10039–44.

Darwin, C. 1859. *On the Origin of Species by Means of a Natural Selection, or the Preservation of Favored Races in the Struggle for Life.* London: Murray.

Davies, P.C.W. 2007. *The Goldilocks Enigma: Why Is the Universe Just Right for Life?* London: Penguin.

Davies, P.C.W. 2013. Directionality Principles from Cancer to Cosmology. In *Complexity and the Arrow of Time.* Cambridge: Cambridge University Press.

Dawkins, R. 1986. *The Blind Watchmaker*. London: Penguin, 1991.

Dawkins, R. 1995. *River out of Eden: A Darwinian View of Life*. London: Weidenfeld & Nicolson.

Dawkins, R. 1996. *Climbing Mount Improbable*. London: Viking.

Dawkins, R. 2016. *The Ancestor's Tale: A Pilgrimage to the Dawn of Life*, 2nd edn. London: Weidenfeld & Nicolson.

Dennett, D.C. 1995. *Darwin's Dangerous Idea: Evolution and the Meanings of Life*. London: Allen Lane.

Descartes, R. 1983. *Principles of Philosophy*, transl. R.P. Miller and V.R. Miller. Dordrecht: Reidel.

Dingle, K., Schaper, S. and Louis, A. A. 2015. The Structure of the Genotype-Phenotype Map Strongly Constrains the Evolution of Non-Coding RNA. *Interface Focus*, 5: 20150053.

Dobler, S., Dalla, S., Wagschal, V., et al. 2012. Community-Wide Convergent Evolution in Insect Adaptation to Toxic Cardenolides by Substitutions in the Na,K-ATPase. *Proceedings of the National Academy of Sciences USA*, 109: 13040–45.

Dostoyevsky, F. 1992. *The Brothers Karamazov: A Novel in Four Parts with Epilogue*, transl. R. Peaver and L. Volokhonsky. London: Vintage.

Dunbar, R.I.M. 2004. *The Human Story: A New History of Mankind's Evolution*. London: Faber and Faber.

Dunbar, R.I.M. 2016. *Human Evolution: Our Brains and Behaviour*. Oxford: Oxford University Press.

Durant, J. 1985. *Darwinism and Divinity: Essays on Evolution and Religious Belief*. Oxford: Blackwell.

Edwards, J. 1696. *A Demonstration of the Existence and Providence of God, from the Contemplation of the Visible Structure of the Greater and the Lesser World*. London.

Ekstrom, L.W. 2013. A Christian Theodicy. In *The Blackwell Companion to the Problem of Evil*, ed. D. Howard-Snyder and J.P. Mcbrayer. Hoboken, NJ: John Wiley & Sons.

Emerton, N. 1989. The Argument from Design in Early Modern Natural Theology. *Science and Christian Belief*, 1: 129–47.

Emery, N.J. and Clayton, N.S. 2005. Evolution of the Avian Brain and Intelligence. *Current Biology*, 15: R946–50.

Emery, N.J. and Clayton, N.S. 2015. Do Birds Have the Capacity for Fun? *Current Biology*, 25: R16–20.

Fernald, R.D. 2006. Casting a Genetic Light on the Evolution of Eyes. *Science*, 313: 1914–18.

Fortna, A., Kim, Y., Maclaren, E., et al. 2004. Lineage-Specific Gene Duplication and Loss in Human and Great Ape Evolution. *PLoS Biology*, 2: E207.

Francioli, L.C., Polak, P.P., Koren, A., et al. 2015. Genome-Wide Patterns and Properties of De Novo Mutations in Humans. *Nature Genetics*, 47: 822–26.

Freeland, S.J. and Hurst, L.D. 1998. The Genetic Code Is One in a Million. *Journal of Molecular Evolution*, 47: 238–48.

Freeland, S.J., Wu, T. and Keulmann, N. 2003. The Case for an Error Minimizing Standard Genetic Code. *Origins of Life and Evolution of the Biosphere*, 33: 457–77.

Futuyma, D.J. 1998. *Evolutionary Biology*, 3rd edn. Sunderland, MA: Sinauer Associates.

Gavelis, G.S., Hayakawa, S., White, R.A., 3rd, et al. 2015. Eye-Like Ocelloids Are Built from Different Endosymbiotically Acquired Components. *Nature*, 523: 204–7.

Gerstein, A.C., Lo, D.S. and Otto, S.P. 2012. Parallel Genetic Changes and Nonparallel Gene-Environment Interactions Characterize the Evolution of Drug Resistance in Yeast. *Genetics*, 192: 241–52.

Gherardini, P.F., Wass, M.N., Helmer-Citterich, M., et al. 2007. Convergent Evolution of Enzyme Active Sites Is Not a Rare Phenomenon. *Journal of Molecular Biology*, 372: 817–45.

Giardino, D., Corti, C., Ballarati, L., et al. 2009. De Novo Balanced Chromosome Rearrangements in Prenatal Diagnosis. *Prenatal Diagnosis*, 29: 257–65.

Giberson, K. (ed.) 2016. *Abraham's Dice: Chance and Providence in the Monotheistic Traditions*. New York: Oxford University Press,.

Gilis, D., Massar, S., Cerf, N.J., et al. 2001. Optimality of the Genetic Code with Respect to Protein Stability and Amino-Acid Frequencies. *Genome Biology*, 2: 1–49.

Gowik, U. and Westhoff, P. 2012. The Path from C3 to C4 Photosynthesis. *Plant Physiology*, 155: 56–63.

Guessoum, N. 2011. *Islam's Quantum Question: Reconciling Muslim Tradition and Modern Science*. London: I. B. Tauris.

Gunton, C.E. 1998. *The Triune Creator: A Historical and Systematic Study.* Grand Rapids, MI: Eerdmans.

Gunton, C.E. 2005. *Christ and Creation.* Eugene, OR: Wipf and Stock.

Hall, J. 1649. *An Humble Motion to the Parliament of England Concerning the Advancement of Learning and the Reformation of the Universities.* London.

Hamilton, G. 2006. Virology: The Gene Weavers. *Nature*, 441: 683–85.

Hannam, J. 2009. *God's Philosophers: How the Medieval World Laid the Foundations of Modern Science.* London: Icon Books.

Harrison, P. 1998. *The Bible, Protestantism, and the Rise of Natural Science.* Cambridge: Cambridge University Press.

Harrison, P. 2002. Voluntarism and Early Modern Science. *History of Science*, 40: 63–89.

Harrison, P. 2007. *The Fall of Man and the Foundations of Science.* Cambridge: Cambridge University Press.

Harrison, P. 2010. The Cultural Authority of Natural History in Early Modern Europe. In *Biology and Ideology from Descartes to Dawkins*, ed. D.R. Alexander and R.L. Numbers. Chicago, IL: University of Chicago Press.

Harrison, P. 2015. *The Territories of Science and Religion.* Chicago: University of Chicago Press.

Haught, J. 2008. *God After Darwin: A Theology of Evolution.* Boulder, CO: Westview Press.

Heim, N.A., Knope, M.L., Schaal, E.K., et al. 2015. Animal Evolution: Cope's Rule in the Evolution of Marine Animals. *Science*, 347: 867–70.

Henson, S. 2016. Throwing Dice? Thoughts of God in a Quantum World. In *Abraham's Dice: Chance and Providence in the Monotheistic Traditions*, ed. K.W. Giberson. New York: Oxford University Press.

Herrmann, R.L. 2004. *Sir John Templeton: Supporting Scientific Research for Spiritual Discoveries.* Philadelphia: Templeton Foundation Press.

Herron, M.D. 2009. Many from One: Lessons from the Volvocine Algae on the Evolution of Multicellularity. *Communicative & Integrative Biology*, 2: 368–70.

Hiebert, T. 2008. Air, the First Sacred Thing: The Conception of Ruah in the Hebrew Scriptures. In *Exploring Ecological Hermeneutics*, ed. N.C. Habel and P.L. Trudinger. Leiden: Brill.

Hooke, R. 1665. *Micrographia: Or Some Physiological Descriptions of Minute Bodies Made by Magnifying Glasses.: With Observations and Inquiries Thereupon.* London: Printed by Jo. Martyn, and Ja. Allestry, printers to the Royal Society, and are to be sold at their shop at the Bell in S. Paul's Church-yard.

Hooykaas, R. 1974. *Scientific Progress and Religious Dissent,* Milton Keynes: Open University Press.

Hume, D. 1990. *Dialogues Concerning Natural Religion,* ed. J.M. Bell. London: Penguin.

Hunt, G.R. and Gray, R.D. 2004. Direct Observations of Pandanus-Tool Manufacture and Use by a New Caledonian Crow (Corvus Moneduloides). *Animal Cognition,* 7: 114–20.

Ilardo, M., Meringer, M., Freeland, S., et al. 2015. Extraordinarily Adaptive Properties of the Genetically Encoded Amino Acids. *Scientific Reports,* 5: 9414.

Iqbal, M. 2002. Islam and Modern Science: Questions at the Interface. In *God, Life, and the Cosmos: Christian and Islamic Perspectives,* ed. T. Peters, M. Iqbal and S.N. Haq. Aldershot: Ashgate.

Johnson, D.R., Ecklund, D.H. and Matthews, K.R.W. 2016. Responding to Richard: Celebrity and (Mis)Representation of Science. *Public Understanding of Science,* DOI: 10.1177/0963662516673501.

Johnson, E.A. 2014. *Ask the Beasts: Darwin and the God of Love.* London: Bloomsbury.

Jonas, H. 1996. *Mortality and Morality: A Search for the Good after Auschwitz,* ed. L. Vogel, Evanston, IL: Northwestern University Press.

Jones, G. 2010. Molecular Evolution: Gene Convergence in Echolocating Mammals. *Current Biology,* 20: R62–64.

Karam, P.A., Leslie, S.A. and Anbar, A. 2001. The Effects of Changing Atmospheric Oxygen Concentrations and Background Radiation Levels on Radiogenic DNA Damage Rates. *Health Physics,* 81: 545–53.

Keeling, P.J. and Palmer, J.D. 2008. Horizontal Gene Transfer in Eukaryotic Evolution. *Nature Reviews Genetics,* 9: 605–18.

Keller, J.A. 2013. Process Theism and Theodicies for Problems of Evil. In *The Blackwell Companion to the Problem of Evil,* ed. D. Howard-Snyder and J.P. Mcbrayer. Hoboken, NJ: John Wiley & Sons.

Keller, T.J. 2013. *Walking with God through Pain and Suffering.* London: Hodder & Stoughton.

Kepler, J. 1604. Astronomiae Pars Optica. Manuscript Presented to Rudolf II, Holy Roman Emperor.

Keya, K. and Priya, S. 2016. A Study of Phylogenetic Relationships and Homology of Cytochrome C Using Bioinformatics. *International Research Journal of Science and Engineering*, 4: 65–75.

Koestler, A. 1967. Kepler, Johannes. *Encyclopedia of Philosophy*, ed. Paul Edwards. New York: Macmillan.

Kong, A., Frigge, M.L., Masson, G., et al. 2012. Rate of De Novo Mutations and the Importance of Father's Age to Disease Risk. *Nature*, 488: 471–75.

Koonin, E.V. and Novozhilov, A.S. 2009. Origin and Evolution of the Genetic Code: The Universal Enigma. *IUBMB Life*, 61: 99–111.

Laland, K., Uller, T., Feldman, M., et al. 2014. Does Evolutionary Theory Need a Rethink? *Nature*, 514: 161–64.

Land, M.F. and Fernald, R.D. 1992. The Evolution of Eyes. *Annual Review of Neuroscience*, 15: 1–29.

Laplace, Pierre Simon de. 1951. *A Philosophical Essay on Probabilities*. New York: Dover Publications.

Lindberg, D.C. 1992. *The Beginnings of Western Science: The European Scientific Tradition in Philosophical, Religious and Institutional Context, 600 BC to AD 1450*. Chicago: University of Chicago Press.

Livingstone, D.N. 1987. *Darwin's Forgotten Defenders: The Encounter between Evangelical Theology and Evolutionary Thought*. Grand Rapids, MI: W.B. Eerdmans; Edinburgh: Scottish Academic Press.

Louis, A.A. 2016. Contingency, Convergence and Hyper-Astronomical Numbers in Biological Evolution. *Studies in History and Philosophy of Biological and Biomedical Sciences*, 58: 107–16.

Lyons, T.W., Reinhard, C.T. and Planavsky, N.J. 2014. The Rise of Oxygen in Earth's Early Ocean and Atmosphere. *Nature*, 506: 307–15.

Malfavon-Borja, R., Wu, L. I., Emerman, M., et al. 2013. Birth, Decay, and Reconstruction of an Ancient Trimcyp Gene Fusion in Primate Genomes. *Proceedings of the National Academy of Sciences USA*, 110: E583–92.

Marsden, G.M. 1984. Understanding Fundamentalist Views of Science. In *Science and Creationism*, ed. A. Montagu. Oxford: Oxford University Press.

Marshall, L.G. 2012. The Great American Interchange: An Invasion Induced

Crisis for South American Mammals. In *Biotic Crises in Ecological and Evolutionary Time*, ed. M.H. Nitecki. Orlando, FL: Academic Press.

Martin, A. and Orgogozo, V. 2013. The Loci of Repeated Evolution: A Catalog of Genetic Hotspots of Phenotypic Variation. *Evolution*, 67: 1235–50.

Masood, E. 2009. *Science & Islam: A History*. London: Icon.

Mathisen, R.R. 2006. *Critical Issues in American Religious History*, Waco, TX: Baylor University Press.

May, R.M. 1976. Simple Mathematical Models with Very Complicated Dynamics. *Nature*, 261: 459–67.

Mcfadden, B.J. 1992. *Fossil Horses: Systematics, Paleobiology and Evolution of the Family Equidae*. Cambridge: Cambridge University Press.

Mele, A.R. 2015. *Surrounding Free Will: Philosophy, Psychology, Neuroscience*. Oxford: Oxford University Press.

Mendes, N., Hanus, D. and Call, J. 2007. Raising the Level: Orangutans Use Water as a Tool. *Biology Letters*, 3: 453–55.

Meringer, M., Cleaves, H.J., 2nd and Freeland, S.J. 2013. Beyond Terrestrial Biology: Charting the Chemical Universe of Alpha-Amino Acid Structures. *Journal of Chemical Information and Modeling*, 53: 2851–62.

Mills, R.E., Bennett, E.A., Iskow, R.C., et al. 2007. Which Transposable Elements Are Active in the Human Genome? *Trends in Genetics*, 23: 183–91.

Moltmann, J.R. 1985. *God in Creation: An Ecological Doctrine of Creation*. London: SCM.

Monod, J. 1997. *Chance and Necessity: An Essay on the Natural Philosophy of Modern Biology*. London: Penguin.

Moore, A. 1891. The Christian Doctrine of God. In *Lux Mundi: A Series of Studies in the Religion of the Incarnation*, ed. C. Gore, 12th edn. London: John Murray.

Moore, J. 1981. *The Post-Darwinian Controversies: A Study of the Protestant Struggle to Come to Terms with Darwin in Great Britain and America, 1870–1900*. Cambridge: Cambridge University Press.

Murray, M.J. 2008. *Nature Red in Tooth and Claw: Theism and the Problem of Animal Suffering*. Oxford: Oxford University Press.

Nowak, M.A. 2006. Five Rules for the Evolution of Cooperation. *Science*, 314: 1560–63.

Nowak, M.A. and Coakley, S. 2013. *Evolution, Games, and God: The Principle of Cooperation,* Cambridge, MA: Harvard University Press.

Nowak, M.A. and Highfield, R. 2011. *Supercooperators: Altruism, Evolution, and Why We Need Each Other to Succeed.* New York: Free Press.

Oakley, T.H. 2003. On Homology of Arthropod Compound Eyes. *Integrative and Comparative Biology,* 43: 522–30.

Ogura, A., Ikeo, K. and Gojobori, T. 2004. Comparative Analysis of Gene Expression for Convergent Evolution of Camera Eye between Octopus and Human. *Genome Research,* 14: 1555–61.

Palacios, M.A. 1930. El "Libro De Los Animales" De Jâḥiẓ. *Isis,* 14: 20–54.

Paley, W. 1883. *The Works of William Paley.* Edinburgh: Peter Brown and Thomas Nelson.

Palmer, T. 2008. Edward Norton Lorenz. *Physics Today,* 61: 81–82.

Pascoal, S., Cezard, T., Eik-Nes, A., et al. 2014. Rapid Convergent Evolution in Wild Crickets. *Current Biology,* 24: 1369–74.

Pauly, D. 2010. *Gasping Fish and Panting Squids: Oxygen Temperature and the Growth of Water-Breathing Animals,* Oldendorf: Ecology Institute.

Pennisi, E. 2013. The Man Who Bottled Evolution. *Science,* 342: 790–93.

Perutz, M.F. 1983. Species Adaptation in a Protein Molecule. *Molecular Biology and Evolution,* 1: 1–28.

Pinto, Y., Gabay, O., Arbiza, L., et al. 2016. Clustered Mutations in Hominid Genome Evolution Are Consistent with APOBEC3G Enzymatic Activity. *Genome Research,* 26: 579–87.

Plantinga, A. 1974. *God, Freedom, and Evil.* New York: Harper & Row.

Poelwijk, F.J., Kiviet, D.J., Weinreich, D.M., et al. 2007. Empirical Fitness Landscapes Reveal Accessible Evolutionary Paths. *Nature,* 445: 383–86.

Randall, I.M. 2015. Evangelical Spirituality, Science, and Mission: A Study of Charles Raven (1885–1964), Regius Professor of Divinity, Cambridge University. *Anglican and Episcopal History,* 84: 20–48.

Ray, J. 1701. *The Wisdom of God Manifested in the Works on the Creation... The Third Edition, Very Much Enlarg'd Throughout. [with a Portrait.].* London: Sam Smith & Benj. Walford.

Ray, J. and Willughby, F. 1678. *The Ornithology of Francis Willughby of Middleton.* London: Printed by A.C. for John Martyn.

Richards, T.A. and Gomes, S.L. 2015. Protistology: How to Build a Microbial Eye. *Nature,* 523: 166–67.

Rodin, A.S., Szathmary, E. and Rodin, S.N. 2011. On Origin of Genetic Code and tRNA before Translation. *Biology Direct,* 6: 14.

Rogozin, I.B. and Pavlov, Y.I. 2003. Theoretical Analysis of Mutation Hotspots and Their DNA Sequence Context Specificity. *Mutation Research,* 544: 65–85.

Rupke, N.A. 2009. *Richard Owen: Biology without Darwin.* Chicago, IL: University of Chicago Press.

Salvini-Plawen, L. and Mayr, E. 1977. On the Evolution of Photoreceptors and Eyes. *Evolutionary Biology,* 10: 207–63.

Sawal, H.A., Harripaul, R., Mikhailov, A., et al. 2016. Biallelic Truncating Scn9a Mutation Identified in Four Families with Congenital Insensitivity to Pain from Pakistan. *Clinical Genetics,* 90: 563–65.

Sayah, D.M., Sokolskaja, E., Berthoux, L., et al. 2004. Cyclophilin a Retrotransposition into Trim5 Explains Owl Monkey Resistance to Hiv-1. *Nature,* 430: 569–73.

Schaper, S. and Louis, A.A. 2014. The Arrival of the Frequent: How Bias in Genotype-Phenotype Maps Can Steer Populations to Local Optima. *PLoS One,* 9: e86635.

Scholl, J.P. and Wiens, J.J. 2016. Diversification Rates and Species Richness across the Tree of Life. *Proceedings of the Royal Society B: Biological Sciences,* 283: 20161334. http://dx.doi.org/10.1098/rspb.2016.1334.

Sedley, D.N. 2007. *Creationism and Its Critics in Antiquity,* Berkeley, CA: University of California Press.

Sender, R., Fuchs, S. and Milo, R. 2016. Revised Estimates for the Number of Human and Bacteria Cells in the Body. *bioRxiv* preprint first posted online 6 January 2016; doi: http://dx.doi.org/10.1101/036103.

Shortt, R. 2016. *God Is No Thing: Coherent Christianity.* London: Hurst & Co.

Shu, H., Wang, L. and Watmough, J. 2014. Sustained and Transient Oscillations and Chaos Induced by Delayed Antiviral Immune Response in an Immunosuppressive Infection Model. *Journal of Mathematical Biology,* 68: 477–503.

Shull, A.F. 1935. Weismann and Haeckel: One Hundred Years. *Science*, 81: 443–52.

Sober, E. 2014. Evolutionary Theory, Causal Completeness, and Theism: The Case of "Guided" Mutations. In *Evolutionary Biology: Conceptual, Ethical, and Religious Issues*, ed. R.P. Thompson and D.M. Walsh. Cambridge: Cambridge University Press.

Sommers, T. and Rosenberg, A. 2003. Darwin's Nihilistic Idea: Evolution and the Meaninglessness of Life. *Biology and Philosophy*, 18: 653–68.

Southgate, C. 2008. *The Groaning of Creation: God, Evolution, and the Problem of Evil*. Louisville, KY: Westminster John Knox Press.

Spencer, N. 2009. *Darwin and God*. London: SPCK.

Stanley, S.M. 2016. Estimates of the Magnitudes of Major Marine Mass Extinctions in Earth History. *Proceedings of the National Academy of Sciences USA*, 113: E6325–34.

Stern, D.L. 2013. The Genetic Causes of Convergent Evolution. *Nature Reviews Genetics*, 14: 751–64.

Stern, D.L. and Orgogozo, V. 2009. Is Genetic Evolution Predictable? *Science*, 323: 746–51.

Stewart, M.Y. 2010. *Science and Religion in Dialogue*. Hoboken, NJ: Wiley-Blackwell.

Stewart, T.A., Smith, W.L. and Coates, M.I. 2014. The Origins of Adipose Fins: An Analysis of Homoplasy and the Serial Homology of Vertebrate Appendages. *Proceedings of the Royal Society B: Biological Sciences*, 281: 20133120.

Su, H., Qu, L. J., He, K., et al. 2003. The Great Wall of China: A Physical Barrier to Gene Flow? *Heredity (Edinburgh)*, 90: 212–19.

Taylor, A.H., Elliffe, D.M., Hunt, G.R., et al. 2011. New Caledonian Crows Learn the Functional Properties of Novel Tool Types. *PLoS One*, 6: e26887.

Templeton, J. and Herrmann, R.L. 1989. *The God Who Would Be Known: Revelations of the Divine in Contemporary Science*. San Francisco: Harper & Row.

Templeton, J. and Herrmann, R.L. 1994. *Is God the Only Reality? Science Points to a Deeper Meaning of the Universe*. New York: Continuum.

Tenaillon, O., Barrick, J.E., Ribeck, N., et al. 2016. Tempo and Mode of Genome Evolution in a 50,000-Generation Experiment. *Nature*, 536: 165–70.

Thomas, K. 1984. *Man and the Natural World: Changing Attitudes in England, 1500–1800*. Harmondsworth: Penguin.

Thomas, R.D., Shearman, R.M. and Stewart, G.W. 2000. Evolutionary Exploitation of Design Options by the First Animals with Hard Skeletons. *Science*, 288: 1239–42.

Tinker, M. 2012. *Intended for Good: The Providence of God*. Nottingham: Apollos.

Tokita, M., Kiyoshi, T. and Armstrong, K.N. 2007. Evolution of Craniofacial Novelty in Parrots through Developmental Modularity and Heterochrony. *Evolution & Development*, 9: 590–601.

Topham, J. 2010. Biology in the Service of Natural Theology: Paley, Darwin, and the Bridgewater Treatises. In *Biology and Ideology: From Descartes to Dawkins*, ed. D.R. Alexander and R.L. Numbers. Chicago, IL: University of Chicago Press.

Van Woudenberg, R. 2013. A Brief History of Theodicy. In *The Blackwell Companion to the Problem of Evil*, ed. D. Howard-Snyder and J.P. Mcbrayer. Hoboken, NJ: John Wiley & Sons.

Vermeij, G. J. 1973. Biological Versatility and Earth History. *Proceedings of the National Academy of Sciences USA*, 70: 1936–38.

Virgen, C.A., Kratovac, Z., Bieniasz, P.D., et al. 2008. Independent Genesis of Chimeric Trim5-Cyclophilin Proteins in Two Primate Species. *Proceedings of the National Academy of Sciences USA*, 105: 3563–68.

West, G.B., Brown, J.H. and Enquist, B.J. 1997. A General Model for the Origin of Allometric Scaling Laws in Biology. *Science*, 276: 122–26.

White, R.S. 2014. *Who Is to Blame? Disasters, Nature, and Acts of God*. Oxford: Monarch Books.

Whiteman, N.K. and Mooney, K.A. 2012. Evolutionary Biology: Insects Converge on Resistance. *Nature*, 489: 376–77.

Wiser, M.J., Ribeck, N. and Lenski, R.E. 2013. Long-Term Dynamics of Adaptation in Asexual Populations. *Science*, 342: 1364–67.

Wittgenstein, L. 1968. *Philosophical Investigations*, transl. G.E.M. Anscombe. Oxford: Basil Blackwell.

Wong, J.T., Ng, S.K., Mat, W.K., et al. 2016. Coevolution Theory of the Genetic Code at Age Forty: Pathway to Translation and Synthetic Life. *Life (Basel)*, 6.

Wray, G.A. 2007. The Evolutionary Significance of Cis-Regulatory Mutations. *Nature Reviews Genetics*, 8: 206–16.

Yarus, M., Caporaso, J.G. and Knight, R. 2005. Origins of the Genetic Code: The Escaped Triplet Theory. *Annual Review of Biochemistry*, 74: 179–98.

Yarus, M., Widmann, J.J. and Knight, R. 2009. RNA-Amino Acid Binding: A Stereochemical Era for the Genetic Code. *Journal of Molecular Evolution*, 69: 406–29.

Zhang, Z., Harrison, P.M., Liu, Y., et al. 2003. Millions of Years of Evolution Preserved: A Comprehensive Catalog of the Processed Pseudogenes in the Human Genome. *Genome Research*, 13: 2541–58.

Zhen, Y., Aardema, M.L., Medina, E.M., et al. 2012. Parallel Molecular Evolution in an Herbivore Community. *Science*, 337: 1634–37.

Zhu, S., Zhu, M., Knoll, A.H., et al. 2016. Decimetre-Scale Multicellular Eukaryotes from the 1.56-Billion-Year-Old Gaoyuzhuang Formation in North China. *Nature Communications*, 7: 11500.

Index

Figure acknowledgments

p. 61, Figure 1: from "Many from One: Lessons from the Volvocine Algae on the Evolution of Multicellularity" in *Communicative & Integrative Biology*, Vol. 2, pp. 368–70. © 2009 M. D. Herron. Reproduced by permission of the publisher Taylor & Francis Ltd.

p. 63, Figure 2: Albert Mestre/Wikipedia Creative Commons, 2008.

p. 66, Figure 3: © 2013 Brian D. Baer/MSU. Used by permission.

p. 71, Figure 4: from "Form, Function, and Evolution of Living Organisms" in *Proceedings of the National Academy of Sciences USA*, Vol. 111, pp. 3332–37. © 2014 J. R. Banavar, T. J. Cooke, A. Rinaldo, et al.

p. 76, Figure 5: from "Pax-6: Where to be conserved is not conservative" by W. A. Harris in *Proceedings of the National Academy of Sciences USA*, Vol. 94, pp. 2098–2100. © 1997, National Academy of Sciences, USA. Used by permission of PNS.

p. 79, Figure 6: Illustration by Oxford Designers & Illustrators, 2018.

p. 82, Figure 7: from "The Great American Interchange - an invasion induced crisis for South American Mammals" by L. G. Marshall in *Biotic Crises in Ecological and Evolutionary Time*, ed. M. H. Nitecki, pp. 133-229. © 1981 Marlene Hill Donnelly. Reproduced by permission of the author and the illustrator.

p. 84, Figure 8A: Didier Descouens/Wikipedia Creative Commons, 2012.

p. 84, Figure 8B: from *Transactions of the Royal Society of South Australia*, Vol. 14, 1890–91. Illustration by Rosa Catherine Fiveash, Lithograph by Harcourt Barrett. Wikipedia Public Domain.

p. 86, Figure 9A: © Dave Watts/Alamy.com.

p. 86, Figure 9B: © PeakMystique/iStockPhoto.com.

p. 88, Figure 10A: © Vladimír Motyčka. Reproduced by permission.

p. 88, Figure 10B: © Dr Robert Asher, University of Cambridge. Reproduced by permission.

p. 88, Figure 10C: © OlyaSolodenko/iStockPhoto.com.

p. 88, Figure 10D: by Sjonge/Wikipedia Public Domain.

p. 95, Figure 12: Illustration by Urban Frank. © The Nobel Committee for Physiology or Medicine. Reproduced by permission.

p. 102, Figure 13: © 2001 Muséum d'Aix-en-Provence. Reproduced by permission.

p. 107, Figure 15: from *Language of Genetics: An Introduction* © 2011 Denis Alexander. Courtesy of Templeton Press.

p. 121, Figure 16: by Randy Olson/Wikipedia Creative Commons.

p. 131, Figure 17: from "Parallel Evolution of IDH2 Gene in Cetaceans, Primates and Bats", *FEBS Letters*, Vol. 588, pp. 450–54. © 2014 W. M. Ai, S. B. Chen, X. Chen, et al. Reproduced by permission of the Licensor through PLSclear.

p. 135, Figure 18: from "Birth, Decay, and Reconstruction of an Ancient Trimcyp Gene Fusion in Primate Genomes" in *Proceedings of the National Academy of Sciences USA*, Vol. 110, pp. 583-92. © 2013 R. Malfavon-Borja, L. I. Wu, M. Emerman, et al. Used by permission of PNS.

p. 165, Figure 19: from "Clusters of Multiple Mutations: Incidence and Molecular Mechanisms" in *Annual Review of Genetics*, Vol. 49, pp. 243–267. © 2015 K. Chan, D. A. Gordenin. Reproduced by permission of the Licensor through RightsLink.